FIVE DOWN AND GLORY

In the pilots' own words, you can experience the climax of breathtaking combat, the thrill of soaring through the air, the fear, and the victories of such famous aces as Rickenbacker, Cochran, and Scott.

FIVE DOWN AND GLORY

also features the only complete record listing every American ace, the number of planes shot down, and the citations of those who won the Congressional Medal of Honor.

FIVE DOWN AND GLORY

Other *War Library* Titles
Published by Ballantine Books:

INSIDE THE SAS
by Tony Geraghty

SHARKS AND LITTLE FISH
by Wolfgang Ott

KAMIKAZE
by Yasuo Kuwahara and Gordon T. Allred

AIRCRAFT CARRIER
by Joseph Bryan III

U-BOATS AT WAR
by Harold Busch

THE ROCK
by Warren Tute

GOODBYE TO SOME
by Gordon Forbes

MIDWAY: THE BATTLE THAT
    DOOMED JAPAN
by Mitsuo Fuchida and Masatake Okumiya

H. M. S. TRIGGER
by Antony Melville-Ross

GALLIPOLI
by Alan Moorehead

FIVE DOWN AND GLORY

by Gene Gurney

edited by Mark P. Friedlander, Jr.

with a foreword by Capt. Eddie Rickenbacker

BALLANTINE BOOKS • NEW YORK

Library of Congress Catalog Card Number: 57-14525

ISBN 0-345-30799-2

Manufactured in the United States of America

First Ballantine Books Edition: May 1958
Third Printing: January 1983

CONTENTS

APPENDICES:

The Air Service in particular is one of such peril that membership in it is of itself a high distinction. Physical address, high training, entire fearlessness, iron nerve and fertile resourcefulness are needed in a combination and to a degree hitherto unparalleled in war. The ordinary air fighter is an extraordinary man; and the extraordinary air fighter stands as one in a million among his fellows.

—Theodore Roosevelt

ACKNOWLEDGMENTS

THIS BOOK HAS been six years in the making, and over this period many people in and out of the Air Force have gone out of their way to be helpful in the collection, investigation, and compilation of the data which have gone into the finished manuscript. I am very much indebted to these people and wish in this space to express my appreciation for the invaluable assistance they have given me.

I particularly want to thank Mr. Falk Harmel, the Pentagon's authority on aces, who spent his own off-duty time over a period of many months aiding me in the tabulation of the individual ace records from the Daily Fighter Victory Credit Board Results. And Mr. Adrian O. Van Wyen of the Naval Aviation Historical Research Section, Department of the Navy, for his help in compiling the data on Marine and Navy aces.

I am greatly indebted to Dr. Albert F. Simpson, Dr. Robert F. Futrell and Mr. Robert T. Finney of the Research Studies Institute, USAF Historical Division, Archives Branch, Maxwell AFB, Alabama, and in particular to Mr. John K. Cameron, Chief Bibliographic Assistance and Reference Section, Air University Library, who was the man who knew just where to put his finger on those otherwise elusive bits of information.

I am indebted, also, to Major George C. Bales, Chief, Historical Properties Office, Secretary of the Air Staff, for his valuable contribution of ace material from the final, official Air Record of Korean and top World War II Ace Listings—the results of 1956-57 special board meetings of which Major Bales was a member.

Further, I wish to thank the many top military aces who personally supplied invaluable material for the preparation of the manuscript, and in particular Colonel Chesley Peterson, Colonel Gerald W. Johnson, Colonel Glen T. Eagleston, Major John J. Voll, and especially Colonel "Hub" Zemke who reviewed the manuscript and added some fine touches. I am grateful, too, for the information given to me by the late Colonel David C. Schilling.

In addition I wish to acknowledge with thanks the helpful material and information supplied to me by the many combat pilots and airmen who knew of the work I was doing on this book. In particular I would like to thank Mr. Roland H. Neel of Macon, Georgia, a decorated flyer of World War I, who reviewed the World War I portion of the manuscript and made many helpful suggestions.

Thanks are due to former 8th Air Force Deputy Fighter Command Chief, Major General Robert W. Burns, presently commander, Air Proving Ground Command, for his helpfulness, and to Lieutenant General William E. Kepner, former 8th Air Force, World War II, Fighter Command Chief (retired and presently Chairman of the Board for Radiation, Inc.) for his encouragement. My appreciation, also, for the hard work performed by the many typists, who over the past six years have helped put this manuscript into legible form.

And finally, my deepest appreciation to Captain James F. Sunderman and the Air Force book program which he directs through the Magazine and Book Branch, Office of Information Services, in the Pentagon. Captain Sunderman took the project, which ultimately resulted in this publication, under wing while it was still in the crawling stage, helped it through its growing pains to a final, completed form in the hands of the publisher. It was primarily through his good offices that this history of American military aces has found its way to the bookshelves.

GENE GURNEY

1957

FOREWORD

IN READING CAPTAIN Gene Gurney's *Five Down and Glory*, you will find that none of our surviving aces were reckless daredevils. None of them was motivated alone by a burning, all-consuming hatred for the people they were fighting. None of them achieved Acedom through selfish egotistical drive for personal glory. None of them was introverted.

They were all warmly human individuals with close ties among their Squadron mates. None of them became Aces because they were concerned only with fighting *against* an ideology—nor *for* an ideology. They fought for other people and for their own survival.

It is suggested by some in these days of ultimate weapons, of ballistic missiles—of electronic devices that take the control of an airplane away from the pilot to make a once deadly game a mere mechanical hunt—that there will be no more Aces.

I pray they are right. I pray there will be no need for any more Aces, because my most fervent prayer is that there will never be another war.

I pray that the airplane, which is evolving at an incredible pace, will be the Angel of Mercy and Peace that God intended it to be. I pray that it will be used to foster understanding among peoples, no longer to further hostilities.

But, I also pray that this Nation, and others throughout the world, will be blessed with men possessing the qualities of these Aces. Qualities to overcome their fears, to overcome their aloneness and, disregarding the odds against them—if need be—to strike out alone for the good of their countries and their loved ones.

Captain Gurney's *Five Down and Glory*, to my knowledge, is the first attempt to put between the covers of one book a chronology of the exploits of all the Aces to date in American Aviation, and I recommend it highly as an historical record.

CAPTAIN EDDIE RICKENBACKER
Chairman of the Board
Eastern Air Lines, Inc.

A DEFINITION:
THE ACE

IN ITS SIMPLEST terms the word *ace* as applied to military aviators is the unofficial title of honor given to a fighter pilot who is officially credited with shooting down five or more enemy aircraft.

The use of ace as a designation for superior fighter pilots originated with the French Air Service in World War I, the term ace itself coming from the French *l'as*—the highest card in a suit. As applied to flyers it was first merely the informal appellation for a pilot of supreme skill and daring. As the French flyers became weaned to the novel art of aerial warfare they set a standard of five enemy aircraft destroyed in combat as a more exact measure of the ace.

The various belligerents adopted the French idea and each estabished their own criterion for the ace designation. The American Air Service accepted the French system and in World War I a fighter pilot became an ace when he had shot down five enemy aircraft. It should be noted that the term enemy aircraft was not restricted to enemy airplanes, but included any type of aerial vehicles such as dirigibles, observation balloons and in World War II even a few buzz bombs.

In the Second World War the American system of designating aces was complicated by the peculiarities of the various areas of operation. The Flying Tigers in China and the Eagle Squadrons in Britain counted only airplanes shot down in air-to-air combat; but the American units taking over the Flying Tigers' job in the China-Burma-India theater and the 8th Air Force absorbing the Americans of the Eagle Squadrons in Britain credited toward acedom enemy airplanes destroyed on the ground as well as those shot from aloft. The reasons in both instances were that the enemy—both the Japanese and the Germans—with their backs to the wall would often refuse to send their fighters up to meet the American aviators, saving their planes for special combined missions. Consequently it became necessary for the Americans to change their tactics—strafing and attacking the enemy planes parked at the airdromes. Oddly enough, because of the intensity of flak and anti-aircraft defenses, the dangers of attacking the planes at the airdromes were much greater than in actual air-to-air battles. At the same time an enemy plane destroyed on the ground was in many instances as big a loss to the enemy as the plane flamed from the sky.

The other numbered U. S. Air Forces in World War II, as well as the Navy and Marine Corps, only credited the flyers with air-to-air kills.

In the Korean conflict the Air Force gave official credit to the aviators for all enemy aircraft destroyed, both on the ground and in the air, but only credited those demolished in the air toward acedom. The Navy and Marine Corps flyers of the Korean conflict, as in World War II, could only become aces through air-to-air kills.

In World War I it was the confirmation by a balloon observer or the remains of the wrecked aircraft found by the ground forces behind the Allied lines that most often gave official credit for a confirmed enemy kill to the American flyer, although the observations by three disinterested parties was in some units considered sufficient proof of a victory.

The title of ace is a quasi-official designation and throughout all military organizations it is recognized and proudly regarded. Nevertheless, there is often seemingly contradictory data and information disseminated from various sources in regard to American aces. In the military air units the final word on aircraft destroyed by individuals is the Fighter Victory Credit Board, originally established to appraise fighter kills.

A pilot may return from a mission certain that he had downed a given number of planes, and report this positive knowledge in his intelligence report and occasionally to an inquiring newspaper reporter. Many days later when his gun-camera film had been developed and carefully analyzed some of the enemy aircraft he thought were "sure kills" turned out to be "probably destroyed" or "damaged" —where the film showed only engine fire instead of the required "intensity of flames or extent of damage to preclude chance of successful landing." Since the aviator himself received his impressions during flashing instants in the heat of battle it is quite easy to understand his inability to carefully analyze and evaluate the destruction he inflicts upon each enemy aircraft he engages. On the other hand, the film from his gun camera, watched from the comfort of a quiet projection room, has produced a better gauge, leaving no doubt as to the authenticity of "official" confirmations. Nevertheless, the Fighter Victory Credit Board has in many instances, in the absence of gun-camera proof —for example when the camera jammed or was shot up— given official credit upon testimony of a witness.

The gunners on America's bombers, who destroyed untold numbers of enemy aircraft, are not normally considered on the ace lists—the term ace generally being considered an appellation belonging solely to pilots. However, this rule has a number of exceptions, as will be noted from time to time in this book. Those occasional gunners who *are* listed among the aces are so listed because within that particular theater, on that particular occasion, that particular gunner was officially listed as an ace. And even these gunners were not always given full credits for their victories, for without gun cameras their kills were difficult, if not impossible, to prove.

In a final summation, it must be remembered that in all of the many aerial combat units the maintenance of accurate records of the raging air battles was at best a difficult and often a very touchy problem. Within recent years a board of officers was convened by Headquarters, USAF, to give a final, official consideration to the ace list for the Korean Conflict. One of the by-products of this board was the official determination that only a pilot who destroys five or more enemy aircraft in air-to-air combat is to be considered an ace. If this rule were to be applied retrospectively many of the lists in this book would be entirely different. This publication, however, being a history, is obliged to record the events as they occurred and to give credit for acedom to those Americans given this honor under the definitions under which their particular theater was operating at the time.

With all the preceding conditions and seeming contradictions in mind every effort has been made in the preparation of this book to arrive at the final and most accurate figures

7

for each of America's aces. The Fighter Victory Credit Board has, wherever applicable, been considered the final, official record of aircraft destroyed. And in the end, with all possible records having been sifted through, it is felt that this compilation contains the most up-to-date and accurate figures available on this sometimes elusive subject.

1

IN THE BEGINNING

At the Hague Peace Conference in the year 1899, the worldly men who dreamed of peace made rules for war. The airplane had not been invented, but observation balloons and the various types of lighter-than-air craft had already seen limited use as weapons during the American Civil War and the Franco-Prussian War. So the Conference prohibited by international law any aircraft, either present or projected, from taking a combatant part in war. Neither the dropping of bombs nor the firing of guns from the air was permissible, and all types of flying vehicles were, by agreement, limited to reconnaissance or communications flights.

These ideas were not entirely original, since the military uses of aircraft had occupied a large place in men's thoughts ever since the first speculations of Count Ferdinand von Zeppelin and Alberto Santos-Dumont. The military development of lighter-than-air craft was indefinite and unsatisfactory, so the great military powers did not care about the Conference's harmless prohibition.

This unheeded wisdom of the Conference—in the dusk of that tired century—was but, at most, a feeble warning to the youth and vigor of the wondrous new century then dawning, a neglected admonition to mankind who would in less than half a century have developed devices of war more horrible and deadly than ever dreamed by the most murderous villain. And oddly enough, the only vehicles that would make this mass destruction possible—the only vehicles which could deliver these terrible weapons—were the vessels of the air so futilely curtailed at that Peace Conference in 1899.

Men were not ready for peace and only a few years later at the Conference of 1907, when the real heavier-than-air ships had been developed and the importance of the airplane was becoming more apparent, there was a marked decrease in the opposition by the world powers to the military uses of airplanes. Farsighted military men were now predicting the airplane's use, not only for reconnaissance, photography, mapping or artillery spotting, but also for such active combatant roles as bombing, machine-gunning enemy troops, and attacking opposing aircraft. But that day was yet to come. As the war drums began to throb on the Continent the airplane was considered by the serious planners as little more than a useful auxiliary for observation and communication.

In America when an air-minded Army officer pleaded with Congress for funds for the purchase of aircraft, a Congressional spokesman laughed off such foolish extravagance by pointing out that the Army already had an airplane.

Such shortsightedness hindered the military's aerial progress, but did not stop it. A small group of young men, with a feeling for flight, evidenced their interest in aviation by joining civilian flying clubs. One such club was the Aero Club of America, and it is interesting to note that five of the first seven recipients of the Aero Club's Expert Aviator Certificates were youthful Army officers. The impressive roster of those first seven men read: Max T. Tillie, Glenn L. Martin, Lieutenant T. DeW. Milling, Lieutenant H. H. Arnold, Captain C. deF. Chandler, Captain P. W. Beck, Lieutenant B. D. Foulois—names which are now a famous part of aviation history.

At the annual banquet of this club in New York in January 1912, one of the members, Mr. Clarence H. Mackay, offered a large silver trophy to the War Department for annual competition by Army pilots. Brigadier General James Allen, Chief of the Signal Corps and a staunch advocate of air power, accepted this trophy on behalf of the Secretary of War. The first requirements, which were to be made progressively more difficult each year, included "a cross-country flight of at least twenty miles at an altitude of not less than 1500 feet, with reconnaissance of a triangle of ten miles on each side for the purpose of locating troops somewhere within the area, an accurate landing and a report as to the location and composition of the troops."

On October 12 of that same year a fiery young lieutenant,

H. H. Arnold, who was later to rise to the rank of general and to command one of the greatest aggregates of air power in history, won the first Mackay Trophy.

America's competitions, trophies, and clubs, however, were little more than pleasant Sunday hobbies compared to the military air progress being made in Europe. The young German nation, feeling her expanding strength and hungering for conquest and colonies in Europe, was mass-producing airplanes for war. When the German army marched into Belgium, Marshal Paul von Hindenburg had five hundred military planes, called, ironically, *Tauben* (doves), ready to demonstrate that the infantry and artillery had new and penetrating eyes. France had even more aircraft, but these were of a bewildering variety, largely unsuited for war. England had half that number, and only a small portion of these were adaptable for military use.

As the German armies poured into France the *Tauben* darted around high and low poking their blunt noses into all the Allied business, with nothing to hinder their free flight except small-arms fire from the ground—a minor hazard. They spotted targets and mapped enemy defenses, calling down murderous fire on forts and troop concentrations, and found weak points for the advancing army to smash through.

The French and British flyers, too, rose to aid the defending Allies. The Prussian advance was stopped at the Marne, saving Paris, because French observers in Nieuports, single-seat monoplanes, discovered the approaching enemy units early enough to give warning.

Back and forth across no man's land the planes darted, gathering intelligence and spotting for the artillery. It was a gay and exciting game for the pilots, who, freed from the earth and the ugliness of war, felt a common bond with the fellow airmen of the enemy nations. War was fun; military flying an adventurous sport. The aviators on both sides would often, when passing each other hurrying to and fro over the battlefields, wave and shout greetings.

Below in the mud and the filth of the trenches, war was not so grand or glorious. Trenches became grim and deadly, and the casual comradeship of the German and Allied flyers soon waned and vanished. It was now 1915 and a patriotic young English pilot named F. Vessy Holt was in a mood for fighting. While on a routine spotting mission he

11

flew his British Scout just above a German reconnaissance plane and rolling his ship into a steep, uncoordinated bank, rested his service revolver on the edge of the cockpit and fired at the German below. The bouncing airplane was a poor platform for a pistol shot and the bullet whizzed wide of its mark. But being fired at from the air so unnerved the German that he dove for the ground, landed in the nearest open field, and ran from his aircraft into the surprised arms of Allied foot soldiers. This was the first known air-to-air victory, and a new type of war was born. Thereafter, automatics and rifles were used with small success in aircraft and soon were abandoned for the fixed and mobile mounted machine guns.

Even before the war the various nations had experimented with the use of the aerial machine gun, but the development was slow and ineffective. In America, as early as 1912, Colonel Isaac N. Lewis had developed and successfully tested his air machine gun, the Lewis gun. This weapon was first mounted and tested from the Wright brothers' aeroplane at College Park, Maryland, and then accepted and used by the Army for ground use as an infantry machine gun. Other nations, too, had considered the air machine gun, but it took the impetus of war to speed the practical growth of airborne firearms. Now the race for fire power was on, and as quickly as one mounted machine gun became a useful weapon, the other side rushed improvements and modifications into combat.

Both the Allies and the Germans experimented with the firing of a machine gun through the revolutions of the propeller, but most of the early efforts had been rewarded with shattered propeller blades. In 1915 a French combat flyer, Roland Garros, built a deflection plate for the blade of the propeller so that the bullets which did not go between the blades would be deflected without damaging the prop. This simple device was a secret weapon which enabled Garros to shoot down many unsuspecting Germans who never realized that the French airplane could shoot forward.

Garros' luck did not last and shortly thereafter he was shot down and his secret weapon fell into the hands of the Germans. Anthony Fokker, a brilliant Dutch-born air inventor—as the early aeronautical engineers were then labeled —was called in to study Garros' machine. He improved upon the deflection plate and added a synchronization gear on the end of the engine crankshaft. This simple device was called an interruptor gear and by mechanical timing allowed the machine-gun bullets to fire through the propeller arc.

The interruptor gear, with various modifications, was developed almost simultaneously by all the belligerents and gave added momentum to the period of large-scale aerial combat that followed.

The French Aviation Service was the only air unit in World War I to use the air cannon. French records reveal that it was such a secret weapon that only three pilots were "cleared" to use it—Guynemer, Nungesser and Fonck. Fonck was the top French ace of World War I and he claimed that the air cannon was responsible for most of his German victories. Guynemer used it on a dozen flights, shooting down three Germans with it. On his twelfth flight the cannon misfired, there was an explosion in the breech, and his upper body was seriously burned.

In general the air cannon was not a revolutionary success and it was the machine gun that won the air battles that raged over France. As the competitive cycle for the development of superior fire power spiraled upward, so likewise did the development of the military airplane. As General H. H. Arnold, then a major in the U. S. Army, described this cycle:

One country would bring out a plane that could climb to a high altitude for fighting, only to see the plane of a hostile country far above it during a patrol. A designer in England would produce a plane having a speed of 115 miles an hour and believe that it was the fastest fighter on the battle front, only to hear that a German plane was much faster in a chase. Fighting in the air caused the production of very maneuverable, rapid-climbing, extra strong planes. Bombing brought out large planes with a long radius of action, capable of carrying heavy loads. The types changed so fast that the best plane on the line one day might very well be called obsolete the next day. The resources of almost the entire world were engaged in producing the best possible aircraft, and the results achieved certainly justified the efforts expended.

13

The increase in efficiency and the improvement in performance were obtained by taking advantage of all possible refinements in design and in securing better and more powerful engines. The airplanes at the end of the war by their performances dwarfed into insignificance those produced before the war as a result of employing more efficient wing sections, a substantial reduction of head resistance, a decrease in the dead weight resulting from the use of stronger and lighter materials of construction, and as a result of having more reliable engines that weighed less per horsepower and using engines of much greater power.

When a forced landing meant either the capture or death of the occupants of a plane, reliability was the principal qualification of an engine. Airplanes went out on missions and were continuously shot at by enemy planes and anti-aircraft artillery. The strength of planes was increased to permit their having a good chance of returning safely even though some parts of the plane were destroyed. This necessitated an increase in the structural factor of safety. Bombers were sent on missions many hundred miles away from their bases, requiring large fuel capacity to insure returning against adverse winds. Fighters were accustomed to attacking enemy planes under any and all conditions requiring the best possible performance in speed and climb. Thus, as a result of military necessities, five desirable qualifications of an airplane were improved: speed, reliability, great strength for a minimum of weight, low gross weight, and high-powered engines.

The Central Powers and the Allies had been slugging it out for three years before the United States actually began mobilizing its vast resources for an air war. Though a late starter, the air records of the Americans in World War I astonished the world.

Even before America actually entered the war, the prowess of American flyers was being demonstrated to the German aviators. Many young Americans had gone to France to fly and fight with the French Air Service. Their record was so outstanding that they acquired a unit of their

14

own within the framework of the French organization. This unit was the Lafayette Escadrille, which, as a part of the French Air Service and later after its incorporation into two American air squadrons, set the stage and the pattern of proud performance to be followed by American airmen down through our military aviation's short but creditable history.*

When the American squadrons arrived in Europe they were equipped with the old Nieuport single-seat monoplanes, which in most cases had neither instruments nor guns. They could fight only a cautious patrol war until early in 1918 when both instruments and guns were provided for all their aircraft. As the war progressed the American units grew in manpower and equipment. The obsolete Nieuports were replaced with Spads, the craft the French produced to outperform the best German fighting machine, the Fokker. The Spad was faster in a climb or in level flight, but the Fokker had the edge in maximum ceiling and diving speed. Nevertheless, the Spads evened out the odds, and the Americans began to prove that they could outfly, outshoot, and outlast the enemy.

That they did so was attested later by General Billy Mitchell, who wrote in his war diary:

> My figures show that from the time that American air units entered into combat on the front—that is, from March 1918, to November 11, 1918—our men shot down and received official confirmation for 927 enemy airplanes or balloons. During the same time we lost, due to operations of the enemy, 316 of our airplanes or balloons.
>
> This ratio of three to one was a remarkable thing, and was much greater in proportion than the victories achieved by any of our allies. The reason was that we had remarkable pilots and that our tactics and strategy were superior to any of those employed elsewhere.

Then came the Armistice and the war on the Continent was over. From the turmoil and the strife had come a new concept of modern warfare—air power. In less than a generation air armadas would blacken the heavens and air forces would vanquish foes previously protected by impassable boundaries. In this short space of years the United States itself would begin and end a war with aerial bombardment. 1899 had been too soon to take serious note of air power; 1919 was too late to ignore it. The age of the aerial warrior had arrived.

2

LAFAYETTE ESCADRILLE

A MONTH AFTER the war in Europe had begun, a handful of American adventurers arrived in Paris to enlist in the French Foreign Legion. Their ambition was to fly in the French Air Force, but because of French laws and America's neutrality their only route to this ambitious goal was through the Foreign Legion. In this group were Raoul Lufbery, William Thaw, Victor Chapman, Kiffin Rockwell and Bert Hall, all of whom were destined to find their way together years later as a part of the proud Lafayette Escadrille.

While the other four Americans spent their first year in France fighting with the infantry in the trenches, Raoul Gervail Lufbery was transferred directly to the French Air Service through the special efforts of his close personal friend, Marc Pourpe, the famous French airman. Lufbery served his friend as airplane mechanic, giving special and highly skilled attention to his companion's flying machine, while Pourpe made French aviation history with seventeen air-to-air victories.

On 2 December 1914 Marc Pourpe was killed in aerial combat. Lufbery was greatly grieved at the loss of his friend and in his grief he became determined to get into the air to take up where Pourpe left off. Taking advantage of his fluent French he feigned French citizenship and entered pilot training. Four years later, Raoul Lufbery became the first man to win the proud, but unofficial, title of "Ace of Aces." French national records indicate that beyond his official record of seventeen kills made within the "sight" of Allied balloonmen, Lufbery had shot down twenty-three more German aircraft behind the enemy lines.

As the war went into its second year, the American flyers, scattered throughout the various units of the French military forces, began to urge the formation of an American flying combat unit. Such other Americans as Dr. Edmund L. Gros, an American physician who had lived in Paris for many years; Frederick H. Allen, a New York lawyer active in French relief work; Colonel Thomas Bentley Mott and Charles Sweeney, were all instrumental in winning over the French Government to the idea and prodding them into the passage of a special law enabling the Americans to be received in the French aviation service.

On 8 July 1915 General Hirschauer, Chief of French Military Aeronautics, finally set into motion the formation of the American flying unit within the French Aviation Corps, which he called the Franco-American Flying Corps. Several months later Americans were accepted into the French flying schools for training.

On 16 April 1916 at Luxeuil-Les-Bains, with the men fully trained, the American unit was officially formed and recognized as the *Escadrille de Casse Nieuport 124,* which was later changed to *L'Escadrille Américaine,* under the command of a French officer, Captain Georges Thenault. An attempt was made at that time to bring all the Americans serving with the French air service into the squadron, but many had become so devoted to their French units that they declined the offer. The original seven Americans to be formed into the Escadrille were Victor Chapman, Kiffin Rockwell, William Thaw, Bert Hall, James Roger McConnell, Elliot Cowdin, and Norman Prince. Hall, a soldier of fortune, was one of the early barnstorming aviators who had given exhibitions in Europe before the war, and during the Balkan Wars had acted as a one-man air force for the Turks and later for the Bulgarians. As a result of his professional soldiering for both belligerents in that war, he was watched closely by French Secret Service; but his outstanding record with the Escadrille quickly allayed their doubts of his loyalty.

Norman Prince and Elliot Cowdin had left Harvard University to take flying lessons for the purpose of enlisting in the French Aviation Corps.

William Thaw, a dashing "sportsman" in his earlier days, had accumulated five hundred flying hours and was an extremely experienced pilot before entering the French flying school in the autumn of 1915. He was blind in one eye, but he felt that his flying experience would more than compen-

18

sate his lack of two good eyes. When he came before the French medical examiner he pulled a sleight-of-hand trick, placing the black cardboard over his bad eye for each eye reading, and was thus entered on the medical records with perfect 20/20 vision in both eyes.

On his first day in cadets he boldly set out to demonstrate his superior flying ability to his flight instructors. Not realizing that the larger military planes didn't handle as easily as the small civilian aircraft he had mastered, he applied full throttle and the airplane roared across the field. The torque of the high-powered engine fooled him, the airplane got away from him, and he flew straight into a bakery on the far side of the field.

The commander of the French airfield came running across the meadow as Thaw climbed uninjured but slightly embarrassed from the wreck. Smiling with approval at the unshaken Thaw and the mangled airplane, the commander remarked: "You're a terrible pilot, but you've got guts. We can teach you to fly." Thaw's achievement of "acedom" gave ample testimony to the correctness of the French commander's judgment.

The men of the Escadrille were trained by the French government at the expense of patriotic Americans in France. The candidates came at first, of course, from those Americans already fighting in France; but later recruits were drawn from the United States, with no requirements of education, only that they be mentally and physically fit to fly and be qualified to take their places as officers and gentlemen. The test of these qualifications was made by observation. (The French government also imposed the condition that the flyers have no German parents or grandparents.) The candidates from the States were sent to the Curtiss School at Old Point Comfort, Virginia, for their air tests, and if they passed satisfactorily were sent to France to begin a six-months' course of aviation training with the pay of five cents a day. The Escadrille itself paid $30 a month plus quarters. A bonus of $250 and two days' leave in Paris was added for every enemy aircraft shot down. The members of the Escadrille bought their own uniforms and had to supply the money for their personal needs; however, nowhere in France would anyone accept money from these Americans, regardless of the purchase.

Immediately after its formation the *Escadrille Américaine*

moved into combat in the Battle of Verdun. The original seven pilots were joined by Raoul Lufbery, whose American citizenship had been discovered but overlooked because of his great renown among French airmen as "a pilot whose attack was like lightning, whose marksmanship was uncanny and whose nerve was never shaken."

Six more American pilots soon arrived at Verdun to join the eight flyers in the Escadrille: Chouteau Johnson, Clyde Balsley, Dudley Hill, Lawrence Rumsey, Didier Masson and Paul Pavelka.

In combat the Escadrille at once made such an outstanding record that the German Ambassador in Washington, Count Bernstorff, protested to the State Department that the *Escadrille Américaine* violated American neutrality. To smooth ruffled feathers and to avoid any embarrassment to the American government, the French Embassy suggested deleting the word *Américaine,* and changing the organization's name to *Escadrille Lafayette* or the Lafayette Flying Corps in honor of the French patriot who so generously and gallantly served America in the Revolutionary War.

On the fourth day of operation, 18 May 1916, Kiffin Rockwell shot down the Escadrille's first German plane. At 6000 feet over the French city of Thann he spotted and dove upon a German reconnaissance plane. As he pulled within 50 feet of the *Boche,* he fired a short burst (only four rounds of ammunition) which killed the pilot and observer and sent the plane down in a spin. It crashed in the German trenches and burned.

He later wrote of this victory:

This morning I went over the lines to make a little tour. I was a little the other side of the lines when my motor began to miss a bit. I turned around to go to a camp near the lines. Just as I started to head for there, I saw a Boche machine about seven hundred meters under me and a little inside our lines. I went for him. He saw me at the same time, and began to dive towards his lines. It was a machine with a pilot and a *mitrailleur* [observer gunner], with two *mitrailleuses* [machine guns], one facing the front and one in the rear that turned on a pivot, so he could fire in any direction. He immediately opened fire on me and my machine was hit, but I didn't pay any attention to that and kept going straight for him, until I got within 25 to 30 meters of him. Then, just as I was afraid of running into him, I fired four or five shots, then swerved my machine to the right to keep from running into him. As I did that, I saw the *mitrailleur* fall back dead on the pilot, the *mitrailleuse* fell from its position and pointed straight up in the air, the pilot fell to one side as if he was done for also. The machine itself fell first to one side, then dived vertically toward the ground with a lot of smoke coming out the rear. I circled around, and three or four minutes later saw a lot of smoke coming up from the ground just beyond the German trenches. I had hoped that it would fall in our lines, as it is hard to prove when they fall in the German lines. The post of observation [balloon observer] signalled seeing the machine fall, and the smoke. . . .

Victor Chapman received a serious scalp wound on 17 June 1916, but he begged not to be taken out of action. His wish was granted and on 23 June he tangled with two German pursuit ships in a nip-and-tuck dogfight. He shot down one German and was maneuvering into position for the second when the wings of his Nieuport buckled and, spinning wildly out of control, his airship plummeted to the ground. He became the first Escadrille American to die in combat. His death was more than an obituary notice, for the Escadrille had won great popularity throughout France, and thousands of mourners attended his funeral. Victor was the great-great-grandson of John Jay, one of the signers of the Declaration of Independence, and the son of John Jay Chapman, an American poet, who when told of Victor's death replied sadly, "Very well. He died for a noble cause."

The men of the Escadrille returned from their patrols during their first operations with their planes riddled, big holes in the fabric, wires and braces cut, the controls and struts shot away. But the Escadrille, sparked by William Thaw's fierce aggressiveness, was on the offensive. In one of the early battles Bert Hall attacked a German plane at 12,000 feet, worked it down to 3,000 and then shot it down over the French front-line trenches. Elliot Cowdin, flying wing with Hall, attacked simultaneously two German planes and forced them both to the ground. But this method of singlehanded combat exacted a mounting toll of deaths.

Chapman had been killed in single combat and Rockwell was to die a short time later operating as a "lone wolf." The men of the Escadrille quickly learned from their high-priced lessons the need for close aerial teamwork. Offensive and defensive group combat tactics were developd and practiced in training sessions. The flyers who insisted on making grandstand plays or who, by temperament, found it hard to follow their leaders' instructions did not last long against the enemy's newly developing formations.

Extensive formation flying was originally introduced by the German ace, Baron Manfred von Richthofen, who headed a squadron of flyers known as the Tango Circus. Although he personally delighted in solo flying, he devised for the German Air Force the V-shaped or "wild-goose" formation which was quickly adopted by the Allies.

Raoul Lufbery contrived a defensive maneuver called the Lufbery Show or Lufbery Circle for his airmen, to be used whenever encountering a larger formation of German pursuit ships. When thus attacked by vastly superior numbers, the Escadrille flyers would form a circle, with each plane protecting the plane in front, gradually moving the circle toward their own territory. The observers in the two-place aircraft picked off the enemy airplanes as they tried to enter the circle, in much the same manner as pioneers in covered wagons fought the Indians in America's early frontier days. The Germans likewise adopted this technique for defense and escape. This tactic found employment by both the Japanese and Americans in World War II, and by the Communist Chinese as part of their tactics in Korea.

Another fighter maneuver developed by Lufbery against the crack German Tango Circus was the reversement. Richthofen had perfected the diving formation sweeps that rained heavy fire upon the Allied flyers. The reversement was a countermeasure in which the attacked American pilot would pull up into a stall and kick right or left rudder to throw his ship into a spin. The airman would let the ship fall through a half-spin and recover, putting his plane in a reversed position ready to fire at the oncoming planes. By the time the enemy formation could wheel around in a flat formation turn, the Allied aviator could gain back his speed and altitude.

Of Baron von Richthofen's limitless bag of tricks his favorite was the "decoy," and many of his victories were

22

attributed to this stratagem. Kiffin Rockwell was one of the American victims of this trap.

On 23 September of the year 1916, Kiffin Rockwell and Raoul Lufbery made the Escadrille's first flight in the new Nieuport 160 (meaning 160 square feet of wing area). This model had the modern Vickers gun which, in conjunction with the recently developed interruptor gear, could fire two hundred rounds through the propeller arc as opposed to the old Lewis gun's mere forty-seven rounds from a mounted position. On this flight Rockwell and Lufbery became separated and Rockwell decided to "lone wolf" it.

From 7,000 feet he spotted and attacked a reconnaissance plane below him at 1,000 feet. As he came within 50 feet, two Fokkers, waiting above in the sun, pounced upon him. With a combined blast of bullets they snapped off a wing and sent his plane spinning to the earth. He was found in the wreckage with a dumdum bullet exploded in his stomach; he had been killed at the instant of the attack —a victim of the Red Baron's "decoy."

Rockwell had requested to be buried where he fell, so he was buried at Luxeuil. His squadron, in tradition, dropped flowers by plane over his grave. At his death Rockwell had four official victories and that number again not confirmed by balloon observers.

In 1914 only one American was serving in the French Air Service, Raoul Lufbery; in 1915 there were eight; by 1916 there were thirty-two; and on 17 April 1917, when the French stopped accepting Americans, there were 148.

Four of the Escadrille's seven original members were killed during their first year of operation, and eleven replacements to the unit fell in combat before the United States entered the war.

The following winter, on 18 February 1918, the Lafayette Escadrille transferred to the American Army Air Service and became the 103rd Pursuit Squadron with all its pilots becoming officers in the United States Army. Lufbery and Thaw became majors; Soubiran a captain; and Dugan a first lieutenant. Some of the men were sent to the other combat outfits to form the experienced backbone of America's new Air Service.

Lufbery, who had valiantly commanded the Lafayette Escadrille, was at once put in command of the 103rd's sister pursuit squadron, the 94th. Then in the late spring of that year, 19 May 1918, flying a Nieuport 28, in his first combat experience over *friendly* territory, Major Raoul Lufbery was killed. He died unable to heed his own advice. He had always instructed his pilots: "If your plane catches fire, don't jump. Stick with it and you may have a chance. If you jump there is no chance whatever." Major Lufbery jumped from his burning aircraft.

Eddie Rickenbacker in his book, *Fighting the Flying Circus,* described Lufbery's last flight as follows:

As Lt. Gude, returning home, crossed over the front lines, "Archy" batteries in the neighborhood again took up the battle and poured up a violent barrage, which surrounded and encompassed this lone enemy on every side. But all to no purpose. The Albatros continued steadily on its retreat, climbing slightly and setting a course in the direction of Nancy.

In the meantime, Major Lufbery, who had been watching the whole show from his barracks, jumped on a motorcycle that was standing in the road and rushed to the hangars. His own plane was out of commission. Another Nieuport was standing on the field, apparently ready for use. It belonged to Lieutenant Davis. The mechanics admitted everything was ready and without another word Lufbery jumped into the machine and immediately took off.

With all his long string of victories, Lufbery had never brought down an enemy aeroplane within the Allied lines. All seventeen of his early successes with the Escadrille Lafayette and his last success—when he had gone out to avenge Jimmy Hall—all had been won across the German lines. He had never seen the wreckage of a single one of his victories. Undoubtedly he seized this opportunity of engaging in a combat almost within sight of our field with impetuous abandon. Knowing nothing of the condition of his guns nor the small peculiarities of his present mount, Lufbery flew into the attack.

With far greater speed than his heavier antagonist, Major Lufbery climbed in pursuit. In approximately five minutes after leaving the ground he had reached 2,000 feet and had arrived within range of the Albatros six miles away. The first attack was witnessed by all our watchers.

Luf fired several short bursts as he dived in to the attack. Then he swerved away and appeared to busy himself with his gun, which evidently had jammed. Another circle over their heads and he had cleared the jam. Again he rushed the enemy from their rear, when suddenly old Luf's machine was seen to burst into roaring flames. He passed the Albatros and proceeded for three or four seconds on a straight course. Then to the horrified watchers below there appeared the figure of their gallant hero emerging in a headlong leap from the midst of the fiery furnace! Lufbery had preferred to leap to certain death rather than endure the slow torture of burning to a crisp. His body fell in the garden of a peasant woman's house in a little town just north of Nancy. A small stream ran by about a hundred yards distant and it was thought later that poor Lufbery, seeing this small chance for life, had jumped with the intention of striking this water. He had leaped from a height of 200 feet and his machine was carrying him at a speed of 120 miles per hour! A hopeless but a heroic attempt to preserve his priceless life for his needy country!

Major H. H. Arnold wrote of Lufbery's death: "One of our modern parachutes would have saved the life of this brave airman who died so heroically, the victim of inadequate equipment rather than defeat by the enemy."

It was one of the mysteries of that early war—that our pilots did not wear parachutes. The main reason for this failure is not to be found in the records, although it is known that many of the young Americans considered them sissy and fought strongly against their use. The enemy pilots, however, eagerly accepted the life-saving devices. The records reveal that over one hundred German aviators returned to fight again by the simple yet sane use of parachutes.

(Nevertheless, it should be noted that the balloon arm of our Air Service had and used parachutes. Many balloonmen were obliged to jump for their lives, and there is only one case on record where a balloonist failed to save his life when using a parachute. This one incident occurred on

26 September 1918 when First Lieutenant C. J. Ross of the 8th Balloon Company jumped from his balloon which had been set afire by enemy aircraft. The rip cord pulled too soon and he fell to his death when the opening chute caught fire from the flaming balloon.)

One hundred and eighty pilots were the total that flew with the French Army serving in ninety-three different French pursuit, observation and bombardment squadrons. Fifty-one were killed in action, six killed in school accidents, five died of illness. Fifteen were taken prisoner; ninety-three transferred to the United States Air Service; twenty-six to the United States Naval Aviation, and thirty-three remained with French Aviation. The pilots were credited with official destruction of 199 German aircraft. Some flew on the Macedonian front against the Serbs and Bulgars. Paul Pavelka died there at Salonika, Greece, on 11 November 1917 from injuries received from a fall while riding a British Cavalry charger in his spare time, a strange end for this Connecticut soldier of fortune who had flown over a hundred combat missions and survived many serious air accidents.

After the war, William Thaw settled in Pittsburgh and was active in aeronautical affairs in the United States and at one time commanded the United States Third Pursuit Group.

A letter of commendation to the men of the Lafayette Escadrille in the form of a General Order is on file at Headquarters, U. S. A. F., Washington, D. C. It is presented here in its entirety:

HQ. First Pursuit Wing Air Service, A. E. F.
16 November 1918

GENERAL ORDER 17

1. The One Hundred and Third Aero Squadron, Third Pursuit Group, will hold itself in readiness to move at any moment to join the First Pursuit Group and proceed into Germany.

2. This honor has been conferred upon the One Hundred and Third Aero Squadron for its long and faithful service with French and American armies.

3. The Wing Commander takes the opportunity of expressing his pleasure at having this Squadron under his command. The Lafayette Escadrille, organized long be-

fore the entry of the United States into the European War, played an important part in bringing home to our people the basic issues of the War. To the French people of future generations the names of its organizers and early pilots must mean what the names of Lafayette and Rochambeau mean to us Americans of this generation. To mention only a few, the names of Norman Prince, Kiffin Rockwell, James McConnell, Victor Chapman, Captain James Norman Hall, Major Kenneth Marr, Major David Mck. Peterson, Major Raoul Lufbery, and Lieutenant-Colonel William Thaw are never to be forgotten. In February last the Lafayette Escadrille of the French Army was transferred to the One Hundred and Third Aero Squadron, United States Army. It was the first, and for nearly two months it was the only, American Air Service organization on the Front. The Squadron produced two of America's four Pursuit Group Commanders as well as a very large proportion of the squadron and flight commanders. While giving thus generously of its experienced personnel to new units, the standard of merit of this Squadron has never been lowered. No task was too arduous or too hazardous for it to perform successfully. In the recent decisive operations of the First American Army, the One Hundred and Third Aero Squadron has done its share.

4. The Wing Commander congratulates Captain Robert Soubiran, Squadron Commander, One Hundred and Third Aero Squadron, and all of his personnel, commissioned and enlisted. No other organization in the American Army has a right to such a high measure of satisfaction in feeling its difficult task has been performed. So long as the personnel bears in mind the record the Squadron has established, there can be no other prospect for it than that of a splendid future.

s/B. M. ATKINSON
Lt. Col., Air Service,
U. S. A. Commanding

LAFAYETTE ESCADRILLE ACES

Unofficial credits, on the average, gave the aces almost twice as many kills as the official tallies listed here. This was due to the fact that the Allies would not give a confirmed victory for kills behind the German lines, and although a higher record for the Escadrille aces was later verified by German records, the official records were not changed.

This list represents Escadrille pilots who became aces during their service with the Lafayette Escadrille, or who later became aces by their aggregate of victories both with the Escadrille and with the Allied Air Services.

The Lafayette Escadrille, which was French Squadron 124, was limited to a total of thirty American pilots; therefore, American aces from all French squadrons are listed here.

1.	Lufbery, Raoul Gervail	17
2.	Baylies, Frank L.	12
3.	Putnam, David	12
4.	Baer, Paul F.	9
5.	Cassady, Thomas G.	9
6.	Parsons, Edwin C.	8
7.	Biddle, Charles J.	7
8.	Larner, G. de Freest	7
9.	Connelly, James A., Jr.	6
10.	Ponder, William	6
11.	Peterson, David McKelvey	5
12.	Thaw, William	5

Note:

Those Escadrille aces who later transferred to the American flying units with the Army Air Service will also be found listed with the World War I aces in the next chapter.

American aviators who served with the Lafayette Escadrille (French Combat Squadron 124) from its formation on 16 April 1916 until 8 February 1918 when it was transferred to the United States Air Service.

NAME	DATE OF ENTRY	
Thenault, Georges, Capt.	16 Apr. 1916	French Commander of the Lafayette Escadrille
De Laage de Meux, Alfred, Lt.	16 Apr. 1916	French Second-in-Command, killed in accident 23 May 1917
Chapman, Victor	20 Apr. 1916	Killed in combat 23 June 1916
McConnel, James R.	20 Apr. 1916	Killed in combat on 19 March 1917
Prince, Norman	20 Apr. 1916	Injured in accident 12 October 1916, died of the injuries 15 October 1916
Rockwell, Kiffin Yates	20 Apr. 1916	Killed in combat on 23 September 1916
Cowdin, Elliot C.	28 Apr. 1916	Transferred to the U. S. Air Service
Hall, Bert	28 Apr. 1916	Remained with the French Air Service
Thaw, William	28 Apr. 1916	Transferred to the U. S. Air Service
Lufbery, Raoul	24 May 1916	Transferred to the U. S. Air Service, killed in combat 19 May 1918
Balsley, H. Clyde	28 May 1916	Transferred to the U. S. Air Service, wounded in action —retired
Johnson, Charles Chouteau	29 May 1916	Transferred to the U. S. Air Service
Rumsey, Lawrence	4 June 1916	Failed physical exam. for U. S. Air Service
Hill, Dudley L.	9 June 1916	Transferred to the U. S. Air Service
Massen, Didier	19 June 1916	Remained in the French Air Service
Pavelka, Paul	11 Aug. 1916	Killed in accident 11 November 1917
Rockwell, Robert L.	17 Sept. 1916	Transferred to the U. S. Air Service
Haviland, Willis B.	22 Oct. 1916	Transferred to the U. S. Naval Air Service
Prince, Frederick H., Jr.	22 Oct. 1916	Transferred to the U. S. Quartermaster Corps
Soubiran, Robert	22 Oct. 1916	Transferred to the U. S. Air Service
Heskier, Ronald Wood	10 Dec. 1916	Killed in combat 12 April 1917
Genet, Edmond C.	19 Jan. 1917	Shot down and killed by anti-aircraft fire 16 April 1917
Parsons, Edwin C.	27 Jan. 1917	Remained in the French Air Service

NAME	DATE OF ENTRY	
Bigelow, Stephen	8 Feb. 1917	Wounded in action 20 August 1917
Hinkle, Edward F.	1 Mar. 1917	Released due to illness
Lovell, Walter	1 Mar. 1917	Transferred to the U. S. Air Service
Willis, Harold B.	1 Mar. 1917	Remained in the French Air Service
Dugan, William E., Jr.	30 Mar. 1917	Transferred to the U. S. Air Service
Hewitt, Thomas M., Jr.	30 Mar. 1917	Transferred to the U. S. Infantry
Marr, Kenneth	30 Mar. 1917	Transferred to the U. S. Air Service
Rocle, Marius R.	30 Mar. 1917	Transferred to the U. S. Air Service
Campbell, A. Courtney	15 Apr. 1917	Killed in combat 1 October 1917
Bridgman, Ray C.	2 May 1917	Transferred to the U. S. Air Service
Dolan, Charles H., Jr.	12 May 1917	Transferred to the U. S. Air Service
Drexel, John Armstrong	12 May 1917	Transferred to the U. S. Air Service
Jones, Henry S.	12 May 1917	Transferred to the U. S. Air Service
Hall, James Norman	16 June 1917	Transferred to the U. S. Air Service
MacMonagle, Douglas	16 June 1917	Killed in combat 24 September 1917
Peterson, David McKelvey	16 June 1917	Transferred to the U. S. Air Service, killed in combat 16 March 1918
Doolittle, James Ralph	3 July 1917	Killed in accident 17 July 1917
Zinn, Frederick W.	22 Oct. 1917	Transferred to the U. S. Air Service
Ford, Christopher W.	7 Nov. 1917	Transferred to the U. S. Air Service
Collins, Phelps	7 Jan. 1918	Transferred to the U. S. Air Service, killed in combat 12 March 1918
Baer, Paul F.	10 Jan. 1918	Transferred to the U. S. Air Service
Biddle, Charles J.	10 Jan. 1918	Transferred to the U. S. Air Service
Wilcox, Charles H.	26 Jan. 1918	Transferred to the U. S. Air Service
Turnure, George E., Jr.	8 Feb. 1918	Transferred to the U. S. Air Service

3

AMERICA IN WORLD WAR I

Army Aviation

WHEN AMERICA WENT to war in April 1917, the Air Service had but two small flying fields and no plans for training the thousands of aviators who would be needed in Europe. But greased by the urgencies of war the creaking wheels of military aviation began to spin. By the third week in May, schools of military aeronautics were opened in five universities: the University of California, the University of Illinois, the University of Texas, Cornell University and Princeton University—each school set up to handle over a thousand students.

To these ground schools, and the flying schools to which qualified cadets were to progress, young Americans began to flock. For more than a year after the declaration of war, applications for the Air Service poured into the War Department by the tens of thousands. This had not been expected, although Congress had passed special legislation offering extra pay and rank for flyers in an effort to make the Air Service especially attractive. What had been overlooked was the high spirit and patriotic fervor of the American youth who yearned to emulate the colorful daredevils and dashing American flyers who, fighting in Europe with the French and English, were filling the front pages with their perilous exploits.

During that next year our aerial military might was organized, trained and carried into battle with the American Expeditionary Forces.

In 1918 the American air force lost its tender feet and gained the respect of the world for its prowess in the air. Brigadier General William Mitchell was in immediate command of the air war and to this man must go credit for the strategical and tactical success of the aerial forces. The observation, reconnaissance, bombardment, and pursuit activities were extensive and the entire employment of air forces was still a new element of war that required fresh vision and military ingenuity.

On 14 April 1918 the first U. S. pursuit unit, the 94th Pursuit Squadron, commenced operations in the Toul sector. On that same day two American flyers, Lieutenants Alan F. Winslow and Douglas Campbell, inaugurated the unit by shooting down two German planes. Because of the excitement at the time over this memorable air victory the War Department released Lieutenant Winslow's personal account of the dogfight.

I had not made a complete half-turn, and was at about 250 meters, when, straight above and ahead of me in the mist of the early morning and not more than a hundred yards away, I saw a plane coming toward me and with high black crosses on its wing and tail. I was so furious to see a Hun directly over our aviation field that I swore out loud and violently opened fire. At the same time, to avoid my bullets, he slipped into a left hand reversement and came down firing on me. I climbed, however, in a right-hand spiral and slipped off, coming down directly behind him and on his tail. Again, I violently opened fire.

I had him at a rare advantage which was due to the greater speed and maneuverability of our wonderful machines. I fired twenty or thirty rounds at him and could see my tracers entering his machine. Then, in another moment, his plane went straight down in an uncontrolled nose-dive. I had put his engine out of commission.

I followed in a straight dive, firing all the way. At about six feet above the ground he tried to regain control of his machine, but could not, and he crashed to the earth. I darted down near him, made a sharp turn by the wreck to make sure that he was out of commission, then made a victorious sweep over him—

This dogfight took place at an altitude of 300 meters or 1,000 feet. One minute later Campbell shot down the second German plane for American victory. After they landed,

Winslow rushed for the spot where he shot down his German plane and reported:

> On the way there—it was only half a mile—I ran into a huge crowd of soldiers—blue and khaki—pressing about one man. I pushed my way through the crowd, and heard somebody triumphantly say to the surrounded man in French:
>
> "There he is; now you will believe he is an American." I looked at the man—a scrawny, poorly clad little devil, dressed in a German uniform. It was the Hun pilot of the machine I had shot down. It seems he would not believe that an American officer had brought him down. He looked me all over, and then asked me in good French if I was an American. When I answered "Yes," he had no more to say.

In the following month three more pursuit squadrons, the 103rd, the 27th and the 95th, were ready to be sent into battle and the four squadrons were formed into the 1st Pursuit Group.

In the relatively stalemated Toul sector the Americans fought a cautious war while learning the techniques of combat. The veteran pilots from the Lafayette Escadrille formed an important bank from which the new pilots drew the experience and the combat know-how to prepare themselves for the more vicious engagements that would soon follow.

Early in July the 1st Pursuit Group was transferred into the Marne sector, where the fighting was heavy and the Germans had a superior number of airplanes. They were on hand for the American counteroffensive and the big push at St. Mihiel. General (then Colonel) Mitchell's brilliantly conceived air organization and his novel war plans were put into full operation. The success of the air service in the offensive is now proud history.

The growing complexities of air operations were changing the tactical aspects of pursuit work and the "lone wolf" who ventured into the blue to engage the enemy in single combat was passing into history—and in many cases, the hereafter.

One of the most spectacular of these vanishing heroes was the "American Wonder" aviator, Lieutenant Frank

Luke. Barely twenty years of age when he entered the Army Air Service, he reported for duty with the 27th Squadron near Château-Thierry in late July 1918. His rise to the position of America's second ace with eighteen planes and balloons to his credit was meteoric. Frank was a quiet boy from the frontier country, a college graduate and a citizen-soldier who loved to fly and loved to fight. He didn't care much for the regimentation of military life and more often than not he would wander from a formation to search out the enemy alone. Early in his combat career it occurred to him that it would be a daring move to vanquish German planes far behind their trenches. His first victory was achieved with this in mind, when, on 6 August 1918, he climbed his plane to an altitude of 15,000 feet and flew deep into German territory. Far below he saw a formation of six planes preparing to land at their airdrome. Luke put his plane into a dive and, traveling at a speed of nearly 200 miles an hour, opened fire on one of the enemy planes, sending it crashing to the ground. Remaining at 2,000 feet he took advantage of the air speed he had gained in the dive to carry him safely home ahead of the surprised and angered German pilots.

He later took up what eventually became his specialty: shooting down enemy observation balloons. This was especially dangerous because they were heavily protected by anti-aircraft units. However, he developed what he called the "dusk attack" and played havoc with the German observers.

At sundown, on 15 September 1918, with his close friend and occasional flying companion Lieutenant Wehner, before a prearranged grandstand audience of Brigadier William Mitchell and his staff, the two men shot down two balloons over Verdun. General Mitchell recalled that when he had looked over their planes after their mission he counted over fifty bullet holes in each ship.

Luke was skillful, yet reckless. He never avoided a fight and loved the glory of his deeds. In his duels behind enemy lines he would often lose official credit for his skills so he prepared a blank form which he presented to the Allied observers after each victory. Upon shooting down an aircraft he would land close to the nearest balloon observer and present his blank form to be filled in with the date, type of destroyed aircraft and certifying signature.

On 18 September 1918 Luke and Wehner were busy shooting down balloons when Luke was jumped by six Fokkers. Wehner, seeing this, flew in firing his machine gun. A seventh Fokker lurking above dove in on Wehner and in one pass shot him down in flames. Frank Luke never recovered from the loss of his dearest friend and with vengeance in his sad heart he sought out and destroyed the Germans with a doubled fury.

On 29 September, barely two months and eighteen enemy aircraft after his arrival in combat, he made his last flight. Flying over an American airdrome he dropped a message asking that they watch three distant German observation balloons that he was about to destroy. Good to his word he had downed two of the balloons, when he was attacked by ten German planes. Undaunted by the combined attack, Luke went into the fight sending two of the enemy down in flames. Then, apparently out of control, his own machine dropped; but it was only a ruse for soon he zoomed back to attack the last balloon. His attack was successful, but the heavy anti-aircraft cannons and machine guns protecting the balloons had peppered his plane. Lieutenant Luke was badly wounded, yet with the ferocity of a tiger he continued to lash out at the enemy. For his bravery that day he was awarded the Congressional Medal of Honor, and in the accompanying citation his last deadly blow at the enemy is best described:

. . . Severely wounded, he descended to within 50 meters of the ground; and flying at this low altitude near the town of Murvaux, opened fire upon enemy troops, killing 6 and wounding as many more. Forced to make a landing and surrounded on all sides by enemy who called upon him to surrender, he drew his automatic pistol and defended himself gallantly until he fell dead from a wound in the chest.

Luke Air Force Base in Arizona was named in honor of this man.

Of the aces to emerge from the air war in that year of 1918, the greatest was Captain Edward Rickenbacker, who not only was an extraordinary pursuit pilot, but also had a knack for leadership that made his squadron, as well as himself, famous.

When the United States entered the war, Rickenbacker had offered to recruit racing drivers, believing that they would make outstanding aviators because of their knowledge of engines and high-precision speed. His idea was turned down, and his own enlistment was rejected because of inadequate education and experience. Undaunted, Rick started in France as General Pershing's staff driver and after much begging was allowed to join a flight unit in France. He became an engineering officer and for many months his commanding officer, Major Carl A. Spaatz, refused to allow him to become a combat pilot because his services were so valuable. In March 1918, he was finally assigned as a flyer to the "Hat-in-the-Ring Squadron" under Major Raoul Lufbery. He saw his first enemy for combat on 25 April 1918.

Rickenbacker had patience acquired from his racing-car days. He was daring and fearless, but never reckless.

In Captain Rickenbacker's own words we have a picture of the victorious flyer as a personality. After his first victory he recounted:

No sooner had I altered my line of flight than the German pilot saw me leave the sun's rays. Hall was already half-way to him when he stuck up his nose and began furiously climbing to the upper ceiling. I let him pass me and found myself on the other side just as Hall began firing. I doubt if the Boche had seen Hall's Nieuport at all.

Surprised by discovering this new antagonist, Hall, ahead of him, the Pfalz immediately abandoned all idea of a battle and banking around to the right started for home, just as I had expected him to do. In a trice I was on his tail. Down, down we sped with throttles both full open. Hall was coming on somewhere in my rear. The Boche had no heart for evolutions or maneuvers. He was running like a scared rabbit, as I had run from Campbell. I was gaining upon him every instant and had my sights trained dead upon his seat before I fired my first shot.

At 150 yards I pressed my triggers. The tracer bullets cut a streak of living fire into the rear of the Pfalz tail. Raising the nose of my aeroplane slightly the fiery streak lifted itself like the stream of water pouring from a

36

garden hose. Gradually it settled into the pilot's seat. The swerving of the Pfalz course indicated that its rudder no longer was held by a directing hand. At 2000 feet above the enemy's lines I pulled up my headlong dive and watched the enemy machine continuing on its course. Curving slightly to the left the Pfalz circled a little to the south and the next minute crashed onto the ground just at the edge of the woods a mile inside their own lines. I had brought down my first enemy aeroplane and had not been subjected to a single shot!

Hall was immediately beside me. He was evidently as pleased as I was over our success, for he danced his machine about in incredible maneuvers. And then I realized that old friend Archy was back on the job. We were not two miles away from the German anti-aircraft batteries and they put a furious bombardment of shrapnel all about us. I was quite ready to call it a day and go home, but Captain Hall deliberately returned to the barrage and entered it with me at his heels. Machine guns and rifle fire from the trenches greeted us and I do not mind admitting that I got out quickly the way I came in without any unnecessary delay, but Hall continued to do stunts over their heads for ten minutes, surpassing all the acrobatics that the enraged Boches had ever seen over their own peaceful aerodromes.

Jimmy exhausted his spirits at about the time the Huns had exhausted all their available ammunition and we started blithely for home. Swooping down to our field side by side, we made a quick landing and taxied our victorious machines up to the hangars. Then jumping out we ran to each other, extending flat hands for our first exchange of congratulations. And then we noticed that the squadron pilots and mechanics were streaming across the aerodrome towards us from all directions. They had heard the news while we were still dodging shrapnel and were hastening out to welcome our return. The French had telephoned in a confirmation of my first victory, before I had had time to reach home. Not a single bullet hole had punctured any part of my machine.

There is a peculiar gratification in receiving congratulations from one's squadron for a victory in the air. It is worth more to a pilot than the applause of the whole outside world. It means that one has won the confidence of men who share the misgivings, the aspirations, the trials and the dangers of aeroplane fighting. And with each victory comes a, renewal and re-cementing of ties that bind together these brothers-in-arms. No closer fraternity exists in the world than that of the air fighters in this great war. And I have yet to find one single individual who has attained conspicuous success in bringing down enemy aeroplanes who can be said to be spoiled either by his successes or by the generous congratulations of his comrades. If he were capable of being spoiled he would not have had the character to have won continuous victories, for the smallest amount of vanity is fatal in aeroplane fighting. Self-distrust rather is the quality to which many a pilot owes his protracted existence.

By 1 June 1918, Rickenbacker had become an ace. During the following summer he suffered from a mastoid infection and spent two months in a hospital in Paris. Returning he made his big splurge and became an "ace of aces" alongside Lufbery.

From the beginning the 94th Pursuit Squadron had been commanded by top-flight combat flyers. Major Raoul Lufbery was its first commander and at his death the squadron was taken over by another former Escadrille flyer, Captain James Norman Hall. Captain Hall was shot down 7 May 1918, but was later returned with the prisoners of war after the signing of the Armistice. (After the war Hall and another Air Service pilot, Captain Charles Nordhoff, wrote a number of books, among them the well-read *Mutiny on the Bounty*.)

On 25 September 1918, Lieutenant Colonel Harold Hartney, 1st Pursuit Group Commander, placed Eddie Rickenbacker into this select group by giving him command of the 94th (Hat-in-the-Ring) Pursuit Squadron. He selected Rick over several superiors because he thought Rickenbacker was more mature, had a better knowledge of engines, and was an exceptional aerial fighter. General Mitchell didn't like the idea of Rick jumping men with more time in grade and service, but he gave his approval on Hartney's insistence. Hartney's judgment proved excellent as Rick served well, shooting down twenty more planes and leading his squadron to victories and honor.

By the end of the war Rickenbacker's squadron led all

the others with sixty-nine confirmed victories. He would never ask a pilot under him to go on a mission that he himself would not undertake. Contrary to the practice in other units Rickenbacker made no attempt to stimulate rivalry between members of the group, but rather appealed to the competitive spirit of the group as a whole against other American Pursuit Squadrons.

Rickenbacker was fascinated by the chance to pit his confidence and experience against those of German aviators and beating them at the game. He tried to make combat a sporting proposition, resolving "never to shoot at a Hun who is at a disadvantage, regardless of what he would do if he were in my position." It has been said that in no other squadron in France was there so much loyalty to a leader, so much squadron fraternalism, such subordination of the individual to the organization. Rickenbacker taught and practiced the "buddy system" in combat, believing that his men should learn to look after each other.

In one engagement Rickenbacker discovered Meissner diving after a German plane with a second German plane diving after Meissner. Rickenbacker immediately dived on the second plane, chasing it away and relieving the pursuit. Both weary pursuits escaped.

A few minutes later, Meissner was sent out with a patrol to protect a British bombing squadron returning from behind the German lines. A German patrol of six planes—two biplanes and four monoplanes—suddenly swooped down on the British airmen. The Americans dashed to the rescue and a free-for-all fight ensued five miles behind the German lines.

A German plane collided with Meissner's plane and was damaged so badly, it fell. The top wing of Meissner's plane was torn off, and he started to struggle homeward.

As Meissner was nearing the American line, a German biplane attacked him. He was unable to maneuver and was in grave danger. Rickenbacker, who singlehanded was dogfighting five German planes and winning, saw Meissner struggling to escape his pursuers. Leaving the enemy he had in his sights he drove straight for the Boche, forcing him to the ground and saving Meissner's life for the second time within one hour.

Rickenbacker and his men fought together, forming their skills into precision squadron teamwork. Rick combined courage with a rare appreciation of the fine points of tactical air warfare. He led, rather than drove, his pilots, making his Hat-in-the-Ring Squadron the most lethal pursuit unit at the front, and his own combat record was still growing when the Armistice came.

After the war, Rickenbacker became associated with the automobile business, during which time he returned to the racing world by obtaining control and becoming President of the Indianapolis Motor Speedway. While with Cadillac Motor Division of General Motors Corporation, he was instrumental in their purchasing control of Fokker Aircraft and became active once again in areonautics when he was transferred to that division. He later joined Aviation Corporation as Vice President of American Airways. Then when General Motors took over control of Eastern Air Lines, he returned to that company and in 1934 was made General Manager. In 1938, through untiring efforts he was able to obtain funds to purchase it from General Motors in order to keep it as an entity for the men who had pioneered it from the beginning. Rickenbacker is still head of this vast air line as Chairman of the Board and General Manager.

NAVAL AVIATION

In 1917, United States naval aviation was barely unfolding its fledgling wings. The 1911-12 Naval Appropriation Act included $25,000 for aviation, scarcely more than a promise so far as development was concerned. Two years later, the Aeronautical Board's recommended budget of $1,297,000 was cut by almost three-fourths. Upon our entry into the European conflict, the Navy had thirty-eight pilots and fifty-four planes. Scouting missions over the city of Vera Cruz in 1914 had provided the only "combat" experience. The Navy's war record in aviation began in June 1917, when a small detachment of naval aviators landed at Bordeaux to become the first United States fighting force in Europe. The activity of naval aviation units, necessarily somewhat limited, was in French or British planes until May 1918. Nevertheless, a well-knit, trained and competent air nucleus was born of World War I to grow and to spread its mighty wings like a giant eagle over a world-wide battle arena within twenty-five years.

Captain Washington Irving Chambers, the father of naval aviation, was the first of a long line of great naval aviation leaders. In the early years the Navy was interested in the airplane because of its scouting use. Obviously, an airplane would have to be adapted for flight from the water or from the deck of a vessel. Glenn Curtiss began working on a pontoon for a hydroplane; Chambers worked on the flight from a vessel idea. A wooden take-off platform was constructed over the forward deck of the USS *Birmingham*. A Curtiss contract pilot, Eugene Ely, in November 1910 at Hampton Roads, Virginia, flew the 83-foot length of the deck and dropped from sight. To everyone's amazement the plane reappeared leveling off, touched its wheels to the water once, and bounced into the air to continue skyward to be the first carrier take-off. In January 1911 he accomplished the first landing on the opposite coast in San Francisco Bay. Ely took off from shore and landed on a wooden platform built aboard the USS *Pennsylvania*. Then came Curtiss' development of the hydroplane which was developed with a catapult launching for use aboard smaller ships at sea.

Before the United States entered the war, an intense interest in naval aviation was evidenced in several of the Eastern universities, particularly at Yale and Princeton. Among these interested young men was F. Trubee Davison, who organized the First Yale Unit, a group of college students who trained, learned to fly and eventually became incorporated into the Naval Reserve as an entire unit.

Along with Trubee Davison (who eventually became Assistant Secretary of War for Air) there were several other enthusiastic young men whose work and energy made the existence of the unit possible. Among these were Artemus Gates (who later became Under Secretary of Navy), Robert Lovett (who later became Secretary of Defense) and David Ingalls who became the Navy's only World War I ace (and later Assistant Secretary of Navy for Air).

This unit, which trained itself, purchasing and training in its own airplanes, received official Naval Reserve status under the Appropriations Act of 1916. This act, while giving the unit authorization, provided no funds; nevertheless the young men stuck fast and at their own expense participated in Naval Reserve maneuvers that year in Gravesend

Bay. Early in 1917 the backers of the unit, including the Yale president, pressed the Navy to activate the First Yale Unit. They met with Lieutenant Jack Towers, a young naval airman, who was immediately sold on the cause and proceeded to Washington, D. C., to champion for the Yale flying unit. The top people in the Navy, respecting Towers' judgment, agreed on the merits of the plan but could not see taking immediate action for training on active duty. Towers and his Old Eli backers went to the office of the Assistant Secretary of Navy. The Secretary, a youthful, intelligent man, spoke with them in terms that showed he knew well enough that U. S. entry into the European war was inevitable and he was impressed with the need for units like the Yale flying club on immediate active duty. That secretary, Franklin Delano Roosevelt, ordered the unit into active reserve status and flight training at Pensacola. That was a happy day for the young Yale men, save one, David Ingalls, who, although he was the best pilot of the Yale Unit, was only seventeen years of age.

Young Ingalls went into training with the First Yale Unit as a civilian amidst the naval personnel. He flew on odd hour flights when the regular Navy people weren't close at hand. The First Unit graduated and young Dave took up with the Second Yale Unit in training. The Second Unit graduated, and Dave stayed behind. The Third Unit started training and poor Dave went through the same routine, getting flying time whenever he could. Finally time cured the defect—Dave turned eighteen, and he proceeded through the training as a full-fledged Naval Reservist and became Naval Aviator #85. The tenacity and fortitude displayed by Ingalls marked him as a future Navy great.

Another university group, the First Princeton Naval Unit, which trained with the Royal Flying Corps in the summer at Toronto and in the winter in Texas, had as one of its flyers James Forrestal who was in World War II to become Secretary of the Navy and later to die at his post as the first Secretary of Defense.

When the units went to war with the United States forces in France, the Navy had four squadrons in action, called the Northern Bombing Group which worked the French northern coastal area. The group consisted of a Marine Corps Day Wing and a Navy Night Wing, the Navy

Night Wing commanded by Lieutenant Robert Lovett. Their primary mission other than coastal patrol was to bomb German submarine pens (bases).

The Navy and Marine pilots weren't content with mild coastal patrol missions, so during off-duty hours they went over to nearby French and British pursuit bases and checked out in the hot, single-seater planes. They developed great friendships with the British and French and one thing led to another until one day a Navy night-duty pilot was sneaking in day-combat flights with the French. The French Escadrille were constantly short of pilots and whenever they were short one for a patrol flight, an American would then fill the empty cockpit. Nineteen-year-old David Ingalls was one of these Americans. Dave had been flying Sopwith Camels for British Camel Squadron #213 since April 1918 on a spare-time basis and on 18 July 1918 he shot down a German Rumpler two-seater. Before returning to the field, a thirty-minute flight, the Navy brass on the coast had the report of the kill and upon landing Dave was told to stop his double-shift flying and to his surprise the shift he was to stop was the one with the Navy. He was now officially on TDY (temporary duty) full time with the British 213th Squadron. On 21 July, the teen-aged David Ingalls led a British flight on a bombing and strafing mission of the German airdrome Varsenaere, 20 miles behind the lines. Leadership of such daring flights usually went to old pursuit veterans rather than nineteen-year-old pilots but the British respected ability rather than age in their pilots. (Captain Albert Ball, a British pilot, had shot down forty-three German planes and won the Victoria Cross—equivalent to our Congressional Medal of Honor—at the age of nineteen.) On this mission the ingenious Ingalls had his flight cut their engines and glide the last five miles to the German airdrome. Caught unaware, the German airdrome and its aircraft were severely damaged. That night the British made Ingalls a flight commander of the 213th. On the 24th he got his second kill—an observation balloon. A few days later he got another Rumpler and within a fortnight, two more victories—to achieve acedom.

The Navy had one of its World War I combat airmen receive the Medal of Honor. Ensign Charles H. Hammann, the recipient, received the honor:

For extraordinary heroism as a pilot of a seaplane on 21 August 1918, when with three other planes Ensign Hammann took part in a patrol and attacked a superior force of enemy land planes. In the course of the engagement which followed the plane of Ensign George M. Ludlow was shot down and fell in the water 5 miles off Pola. Ensign Hammann immediately dived down and landed on the water close alongside the disabled machine, where he took Ludlow on board. Although his machine was not designed for the double load to which it was subjected, and although there was danger of attack by Austrian planes, he made his way to Porto Corsini.

MARINE AVIATION

Marine Corps aviation was first organized within the naval establishment in 1915. One year later the Marines had five pilots who were also rated with the Navy. Marine Pilot #1 was Lieutenant Alfred A. Cunningham and Marine Pilot #2 was Lieutenant Bernard I. Smith. By 1917 one more pilot was added to the original five to make a total of six. The Naval Appropriations Act of 1915 had set up a 4 to 1 ratio of Navy pilots to Marine pilots. It also had been established that the primary mission of the Marine air arm was to supply air support to amphibious operations; this was to be conducted from land bases. However, later in World War II the Navy assigned some small escort carriers (Boxer type) for operational use by the Marines. The Naval Air Stations at Corpus Christi, Texas, and Pensacola, Florida, now allow graduating pilots to choose either Navy or Marine Corps service.

Marine Corps pilots saw some activity in World War I. On 30 July 1918, Cunningham, who had been made Commander of Marine Aviation, arrived at Brest, France, with three squadrons of Marine aviators, but alack and alas, no airplanes (or aeroplanes as they were called at that time). While waiting for planes the Marine pilots were assigned to British Squadrons 217 and 218 for proficiency flying. They were formed into the Day Wing of the Northern Bombing Group. The British aviation organization had from three to five wings to a group while the American aviation organization had from three to five groups in a wing. (The British group and the American wing during

World War I were equal in aircraft strength.) After World War II the United States converted to the British designation system.

The United States Marine Day Wing was officially credited with destroying four enemy aircraft in World War I using the DH-4 aircraft exclusively. Two of its flyers, Talbot and Robinson, were awarded the Congressional Medal of Honor.

The award to Talbot read:

For exceptionally meritorious service and extraordinary heroism while attached to Squadron C, First Marine Aviation Force, in France. Second Lieutenant Talbot participated in numerous air raids into enemy territory. On 8 October 1918, while on such a raid, he was attacked by nine enemy scouts, and in the fight that followed shot down an enemy plane. Also, on 14 October 1918, while on a raid over Pittham, Belgium, Lieutenant Talbot and another plane became detached from the formation on account of motor trouble, and were attacked by 12 enemy scouts. During the severe fight that followed, his plane shot down one of the enemy scouts. His observer was shot through the elbow and his gun jammed. Second Lieutenant Talbot maneuvered to gain time for his observer to clear the jam with one hand, and then returned to the fight. The observer fought until shot twice, once in the stomach and once in the hip. When he collapsed, Lieutenant Talbot attacked the nearest enemy scout with his front guns and shot him down. With his observer unconscious and his motor failing, he dived to escape the balance of the enemy and crossed the German trenches at an altitude of 50 feet, landing at the nearest hospital to leave his observer, and then returned to his aerodrome.

Robinson's citation read:

For extraordinary heroism as Observer in the First Marine Aviation Force at the Front in France. In company with planes from Squadron 218, Royal Air Force, conducting an air raid on 8 October 1918, Gunnery Sergeant Robinson's plane was attacked by nine enemy scouts. In the fight which followed, he shot down one

45

of the enemy planes. In a later air raid over Pittham, Belgium, on 14 October 1918, his plane and one other became separated from their formation on account of motor trouble and were attacked by 12 enemy scouts. Acting with conspicuous gallantry and intrepidity in the fight which ensued, Gunnery Sergeant Robinson, after shooting down one of the enemy planes, was struck by a bullet which carried away most of his elbow. At the same time his gun jammed. While his pilot maneuvered for position, he cleared the jam with one hand and returned to the fight. Although his left arm was useless, he fought off the enemy scouts until he collapsed after receiving two more bullet wounds, one in the stomach and one in the thigh.

One of the Marine flyers from the First World War, Lieutenant Colgate W. Darden, Jr., later became Governor of Virginia and after that, president of the University of Virginia.

RECORDS OF U. S. ACES—WORLD WAR I

NAME	RANK	ORGN.	AIRPLANES	BALLOONS	TOTAL	HOME-TOWN
Rickenbacker, Edward V.	Captain	94	22	4	26	Columbus, Ohio
Luke, Frank, Jr.*	2nd Lt.	27	4	14	18	Phoenix, Ariz.
Lufbery, Raoul G.[1]	Major	94	17		17	Wallingford, Conn.
Vaughn, George A.	1st Lt.	17	12	1	13	Brooklyn, N. Y.
Kindley, Field E.*	Captain	148	12		12	Gravette, Ark.
Putnam, David E.*	1st Lt.	139	12		12	Boston, Mass.
Springs, Elliott W.	Captain	148	12		12	Lancaster, S. C.
Landis, Reed G.	Captain	25 (40th-RAF)	9	1	10	Washington, D. C.
Swaab, Jacques M.	Captain	22	10		10	New York, N. Y.
Baer, Paul F.	1st Lt.	103	9		9	Ft. Wayne, Ind.
Cassady, Thomas G.	Captain	28	9		9	Spencer, Ind.
Wright, Chester E.	1st Lt.	93	8	1	9	Cambridge, Mass.
Beane, James D.*	1st Lt.	22	6	2	8	Concord, Mass.
Clay, Henry R., Jr.*	1st Lt.	148	8		8	Fort Worth, Texas
Coolidge, Hamilton*	Captain	94	5	3	8	Boston, Mass.
Creech, Jesse O.	1st Lt.	148	8		8	Washington, D. C.
Donaldson, John Owen	Captain	RAF (22)	7	1	8	Greenville, S. C.
Erwin, William P.	1st. Lt.	1 (Observ.)	8		8	New York, N. Y.
Hamilton, Lloyd A.	1st. Lt.	17	5	3	8	Burlington, Vt.
Hunter, Frank O'D.	1st Lt.	103	7	1	8	Savannah, Ga.
Jones, Clinton	2nd Lt.	22	8		8	San Francisco, Calif.
Meissner, James A.	Major	94	7	1	8	Brooklyn, N. Y.
Wehner, Joseph Fritz*	1st Lt.	27	2	6	8	Boston, Mass.
White, Wilbur Wallace*	1st Lt.	147	7	1	8	New York, N. Y.
Biddle, Charles J.	Major	13	7		7	Andalusia, Pa.
Burdick, Howard	1st Lt.	17	7		7	Brooklyn, N. Y.
Chambers, Reid M.	Major	94	6	1	7	Memphis, Tenn.
Cook, Harvey Weir	Captain	94	4	3	7	Toledo, Ohio
Holden, Lansing C.	1st Lt.	95	2	5	7	New York, N. Y.

RECORDS OF U. S. ACES—WORLD WAR I (continued)

NAME	RANK	ORGN.	AIRPLANES	BALLOONS	TOTAL	HOME-TOWN
Huffer, John	Major	103	7		7	Washington, D. C.
Larner, Defreest Gorman	Captain	103	7		7	Fort Smith, Ark.
Robertson, Wendel A.	1st Lt.	139	7		7	Newark, N. J.
Rummel, Leslie J.	1st Lt.	147	7		7	Indianapolis, Ind.
Schoen, Karl J.*	1st Lt.	139	5	2	7	Bath, Mo.
Sewall, Sumner	Captain	95	7		7	Stovall, Miss.
Stovall, William H.	1st Lt.	13	7		7	Denver, Colo.
Vasconelles, Jerry C.	Captain	27	6	1	7	Milford, Texas
Baucom, B. V.	1st Lt.	1st (ob.)	6		6	Framingham, Mass.
Brooks, Arthur R.	Captain	139	6		6	Mt. Hamilton, Calif.
Campbell, Douglas	Captain	94	6		6	Rochester, N. Y.
Curtiss, Edward Peck	Captain	95	6		6	Port Flagler, Wash.
Esterbrook, Arthur E.	1st Lt.	1st (ob.)	6		6	Mobile, Ala.
Guthrie, Murray K.	1st Lt.	13	6		6	Colfax, Iowa
Hall, James Norman[2]	Captain	94	6		6	San Francisco, Calif.
Hammond, Leonard C.	Captain	91	6		6	New York, N. Y.
Hartney, Harold E.[3]	Lt. Col.	27	6		6	Chicago, Ill.
Hayes, Frank K.	1st Lt.	??	6		6	New York, N. Y.
Hudson, Donald	1st Lt.	27	6		6	
Keating, James A.	Major	??	6		6	Carlinsville, Ill.
Knotts, Howard C.	2nd Lt.	17	6		6	Maderson, N. C.
Lindsay, Robert O.	1st Lt.	139	6		6	Buffalo, N. Y.
McArthur, John K.*	2nd Lt.	27	6		6	
McClure, David M.	1st Lt.	27	6		6	Nogales, Ariz.
O'Neil, Ralph A.	1st Lt.	147	6		6	Mangum, Okla.
Ponder, William T.	1st Lt.	103	6		6	Dowagiac, Mich.
Porter, Kenneth L.	2nd Lt.	147	6		6	Tevin Valley, Minn.
Stenseth, Martinus	Captain	28	6		6	San Antonio, Texas
Tobin, Edgar G.	Captain	103	6		6	

Name	Rank	Sqdn.				Home Town
Vernam, Remington D.*	1st Lt.	22	3	3	6	New York, N. Y.
Badham, William T.	1st Lt.	91	5		5	Birmingham, Ala.
Baer, Herbert L.	1st Lt.	RAF (24)	5		5	Fort Wayne, Ind.
Bissell, Clayton	Captain	148	5	1	5	Kane, Pa.
Buckley, Harold R.	Captain	95	4		5	Agawam, Mass.
Calahan, Lawrence R.	1st Lt.	148	5		5	Chicago, Ill.
Cook, Everett R.	Captain	91	5	1	5	San Francisco, Calif.
Furlow, George W.	1st Lt.	103	5		5	Rochester, Minn.
George, Harold H.	1st Lt.	139	5		5	Niagara Falls, N. Y.
Gray, Charles G.	Captain	213	4	1	5	Chicago, Ill.
Haight, Edward M.	1st Lt.	139	5		5	New York, N. Y.
Healy, James A.	Captain	147	5		5	Jersey City, N. J.
Ingalls, David S.[4]	Ensign		5		5	New York, N. Y.
Knowles, James	1st Lt.	95	5		5	Cambridge, Mass.
Luff, Frederick E.	1st Lt.	25	3	2	5	Cleveland, Ohio
Miller, Zenos R.	1st Lt.	27	4	1	5	Baltimore, Md.
Owens, J. Sidney	2nd Lt.	139	5		5	Honesdale, Pa.
Peterson, David McK.[5]	Captain	9	5		5	Lincoln, Nebr.
Ralston, Orville A.	1st Lt.	148	5		5	Chicago, Ill.
Seerley, John, Jr.	1st Lt.	13	5		5	Evanston, Ill.
Strahm, Victor H.	Major	91	5	1	5	New York, N. Y.
Symonds, Francis M.	1st Lt.	147	4		5	Pittsburgh, Pa.
Thaw, William	Lt. Col.	103	5	1	5	Cincinnati, Ohio
Todd, Robert M.	1st Lt.	17	4		5	Everett, Mass.
Williams, Rodney D.	1st Lt.	17	4	1	5	

* Killed in combat.

1 Lufbery gained his seventeen officially credited victories with the Lafayette Escadrille. All seventeen were shot down over the German lines; he had twenty-three more shot down behind the German lines, but during the war did not receive official credit for them because of the scoring rules used at that time.

2 Hall is co-author of *Mutiny on the Bounty* and *Hurricane.*

3 Hartney received five of his six official victories while flying with the British Expeditionary Forces. Later in the war he was the commander of the 1st Pursuit Group.

4 Ingalls was assigned to a U. S. Coastal Patrol Squadron and flew with the British at the front in his spare time.

5 Peterson gained one of his five official victories while flying with the French Air Forces.

49

4

THE FLYING TIGERS

THE AMERICAN VOLUNTEER Group in China—the Flying Tigers—generated thirty-nine American aces during the short span of its combat history; yet the one man more instrumental in the destruction of enemy aircraft than any one of the individual aces did not himself shoot down a single plane. This man was Claire Chennault.

Claire Chennault left his job as principal of a small Texas high school to enlist in the Army Air Service in 1917. After the war he stayed in the service and served for twenty years in many exciting and useful capacities. He was a daring acrobatic stunt pilot and a recognized leader in the field of precision air-to-air and air-to-ground pursuit maneuvers. Even in the sluggish pace of the peace-time military his thoughts were constantly on the improvement and development of new fighter strategy. During his tour as an instructor with the Air Corps Tactical School at Maxwell Field, Alabama, he wrote a textbook on the subject, *The Role of Defensive Pursuit*, which the school published in 1935. Also while at Maxwell he became the leader of an aerobatic act called "Three Men on a Flying Trapeze." In this act, with Lieutenants Haywood S. Hansell and John H. Williamson and later with Lieutenant William C. McDonald replacing Hansell, Chennault performed at Cleveland's National Air Races in 1934 and 1935.

But the many years of flying in open airplanes had gradually damaged his ears, causing partial deafness; so in 1937 Chennault was retired from active duty in the permanent rank of captain.

With thoughts of more leisurely occupations and of comfortably settling down, Chennault had taken his wife and eight children to Louisiana when he received the amazing offer of full command of the Chinese Air Force.

Six years had passed since the Japanese octopus had begun to stretch and spread its armed tentacles into the provinces of China. In 1931 the Japanese Army had swept into Manchuria; in 1932 Shanghai had fallen; and now in 1937 the Imperial Army of Japan stood poised for her big invasion into the heart of the Chinese mainland.

As early as 1932 Colonel John H. Jouett, a West Point graduate and famous balloon commander in World War I, had begun the work of organizing the Chinese Air Force along a U. S. design, but development had been slow. In 1936 McDonald and Williamson, Chennault's old friends of the "Three Men on a Flying Trapeze," had gone to China at the invitation of Madame Chiang Kai-shek, the National Secretary of Aviation, to organize a flying school. But now the Japanese serpent was coiled to strike, and there was still no Chinese air force to meet the pending onslaught. Under the urgings of McDonald and Williamson, plus another old Air Corps friend, Roy Holbrook, Captain Chennault accepted the Chinese offer and went to the Orient with the Chinese rank of colonel.

He arrived at Kunming Field, located in a valley beneath the She-shan Mountains, in July 1937 slightly behind the Japanese attack on Peiping, to find that his air force was only a miserable handful of obsolete aircraft manned by a few Chinese and professional-international pilots. Nevertheless, their training had been good, and a well-conceived skeleton organization had been established. Colonel Chennault was not discouraged for he was determined to teach and employ his own advanced concepts of aerial warfare, and to build the Chinese organization along the lines of his own theories of pursuit tactics.

Madame Chiang Kai-shek purchased for Chennault's personal use a $50,000 Curtiss-Wright P-36 which he used extensively to observe from the air the training of his men and the development of their dogfight tactics.

To protect his embryo air force from Japanese air raids he instituted a Chinese radio warning system. Radio lookout stations were established along the Japanese bombing route from the advance Japanese air base at Hanoi, Indo-China, to his own Kunming Field. As the stations warned of oncoming enemy bombers, the Chinese planes were air evacuated and dispersed throughout the countryside. This warning system was considered so effective that the United

States War Department reported that "the Chinese headquarters was warned of a raid while the Japanese bombers were still warming up at their bases." It was among the earliest successful early warning air-raid systems.

Among the American people there was a great deal of sympathy for the sufferings of the Chinese people as the victorious Japanese Army overran and ravaged their country. Early in 1941 this sympathy had concrete expression in the granting of a hundred Curtiss-Wright P-40B Tomahawks to China. (Later models used by the United States were the P-40E Kittyhawk and the P-40F Warhawk.) However, the grant made no provision for parts or replacements, so whenever one of the crates containing a wing was dropped into the water during the loading process, it was carefully salvaged for what use could still be made of it. Later a hundred liquid-cooled Allison engines, which had been rejected by the Air Corps because of minor faults, were acquired by the Chinese. Dr. T. V. Soong, head of the Bank of China and brother of Madame Chiang Kai-shek, was in the United States making the arrangements and putting up the financial backing (although the payment eventually came from United States lend-lease funds).

After planes had been secured for China, Colonel Chennault set about acquiring American pilots to fly them. President Franklin D. Roosevelt officially approved the American Volunteer Group's acquisition of military pilots. With the United States Government's blessing, Chennault raided the military services for fighter pilots. He found forty of his old Pursuit Squadron friends and sixty naval and marine fighter pilots who were willing to fly for China against the Japanese. The youngest pilot was Henry Gilbert (21) and the oldest, Louis Hoffman (43), who was later to become an ace. The Chinese Government paid them well; in addition to a basic salary of $600 a month, a bonus of $2,500 was paid to each man as he became an ace. (Actually a rate of $500 was established for each enemy aircraft shot down.) Flight leaders were paid $675 and squadron commanders $750 a month. However, the money was an incidental factor to a majority of the adventurous men who believed in the Chinese cause.

The United States was still maintaining diplomatic relations with Japan, so special arrangements were made to give the pilots recruited by Chennault a release from their respective services. Hundreds of supporting personnel were obtained in the United States to help the fighter pilots perform their mission which technically was "to protect the air over the Burma Road lifeline to the Chinese Army." The first contingent of 150 support personnel included a flight surgeon's unit with two nurses. Chennault stubbornly insisted that his pilots be in top physical condition at all times, so when they weren't flying he usually saw to it that they had a boisterous baseball game going in which Chennault ceremoniously reserved for himself the position of pitcher.

The Americans in this volunteer group had to sign one-year contracts "to manufacture, service and operate aircraft in Asia" with the Central Aircraft Manufacturing Company of China, called CAMCO, and set up to handle the American Volunteer Group.

When the men sailed on 11 July 1941 from San Francisco on the crack Dutch liner *Jaeggersfontaine* the newspapers picked up the story in spite of the cloud of secrecy under which she sailed. They predicted that Japan would never allow her to reach China—the *Jaeggersfontaine* sailed westward while the world waited and watched. West of Honolulu, in dangerous waters, two cruisers suddenly appeared alongside the *Jaeggersfontaine*—American escorts. The ex-carrier boys among the AVG's identified the cruisers as the *Salt Lake City* and the *Northampton;* President Roosevelt had not forgotten the young American aviators.

Both men and planes poured into Rangoon, Burma, during the summer of 1941. Chennault formed his material into three squadrons: the 1st, or "Adam and Eve" Squadron; the 2nd Squadron, called the "Panda Bears"; and the 3rd Squadron, "Hell's Angels." Inspired by a magazine picture of a tiger painted on a British fighter, Chennault had the ground crews paint a row of shark's teeth along the air-intake recess of the nose of all the P-40's. The men added blood-red tongues and fierce eyes to complete the picture of the tiger shark. This was especially symbolic to the Chinese whose national emblem was the tiger—an emblem growing out of the overthrow of the Manchu dynasty and the formation of the Republic in 1911. The nickname, Flying Tigers, quickly sprang up in reference to the Americans in the painted warplanes, and later Walt Disney Studios of Hollywood prepared an official Flying Tiger emblem. The blue-

and-white identification of the Chinese Air Force was never really needed after that.

Training of the new units took place according to the concepts of fighter tactics for which Chennault became world famous. Especially revolutionary was his two-plane element as opposed to the commonly used Air Corps three-plane element. In his two-plane element tactics, Chennault had a third plane fly top cover. Advantage was concentrated on double fire power which accounted for so many ½, ⅓, and ¼ victories being credited to the Flying Tigers. Chennault studied the Japanese first-line fighter, the Zero, and analyzed its superior performance in a dozen categories compared to the P-40's superiority in three categories. During training he stressed to his men the necessity of fighting the Zero on the P-40's most favorable points. He pointed out that if his men had the Zeros they could just as easily fight against the weaknesses of the P-40.

His pilots found the narrow landing gear of P-40 especially troublesome when operated from hard earthen runways. Even the men who had had previous experience in the P-40 had "groundloop" trouble and gear-retraction problems. Still, the Flying Tigers continued to train. Chennault wanted a crack outfit before he would send them into battle with the Japanese.

On 7 December 1941, the Japanese bombed Pearl Harbor and their activity against the Chinese Air Force was stepped up. On December they bombed Kunming at a much higher level than had been used during the raids of the previous spring. The next day their formations struck again but now Chennault was ready for them and the Flying Tigers came prepared to fight.

The radio warning net reported ten twin-engine Japanese bombers of the Mitsubishi-97 type climbing to great altitude out of Hanoi in the direction of the She-shan Mountains where Chennault's Kunming field was located. Unaccustomed to air opposition, the Mitsubishis were unescorted by fighters. Chennault sent four planes of Jack Newkirk's Panda Bear Squadron to intercept the bombers, six other planes to cover the Tigers' home field, and fifteen planes of the Adam and Eve Squadron to cut off any enemy retreat. In this last group Bob Sandell led the six-plane assault formation and Bob Neale the four-plane support group with Bob Little leading the reserve ships. Newkirk's men sent the bombers hurrying for home and into the waiting guns of the Adam and Eve boys. Only four Jap bombers returned to their base at Hanoi. Fritz Wolf, formerly a dive-bomber pilot on the USS *Saratoga*, had the best tally that day with two confirmed Mitsubishis destroyed and one assist. Wolf's report reads:

I attacked the outside bomber in the V. Diving down below him, I came up underneath, guns ready for the minute I could get in range. At 500 yards I let go with a quick burst from all my guns. I could see my bullets rip into the rear gunner. My plane bore in closer. At 100 yards I let go with a long burst that tore into the bomber's gas tanks and engine. A wing folded and the motor tore loose. Then the bomber exploded. I yanked back on the stick to get out of the way and went upstairs. . . . There I went after the inside man (of the Japanese bomber formation). I came out of a dive and pulled up level with the bomber just behind his tail. I could see the rear gunner blazing away at me, but none of his bullets were hitting my plane. At 50 yards I let go with a long burst, concentrating on one motor. The same thing happened and I got No. 2. The bomber burned and then blew up.

A few days later on 23 December, the Japanese bombers attacked Rangoon, which was 1000 miles from Chennault's Kunming Headquarters, but he had his 3rd Squadron, Hell's Angels, at Mingaladon Field to meet them. Six Japanese bombers and four Jap pursuit planes were shot down in that engagement, and the air war was on.

Rangoon was the Burma port which served as the pouring end of the funnel for the supplies flowing up the Burma Road into China. Millions of dollars' worth of goods were centered and stored around this thriving port city. It was an important target and the Japanese were determined to destroy it. On Christmas Day 1941, Chennault's early warning system reported that a large force of over one hundred Japanese planes were headed toward Rangoon.

The 3rd Pursuit Squadron rose to meet the attack. As the Japanese armada swept over—seventy bombers protected by a top cover of thirty-eight fighters—the eighteen Tomahawks of the Hell's Angels, led by Arvid Olson, screamed down out of the blinding sun, surprising and panicking the Japanese by the speed and fury of the attack. In the ensuing fight nine Japanese fighters and fifteen bombers crashed into the rice paddies, and without accomplishing their mission the armada fled for home. Along the way nine additional Jap planes crashed, delayed victims of the fire-breathing tiger sharks.

The Hell's Angels switched locations with the Panda Bears, and on 28 December, the 2nd Pursuit Squadron met the next massive Japanese air assault on Rangoon, exchanging one Flying Tiger for eighteen Japanese planes.

In the next three months, Japanese planes were shot down at a ratio of 20 to 1, with ninety-two Japanese airmen killed for every AVG pilot lost—a record never to be equaled. Chinese morale benefited greatly from the exploits of the Flying Tigers and they became endeared in the hearts of the Chinese people. To Madame Chiang Kai-shek, whom the boys had made the Honorary Commander of their group, they were "my angels, with or without wings."

In April 1942, Claire Chennault was recalled to active duty in the United States Army Air Corps and given the rank of temporary colonel, with permission to remain in his position with the Chinese Government. A few weeks later he was promoted to the rank of brigadier general. In that same month Colonel Robert L. Scott arrived in China to observe and later to take command of the 23rd U. S. Fighter Group which was to be formed from the Flying Tiger unit—the formal transfer taking place on 4 July 1942 when the American Volunteer Group was officially disbanded and replaced with the 23rd. The official score of the AVG at that time was 299 Japanese planes destroyed in seven months and an equal number of probables (not confirmed victories).

Ten AVG pilots and one crew chief had been killed in action (four in air combat, six were hit by ground fire); nine pilots had been killed in accidents. The remaining Flying Tigers with the exception of Chennault and five others (John Bright, Dave Hill, Ed Rector, Charles Sawyer and Frank Schiel) returned to the United States where most of them later rejoined their Navy and Army Air Force units. "Pappy" Boyington and Jim Howard went on to fly their way to more victories, command positions, and

Congressional Medals of Honor. The remaining five men formed the nucleus of the 23rd Pursuit Group under Colonel Scott.

Claire Chennault assumed command of the China Air Task Force which included the 23rd Fighter Group, the 16th Fighter Group and the 11th Bombardment Squadron (Medium). In March 1943, as a major general, Chennault was made the commander of the 14th Air Force which was formed out of the China Air Task Force.

Fresh young men from the AAF cadet schools poured into China to replace the old Flying Tigers and form the new units in America's growing air force. Of these men, General Chennault in January 1944 wrote (in a letter to General H. H. (Hap) Arnold, Chief of the Army Air Force, in regard to the 14th Air Force's outstanding combat record): "It is indicative of what the American youngster, with the fine training he has received under your careful guidance, can accomplish in this vast country." The old pilots had held the enemy until the young Americans could pour through the flying schools to take over a tough job well done.

General Chennault continued his work with fighters and developed the most valuable tactical concept to come out of the war—low-level fighter bombing. He continued, as commander of the 14th Air Force, to perfect to a high degree his ideas of fighter-plane versatility. He conceived the plan for a fragmentation bomb, timed to go off at any altitude, to be carried by fighters to enable them to get above an enemy bomber formation and bomb them with a sort of upside-down flak. This technique was never developed to a precision point, although late in World War II it was feared that the Germans had nearly perfected a similar type weapon. Chennault was also able to watch an idea he had propounded early in 1932 become a useful realization: the paratrooper and the paradropping of artillery and other heavy equipment.

This man, who was known as the Old Man to the men who flew for him, and Old Leather Face to the Chinese people who loved him, was also dubbed Father of Aces for his brillant leadership of the Flying Tigers, whose remarkable performances left a proud entry on the selective pages of aviation history.

LIST OF AVG ACES

NAME	HOME TOWN	FORMER MILITARY UNIT	VICTORIES
Capt. Robert H. Neale	Seattle, Wash.	Navy-Dive Bomber Sq. Aircraft Carrier Saratoga	16
David "Tex" Hill	Hunt, Texas	Navy Pilot	12¼
Maj. Edward F. Rector	Marchall, N. C.		12
William N. Reed	Marion, Iowa		11
George T. Burgard	Sunburg, Pa.	Air Corps—B-17 Sq. MacDill Field	10¾
William D. McGarry[1]	Los Angeles, Calif.	Air Corps, 1st Pursuit Gp. Selfridge Field	10½
Kenneth A. Jernstedt	Yamhill, Ore.	Marine Corps, Quantico	10½
John Van Kuren Newkirk[2]	Scarsdale, N. Y.	Navy-Fighter Sq. Aircraft Carrier Yorktown	10½
Robert L. Little[3]	Spokane, Wash.	Air Corps—8th Pursuit Gp. Mitchel Field	10½
Charles H. Older	Los Angeles, Calif.	Marine Corps—Quantico	10¼
Charles R. Bond	Dallas, Texas	Air Corps—B-17 Sq. MacDill Field	9
Maj. Robert T. Smith[4]	Los, Angeles, Calif.	Air Corps—Flight Instructor Randolph Field	9
Frank Lawler	Coronado, Calif.	Navy-Fighter Sq. Aircraft Carrier Saratoga	8½

58

Name	Hometown	Unit	Score
Maj. Chas. W. Sawyer	Emmett, Idaho	Air Corps—8th Pursuit Gp. Mitchel Field	8
Percy R. Bartelt	Missoula, Mont.	Navy—Dive Bomber Sq. Aircraft Carrier Wasp	7
Capt. Wm. E. Bartling	Middletown, Ind.		7
Capt. Robert Moss	Doerun, Ga.	Air Corps—1st Pursuit Gp. Selfridge Field	7
Lt. Col. Frank Schiel, Jr.	Prescott, Ariz.	Air Corps—23rd Proving Ground Gp. Eglin Field	7
Lt. Col. Jas. H. Howard[5]	St. Louis, Mo.	Navy Pilot	6½
Lt. Col. John "Gil" Bright	Reading, Pa.		6
Robert P. "Duke" Hedman	Webster, S. D.		6
Gregory "Pappy" Boyington[6]	Okanogan, Wash.	Air Corps—1st Pursuit Gp. Selfridge Field	6
Capt. Rob. J. Raines	San Francisco, Calif.	Marine Corps, San Diego	6
Capt. John Richard Rossi	San Francisco, Calif.		6
Lewis S. Bishop[7]	Warrington, Fla.	Navy Pilot	5½
Thos. "Tom" Haywood	St. Paul, Minn.	Marine Corps—Quantico	..
Parker Dupouy	Farmingdale, N. Y.	Air Corps—8th Pursuit Gp. Mitchel Field	5
Capt. G. H. Laughlin	Ashland, Mo.		5
Joseph Camille Rosbert	Seattle, Wash.		5
Edward Overend	Coronado, Calif.	Navy Pilot	5

NAME	HOME TOWN	FORMER MILITARY UNIT	VICTORIES
Maj. John Petach[8]	Perth Amboy, N. J.	Navy Pilot	5
Louis Hoffman[9]	San Diego, Calif.		5
Robert J. Sandell[10]	St. Louis, Mo.	Air Corps—Pursuit Instructor Craig Field	5
Maj. Robert H. "Snuffy" Smith	Eagle River, Wisc.	Air Corps—1st Pursuit Gp. Selfridge Field	5
George McMillan	Winter Garden, Fla.	Air Corps—23rd Proving Ground Gp. Eglin Field	5
Capt. R. W. Prescott	Ft. Worth, Texas		5
Noel R. Bacon	Norfolk, Va.		5
Fritz E. Wolf	Shawano, Wisc.	Navy—Diver Bomber Sq. Aircraft Carrier Saratoga	5

1 William D. McGarry, former Army pilot, was downed by ground fire on 24 March 1942, over Indo-China and interned.
2 John V. K. Newkirk, former Navy pilot, was killed by ground fire while strafing on 24 March 1942, near Chiengmai, China.
3 Robert L. Little, former Army pilot, was killed while strafing on 22 June 1942, near Yunman, China.
4 Robert T. Smith was first American pilot to become an "ace" in one combat flight.
5 James H. Howard went to the Air Corps and later single-handedly attacked 30 German fighter planes for which deed he received the Congressional Medal of Honor.

6 Gregory Boyington went back to the Marines and on to shoot down a total of 28 Japanese planes; he received the Congressional Medal of Honor.
7 Lewis S. Bishop, former Navy pilot, was interned in Indo-China on 28 May 1942.
8 John E. Petach was killed when his plane exploded in mid-air after ground fire set off his bombs on 10 July 1942. His wife was Emma Jane Forter, one of the AVG nurses.
9 Louis Hoffman, former Navy pilot, was the only ace killed in air combat on 26 January 1942, near Rangoon, Burma.
10 Robert J. Sandell, former Army pilot, was killed in an accident on 7 February 1942, near Rangoon, Burma.

5

THE EAGLE SQUADRON

HISTORY WAS REPEATING itself, and as France again took up arms to meet the swift thrust of Germany's new aggression, Charles Sweeney, an American soldier of fortune who had helped organize the Americans in France in 1914, attempted to form a modern Lafayette Escadrille. A scattering of Americans actually did go to France and fight with the *Armée de l'Air,* but the Lafayette Escadrille had lost its allure, and there was little interest in America for his plan when France fell. Those Americans who did go over were trapped in the shattered country. A few of these were able to make their way to England where they joined the American pilots already fighting with the Royal Air Force and later they became a part of the first Eagle Squadron.

On 30 October 1940, in the autumn following Dunkirk and the Battle of Britain, the Eagle Squadron was made operational as the 71st Royal Air Force Pursuit Squadron. This unit was commanded by Walter Churchill, an Englishman, and Charles Sweeney was made Honorary Commanding Officer for his work in helping to organize the unit after his unsuccessful efforts with a new Lafayette Escadrille in France.

The unit was comprised of Americans fighting with various squadrons of the RAF. These men were the transport pilots, crop dusters, stunt flyers, aeronautical engineers and non-aviation people—students, journalists—who had gone to Canada and enlisted in the Royal Canadian Air Force. There they had been given basic flight training and sent to Britain for their operational training. Among these men was a young pilot officer, Robert Sweeney, nephew of the honorary commander.

As the German troops marched through France for the

second time within two decades the British had found a growing need for young pilots. So the Commonwealth of Canada with the approval of Uncle Sam had set up recruiting booths just outside the gates at Randolph Field, Texas, and Maxwell Field, Alabama, where the United States flying cadet examinations and flight training took place. Whenever cadets were rejected for physical reasons or for lack of flying ability and subsequently discharged from the U.S. Army Air Corps, the RCAF people welcomed them with open arms. It worked almost as if the Air Corps had a monthly quota for the RCAF. The Canadian and British air units did not agree with the American flying program policies and were not so concerned whether the young men were yellow-green color-blind or if they needed twelve instead of ten hours to solo. (It is noted that the RCAF didn't get many rejects from the Navy—the Navy believed, as did the RCAF, that anyone who had once started pilot training could learn to fly. If a naval cadet was slow in acquiring flight proficiency, he would, more often, be washed back a class rather than washed out of the training.)

These Americans with the RCAF and the RAF wore the Royal Air Force uniform, but with a distinguishing Eagle Squadron patch on the left shoulder. This emblem became known throughout England, and the English people opened their hearts and their homes to these Americans. Their salary of $76 a month went a long way in this country abounding with the generosity of appreciative people.

The American-comprised 71st RAF Pursuit Squadron did not contain experienced personnel, so to bring the organization up to the fighting effectiveness of the British squadrons they were sent to the north of England for more training under the experienced guidance of their commander, Walter Churchill. When they returned for battle in April 1941, with Super-marine Spitfires and Hawker Hurricanes, the Eagles were ready to take on anything the Germans could send over. In twenty months the Eagle flyers destroyed 73½ planes; the unofficial count was even higher. For this they received twelve Distinguished Flying Crosses and one Distinguished Service Order.

One pilot came home after strafing a supply train with a chunk of telegraph pole in his wing and another returned more than 100 miles from a patrol over the Dutch coast with his crippled Spitfire riddled by three cannon shells and thirty machine-gun bullets, plus a sea gull that had lodged in the carburetor intake.

At the end of its first year, the Eagle Squadron had suffered twelve casualties; eight of its members had been killed, three were missing in action and one had been taken prisoner. At the end of its second year of action only four of the original thirty-four men were left and over a hundred Eagles had been lost over enemy territory.

By that time two other Eagle Squadrons had joined the 71st in the RAF. They were the 121st initially under the command of Jimmy Daley, DFC, later skippered by Donald J. M. Blakeslee. The 133rd was commanded by Carroll McColpin, DFC, and a British squadron formed on Malta consisted almost entirely of Americans.

The original Eagle Squadron, the 71st, had had seven commanders. The first, Walter Churchill, was followed by W. E. G. Taylor, an ex-U. S. Navy pilot who had been flying with the RAF. He was released at thirty-six because it was felt he was too old for active flying duties, and was followed by H. de G. A. Woodhouse, an English officer. The next commander, E. R. Bitmead, did not actually lead the Eagles in battle because of ill-health and he was soon replaced by S. T. Mears, another Englishman. The last two commanders were American flyers, Chesley Gordon Peterson and Gus Daymond, both aces of the Eagle Squadron.

Colonel Chesley Peterson was the most colorful of the Eagle Squadron commanders. The new men in the outfit had a tendency to underrate the soft-spoken, sandy-haired man with the long, careless legs who had been pictured to them beforehand as the "tiger" and the "killer." They quickly learned, however, that their easy-going commander with the briar pipe was a Jekyll and Hyde who could make an airplane sit up and talk a language the Germans did not care to hear.

He was the same quiet tiger who at nineteen had changed his birth certificate to make himself twenty-one and eligible to join the U. S. Air Corps. His certificate was accepted and he completed his primary flight training at Lindbergh Field in San Diego, California. From there he went to Randolph Field in Texas for basic flight training, where he was washed out of pilot school for "lack of flying ability." Only four years later this "wash-out" cadet was, at twenty-three, a fighter-group commander in the 8th Air Force and the youngest colonel in the U. S. Military. In cadet school Peterson was constantly concerned about his age and his slowness in picking up some of the finer points of flying. As he expressed his feelings: "I was there a month getting more scared every day because I thought I wasn't going to make it. I should have worried; I didn't. When I saw the formula, 'lack of flying ability' I thought, 'My God, maybe they're right.' Then and there I swore I'd never step into a plane again."

Leaving the Air Corps he went to work at Douglas Aircraft in Santa Monica. When he heard that Colonel Charles Sweeney was organizing a squadron to fight in France, he decided to give flying another go.

"All the arrangements were made and we got to Toronto before the whole thing blew sky-high. The Federal police (FBI) nabbed us under some neutrality act and told us to get the hell back."

Back to Douglas Aircraft went the young Peterson, until June 1940, when the legal barriers had been removed and then back to Canada he went for his flight training. When he arrived in England, 1 August 1940, the Germans were throwing everything they had into the sky. Peterson and the other Yanks were given a couple of weeks of operational training and Hawker Hurricanes to fly. The Americans actually didn't get into much of the Battle of Britain (September 1940 when Britain defeated the *Luftwaffe* decisively over England) although they did fly a few sorties.

Colonel Peterson went with the Eagles to the north of England and returned the following April. By autumn he began to make the headlines, winning the British DFC in October 1941. In December he was awarded the British DSO by the King, "for high courage, magnificent leadership and devotion to duty." The next June (1942), taking time out from war for romance, he married Audrey Boyes, South African-born British stage and screen star.

Two months later he came close to being harvested by the Grim Reaper when his plane was severely damaged by machine-gun fire from the rear gunner of a JU-88 which he was "cutting up" during the Dieppe landing. "The guy was good; I fired the same time he did, and he turned over on his back and went right into the sea. But my Spit was burning up so I thought it was a swell time to make a parachute debut." Floating down into the Channel, Pete noticed his new revolver still stuck in his flying jacket. Realizing that he had to get rid of it and remembering that he had never had an occasion to fire it—"What the hell, if I don't fire it now, I may never get the chance—" he pulled it out and blazed away as he came down, heaving it into the Channel before impact. He was in the water barely twenty minutes when he was spotted and picked up by one of the last boats coming back from Dieppe.

By the fall of 1942 the United States Air Corps was beginning to arrive in England, and on 29 September 1942 the Eagle Squadrons from the RAF were transferred to American control. Colonel Peterson took a well-earned two-week leave back home in Santaguin, Utah, where a hero's welcome awaited the quiet Mormon youth who had become one of the RAF's deadliest fighters.

Rested, he returned to combat to fly P-47 Thunderbolts in the USAAF. It was while flying the P-47 that he took his second dive into the chilly Channel and knocked hardest on the pearly gates.

His ship was hit in the engine by an FW-190 during a dogfight over Holland, and he tried to coax his ship across the Channel; but halfway across the plane began dropping out of the sky. "I jumped at about 1000 ft.; the chute streamed, and I took a high dive into the briny. Got two beautiful shiners and drank some of the coldest damned water ever." Free-falling from 1000 feet and hitting the water face first, it was a miracle that he was even alive, but his luck was still good, for a British Walrus rescue aircraft was nearby and immediately picked him up. He was hospitalized for four days with shock, bruises and temporary blindness.

As Group Commander, Colonel Peterson won his highest honor, the American DSC, in July 1943, while leading a fighter-cover formation protecting Flying Fortresses (B-17s) destined for an important target in Germany. Spotting eight enemy planes peeling off for attack, he ordered his formation to stay en route with the Forts while he tore into the enemy planes alone. He got one, damaged another and sent the rest scurrying home. Laughing at the story that the Germans were gunning for him in particular, he commented: "If they can pick me out of the mess that our scrapes usually develop into, they can have me."

At the end of the hostilities his record was nine enemy planes destroyed, seven probably destroyed and five damaged. He had always maintained a discreet silence about his washing out of cadets for "lack of flying ability," but when pressed for a statement he commented: "I've always declared that I left because the authorities discovered that I was under age. But, so help me, I was kicked out."

When the Eagle Squadrons were disbanded in the RAF and incorporated into the USAAF in 1942 slightly more than eighty American flyers were on hand to receive the thanks of the British people for the service they had rendered in those dark days when Britain stood alone against the onslaught of German aggression.

On that day—29 September 1942—of the official transfer Air Chief Marshal Sir Charles Portal spoke at the ceremony and expressed the sentiments of the RAF: "On the occasion of the merging of the Eagle Squadrons with the United States Air Corps, I would like to thank you for all you have done during the past two years. The RAF will never forget how the members of the Eagle Squadrons came spontaneously to this country, eager to help us in the critical weeks and months during and after the Battle of Britain."

And Sir W. Sholto Douglas, speaking for the British people, said: "You joined us readily and of your own free will when our need was the greatest. There are those of your number who are not here today—those sons of the United States who were first to give their lives for their country. For all the subjects of His Highness the King, I give you and your fallen comrades the most heartfelt thanks."

On 24 June 1943 the Duchess of Kent presented plaques commemorating the part played by American Eagle Squadrons in the RAF.

The following men transferred to the USAAF from RAF Eagle Squadrons in September 1942 to form the 4th Fighter Group. This was the only United States Air Group formed entirely of Americans serving in a foreign Air Force.

71st

*Col. Chesley G. Peterson (S/Ldr.), D.S.O., D. F. C
*Maj. Gus Daymond (S/Ldr.), D.F.C. and Bar
Capt. Oscar H. Coen (Flt./Lt.), D. F.C.
Capt. R. S. Sprague (Flt./Lt.)

*Lt. M. G. McPharlin (Flt./Off.)
Capt. S. A Maureillo (Flt./Ldr.)
Lt. T. J. Andrews (Flt./Off.)
Lt. W. T. O'Regan (Plt./Off.)
Lt. H. H. Strickland (Flt./Off.)
Lt. R. D. McMinn (Plt./Off.)
Lt. W. J. Hollander (Flt./Off.)
Lt. H. L. Stewart (Plt./Off.)
*Lt. James A. Clark, Jr. (Plt./Off.)
Lt. W. C. Brite (Sgt./Plt.)
Lt. G. G. Ross (Plt./Off.)
Lt. A. H. Hopson (Plt./Off.)
Lt. Robert Priser (Plt./Off.)

Lt. G. H. Whitlow (Plt./Off.)
Lt. J. F. Lutz (Plt./Off.)
Lt. Howard Hively (Plt./Off.)
Lt. S. M. Anderson (Plt./Off.)
Lt. M. S. Vosberg (Flt./Off.)
*Lt. Henry L. Mills (Plt./Off.)
*Lt. Duane W. Beeson (Plt./Off.)
*Lt. R. C. Care (Plt./Off.)
Lt. R. A. Boock (Plt./Off.)
Lt. J. C. Harrington (Plt./Off.)
Lt. A. J. Seaman (Sgt./Plt.)
*Lt. Victor J. France (Sgt./Plt.)
Lt. Vernon A. Boehle (Sgt./Plt.)
Lt. W. B. Morgan (Plt./Off.)
*Lt. M. W. Dunn

121st

*Colonel Donald J. M. Blakeslee
*Maj. W. J. Daley
*Capt. Shelden R. Edner
Lt. E. D. Beattie
Lt. F. O. Smith
Lt. A. D. Young
Lt. B. A. Taylor
Lt. J. M. Osborne
Lt. Cadman V. Padgett
Lt. Frank M. Fink
Lt. D. K. Willis
Lt. R. G. Patterson
*Lt. K. G. Smith
Lt. J. G. Matthews

Lt. Gilbert Halsey
Lt. G. B. Fetrow
Lt. Frank R. Boyles
Lt. C. A. Hardin
*Lt. George Carpenter
Lt. Paul M. Ellington
Lt. Leon M. Blanding
Lt. R. J. Fox
*Lt. James R. Happel
*Lt. Roy W. Evans
Lt. W. P. Kelly
Lt. J. M. Saunders
Lt. J. T. Slater

133rd

*Maj. C. W. McColpin (Plt./Off.) D. F. C.
Capt. M. E. Jackson
Capt. C. A. Cook, Jr.
Lt. W. H. Baker
Lt. G. B. Sperry
Lt. R. M. Beaty

Lt. Leroy Gover
Lt. D. E. Lambert
Lt. Carl H. Miley

* Aces

67

Lt. L. T. Ryerson
*Lt. Don S. Gentile
*Lt. John T. Godfrey
Lt. D. D. Smith
Lt. G. G. Wright
Lt. G. H. Middletown
Lt. E. L. Miller
Lt. R. E. Smith
Lt. G. P. Neville

Lt. Don D. Nee
Lt. G. J. Smart
Lt. H. L. Ayres
Lt. R. L. Alexander
Lt. W. C. Slade, Jr.
Lt. C. H. Patterson
Lt. Joe L. Bennett
Lt. J. Mitchelweis, Jr.

"EAGLES" ON MALTA WITH THE 185TH, 126TH AND 249TH FIGHTER SQUADRONS

*Maj. Vasseure H. Wynn	Dalton, Ga.
Pilot Off. William Wendt	Hibbin, Minn.
Flight Sgt. James Farrell	Newark, New Jersey
Pilot Off. Claude Weaver III	Oklahoma City, Okla.
James Peck	Berkeley, Calif.
Donald McLeod	Norwich, Conn.
*Maj. Reade Tilley (Col.)	Clearwater, Fla.
Joe Otis	Chicago, Ill.
Lt. Col. John Lynch	Tulsa, Okla.
Ripley Ogden Jones	Cooperstown, N. Y.
Douglas Booth	Brooklyn, N. Y.
Bruce Downs	San Angelo, Texas
Richard McHan	Pocatello, Idaho
Joe Lowry	New York City, N. Y.
Harry Kelly	San Antonio, Texas
**Flight Sgt. Pete Peters	Dallas, Texas

ADDITIONAL EAGLE PERSONNEL (TAKEN FROM LIST ON PLAQUE PRESENTED TO COLONEL PETERSON)

1. Squadron Leader W. Churchill, D. S. O., D. F. C. (British)
2. Flight Lieutenant A. Mamedoff
3. Pilot Officer V. C. Keough
4. Flight Officer E. Q. Tobin
5. Pilot Officer P. H. Lechrone
6. Flight Officer J. H. Tann (British)
7. Flight Lieutenant G. Brown (British)
8. Pilot Officer F. B. Bennett
9. Squadron Leader W. E. Taylor
10. Flight Officer R. Sweeney
11. Pilot Officer L. E. Allen
12. Fight Lieutenant R. C. Wilkinson, D. F. M. (British)
13. Pilot Officer S. M. Kolendorski
14. Pilot Officer B. F. Kennerly
15. Pilot Officer J. L. McGinnis
16. Pilot Officer E. E. Orbison
17. Pilot Officer D. Satterlee

* Aces
** Had formerly flown with the Spanish Loyalists.

18. Pilot Officer R. A. Moore
19. Flight Officer R. Robinson (British)
20. Pilot Officer K. S. Taylor
21. Flight Officer C. E. Bateman
22. Pilot Officer J. B. Ayre
23. Flight Officer W. Nicholls
24. Pilot Officer P. Provenzano
25. Pilot Officer J. K. Alexander
26. Flight Officer V. R. Bono
27. Pilot Officer N. Maranz
28. Pilot Officer P. R. Anderson
29. Flight Lieutenant A. S. Osborne
30. Flight Officer W. A. Becker
31. Pilot Officer C. O. Galbraith
32. Pilot Officer R. E. Tongue (British)
33. Pilot Officer C. F. Ambrose, D. F. C. (British)
34. Flight Lieutenant N. Anderson
35. Pilot Officer J. Flynn
36. Flight Officer T. C. Wallace
37. Pilot Officer T. P. McGerty
38. Pilot Officer R. C. Ward
39. Pilot Officer W. I. Hall
40. Pilot Officer V. W. Olson
41. Flight Officer W. R. Dunn
42. Pilot Officer H. S. Fenlaw
43. Pilot Officer W. Pendleton
44. Flight Officer W. D. Geiger
45. Flight Officer R. L. Mannix
46. Flight Officer C. W. Tribken
47. Squadron Leader H. de C. A. Woodhouse (British)
48. Pilot Officer J. W. Weir
49. Flight Officer M. W. Fessler
50. Flight Officer J. G. DuFour
51. Pilot Officer W. R. Driver
52. Squadron Leader E. R. Bitmead (British)
53. Flight Officer A. F. Roscoe, D. F. C.
54. Pilot Officer F. P. Dowling
55. Squadron Leader S. Meares, D. F. C. (British)
56. Flight Lieutenant H. Gilbert, D. F. C. (British)
57. Pilot Officer R. O. Scarborough
58. Pilot Officer D. Geffene
59. Flight Officer E. T. Miluck
60. Pilot Officer C. Marting
61. Pilot Officer G. C. Daniel
62. Pilot Officer L. A. Chatterton
63. Pilot Officer R. H. Atkinson
64. Flight Officer E. M. Potter
65. Pilot Officer J. M. Kelly
66. Pilot Officer L. S. Nomis
67. Pilot Officer J. J. Lynch, D. F. C.
68. Pilot Officer B. F. Mays
69. Pilot Officer F. G. Zavakos
70. Pilot Officer J. A. Gray
71. Pilot Officer W. B. Inabinet
72. Pilot Officer G. St. M. Maxwell
73. Fight Officer E. Brookes (British)
74. Pilot Officer G. Techiera

75. Pilot Officer J. F. Helgason
76. Pilot Officer R. F. D. Collins (British)
77. Pilot Officer W. D. Taylor
78. Sergeant Pilot J. E. Evans
79. Pilot Officer P. Salkeld (Argentine)
80. Pilot Officer B. J. Hudson (British)
81. Flight Officer D. G. G. Jones (Wales, M. D.)
82. Pilot Officer S. N. Pissanos

6

NAVY—WORLD WAR II

ON 26 NOVEMBER 1941 a Japanese task force—six aircraft carriers, two battleships and a complement of lesser vessels —steamed from Hitakappu Bay in the Kuriles for a rendezvous with history. In the inky darkness that preceded the warm Pacific dawn of 7 December the task force arrived at its predetermined destination 200 miles north of the main Hawaiian Island of Oahu. Exactly on schedule, at 0600 of that fateful morning, the first wave of Japanese planes roared from the carrier decks—fifty fighters, fifty horizontal bombers, fifty torpedo bombers and fifty dive bombers. At 0755 Japanese planes were observed heading for Hickam Field and Pearl Harbor. Within minutes bombs poured from the sky and the United States was plunged into the greatest war in history.

In their attack on Pearl Harbor the Japanese had planned to repeat their victorious stratagem of the Russo-Japanese war when they destroyed the Russian fleet in a surprise attack on Port Arthur, and although at Pearl Harbor they played havoc with Battleship Row they failed to sink a single U. S. aircraft carrier. (The *Lexington* and *Enterprise* which were normally at Pearl Harbor were out on a duty mission that Sunday morning.) In this failure to strike at the naval air units they failed to foresee what they themselves had proved through their own air attack against Pearl Harbor: that aviation was the new and powerful fist of the modern warring navy.

On that day, 7 December 1941, the United States became an active belligerent in the turmoil that encompassed the world, but even prior to that fateful day naval planners had been preparing the Navy and revising their thinking along the more modern lines of twentieth-century warfare. As early as 1920 air commands had been created with the fleet, and although aviation, like other branches of the service, was hampered throughout the twenties and early thirties by lack of funds, the first Chief of the new Naval Air Command (Bureau), Rear Admiral William A. Moffett, by virtue of being a brilliant administrator, was able to channel most of his air funds into experimentation and skeleton forces. The power catapult from battleships and cruisers, the evolution of the aircraft carrier and rigid airships were the developments. In 1922 the *Langley*, converted from the collier *Jupiter* into an experimental carrier, proved so succesful in fleet operations that in 1927 two carriers, the *Lexington* and the *Saratoga*, converted from battle-cruiser hulls upon which construction had been halted as a result of the Washington Treaty of 1929, were commissioned. The *Ranger*, commissioned in 1933, was the first American ship designed as an aircraft carrier from the keel up.

In 1936, the *Langley* was retired as a carrier and converted to a seaplane tender. Prior to Pearl Harbor four other carriers were added to the fleet, the *Yorktown, Enterprise, Wasp* and *Hornet*.

By June 1940, the Navy had 1,741 aircraft and 2,965 pilots.

On 14 June 1940, Congress authorized a limit of 4,500 planes and that night France began to crumble; the next morning Congress changed that to 10,000 planes. France collapsed and Congress gave the Navy a new authorization for 15,000 planes. By the time the authorization reached the President, Congress had again reconsidered, this time giving the Secretary of the Navy a blank check to write his own figure.

The naval air planners were thus already moving in the right direction when the blow was struck in the Hawaiian Islands. Admiral Ernest J. King, Commander-in-Chief of the United States Fleet and Chief of Naval Operations, expressed it thus:

I have come to the conclusion that a great many people in this country . . . are under the impression that the tremendous importance of Naval Aviation as a part of our military organization was discovered on December 7, 1941. . . . The facts of the matter are that the United States Navy pioneered in the development of aircraft as a military weapon . . . we have spared no effort to develop it and fit it into our organization. We have watched it grow and we have grown with it. We took advantage of each and every advance in aviation. . . . We built and tested carriers. We experimented with and developed various types of planes, and we worked out techniques for their tactical development. In short, aviation soon became an integral part of the profession of every Naval officer, regardless of whether or not he himself was an aviator.

In that first year of war that followed Pearl Harbor the aircraft carriers and their squadrons of flying men were probably the most destructive instrument of combat, hitting the enemy blows that he never expected or had dreamed would have been possible after he had laid waste our fleet in the Harbor.

In the Philippines the Navy Patrol Wing 10 fought a valiant withdrawing action. Comprising the only naval air unit in that area, the men of Patwing 10 fought their patrol aircraft against the Japanese first-line fighters, and in the Aleutians, Patwing 4 withstood the initial surge of the enemy into the Alaskan area in June 1942.

In less than two months after the first Japanese assault an American task force under Admiral William Halsey attacked Jap-held Marshall and Gilbert Islands. While surface units shelled enemy fortifications the air groups bombed, torpedoed and strafed the enemy. Just twenty days later another task force—containing the carrier *Lexington* —steamed westward into the Solomons. Spotted near the island of Bougainville, the *Lexington* was raided by Japanese bombers. When the fight was over the Japs had lost eighteen bombers and the Navy had lost two Wildcats, one pilot and had gained its first ace of World War II, Lieutenant Edward H. (Butch) O'Hare.

In the Japanese operations headquarters the word was received that a U. S. aircraft carrier was steaming into Japanese waters. Immediately eighteen twin-engined land-based bombers were dispatched to sink the ship that the Americans were so foolishly bringing within bomber range of the Japanese forces. The *Lexington* was to be sunk.

Aboard the carrier a squadron of Grumman Wildcats led by future Navy ace Lieutenant Commander John S. Thach were ordered aloft to intercept any aircraft that the Japanese might possibly send out. Ready and waiting the Navy flyers had a hot welcome prepared as the Japanese bombers streaked toward the *Lexington*. The Navy flyers flamed five of the first wave but as the second wave swept over only two Wildcats were in position to strike. The two fighters roared into the attack and as they came within range the guns of one of the planes jammed, leaving Butch O'Hare in the lone remaining Navy fighter to carry the attack. With only himself between his carrier and the nine enemy bombers of the second wave, O'Hare bore in on the enemy, flashing in at the tail end of one side of the V formation. In two quick bursts he demolished two bombers, then ducked away on the other side as the enemy gunners fired at his ship—only to dart back into the flock on the other side shooting down three more enemy ships and damaging a fourth. The remaining four bombers dropped their bombs wide of the carrier and hurried homeward from the fray before O'Hare or the other Navy flyers could strike again. The *Lexington* had been saved and O'Hare had become an ace, was promoted to lieutenant commander and awarded the Congressional Medal of Honor.

Four days later Wake Island was bombed and on 4 March Marcus Island was hit by the Navy airmen. A week later squadrons from the *Lexington* and *Yorktown* hit Jap warships, transports and cargo vessels berthed in the harbors of the Salamaua–Lae section of New Guinea. Two heavy cruisers, one light crusier and a destroyer were lost to the Japanese that day. More Jap losses were racked up on Tulagi by planes from the *Yorktown* on 4 May as a prelude to the big naval battle shaping up. Three days later a U. S. task force headed by the *Lexington* and *Yorktown* made contact with a large Jap fleet moving on New Guinea, and for the first time aircraft carriers faced each other in a raging air-sea battle—the Battle of the Coral Sea. The fierce battle continued for two days at the end of which time a battered and beaten enemy was forced to abandon its mission and the Japs had lost one, and probably three carriers, a light cruiser and ninety-one planes while the United States had lost the *Lexington* and twenty-seven planes.

One month later the Japanese massed their strength for what turned out to be one of the most important engagements in history—the Battle of Midway. On this battle hinged the outcome of the Pacific war, and fulfilling their key role in history the gallant airmen of the Navy, Army and Marine Corps turned back the tide of Jap aggression. When the smoke blew clear and the coughing guns and screaming planes were silent the once aroused and determined enemy was limping homeward minus four carriers, two heavy cruisers and three (possibly four) destroyers and an estimated five thousand men. They carried with them two (probably three) badly damaged battleships, three damaged heavy cruisers, and one damaged light cruiser. The Navy paid for this victory with the *Yorktown*, 150 airplanes, and 307 men.

Captain Yasumi Toyama, chief of staff of the 2nd Japanese Destroyer Squadron at Midway, summed up the importance of the American victory in this way:

The loss of five carriers in May and June, with several others damaged, made it necessary to reorganize our striking forces. The loss of the carriers was later felt in our operations. We were unable to use seaplanes for long-range reconnaissance because we had to convert seaplane tenders like the *Chitose* to aircraft carriers. We also had to convert the battleships *Ise* and *Hyuga* to carriers, so they were lost to us for a long time.

After Midway we were defensive, trying to hold what we had instead of expanding.

Meanwhile on the other side of the world in the North African invasion carrier-based planes had opposed land-based planes and had destroyed more than 125 enemy aircraft while suffering only twenty-five aircraft losses themselves.

Thus by 1943 the naval air force had taken a vital role in every major action of the war—Pearl Harbor, Midway, the Aleutians, the Solomons and North Africa.

The fortunes of war had changed and on both sides of the globe the free world was taking the offensive. "The epic advance of our united forces across the vast Pacific, westward from Hawaii and northward from New Guinea, the Philippines and to the shores of Japan was spearheaded by naval aviation. . . . The final phase of the Pacific naval war commenced with the assault of Iwo Jima in February, 1945, closely followed by that on Okinawa in April." [*Aircraft Yearbook for 1946*.] The war was drawing to a close, and although the naval air units were at no time during the war nearly as large or as numerically strong as the Army Air Forces, naval aviation had made a major contribution to the final hard-earned victory.

In helping to bring about the final victory the naval air arm produced nearly 330 aces who shot down a combined total of over 2,400 enemy aircraft. The astounding accomplishments of these top Navy flyers were not, however, given much public attention during the war—the real value of the air ace as a weighty part of the balance of air superiority having not yet been fully appreciated or understood. In a press release in 1944, Rear Admiral Thomas L. Sprague expressed the view that publicity for aviation aces tended to disrupt teamwork and cause a decay of morale. Explained the admiral: "Very few aces are still alive— sooner or later that fellow [the ace] is going to get shot down. Aviators don't last long after they get famous."

This viewpoint, however, was not borne out by the final tabulations of the air war. Actually combat losses among Navy aces were the lowest of any comparable group. The top four Navy aces, for example, all returned safely from the conflict, tallying among the four of them one hundred enemy planes. It wasn't until twelve years later that the fifth ranking naval ace, then serving with the U. S. Air Force, Colonel Patrick Fleming, was killed in the first B-52 accident.

The top Navy ace was Commander David McCampbell from Bessemer, Alabama, who skillfully led Air Group 15, the "Fabled Fifteen," based on the aircraft carrier *Essex*, shooting down thirty-four planes himself and destroying twenty-one on the ground, the highest number ever shot down by an American pilot during a single tour of duty.

Under his leadership, Air Group 15 ranged from the Central to the Far Western Pacific; participated in the attack on Marcus Island in May 1944; in the first strike over Saipan on 11 June 1944; and seven days later, as part of the famous Task Force 58, under command of Vice Admiral Marc A. Mitscher, took part in the opening round of the First Battle of the Philippine Sea, continuing its exploits during this and the Battle for Leyte Gulf (formerly known as the Second Battle of the Philippine Sea).

Within the seven months of operations the Fabled Fifteen compiled a carrier group record of 312 enemy planes destroyed in the air; 348 destroyed on the ground; 388 probably destroyed or damaged in the air and on the ground; a carrier, a destroyer, and a destroyer escort sunk without aid from other air groups; two carriers and a heavy cruiser sunk in co-ordinated attacks with other groups; a battleship and a light cruiser probably sunk in conjunction with attacks by other squadrons; three battleships, a carrier, five heavy cruisers, three light cruisers, and nineteen destroyers damaged in co-ordinated attacks with other air groups.

Commander David McCampbell—who picked up the nickname "Wait-For-Me" from his habit of calling out "Wait for me!" over the radio whenever his boys would take off after some Jap aircraft—shot down his first Jap plane (a Zeke-type Zero) over Pagan in the Marianas on 11 June 1944. After that he began piling up victories at a constant rate.

On 24 October of that same year during the Second Battle of the Philippine Sea Commander McCampbell was leading a group of fighters over hostile waters. Enemy bombers were spotted below through the scattered puffs of clouds. "Five of my seven planes dived on the twenty enemy bombers," explained McCampbell, "leaving Lieutenant Roy Rushing, of McGehee, Arkansas, and myself as top cover. We ran into forty Zeros [the bomber escorts] and made a pass at them, each of us shooting down one. To our surprise the enemy formed a defensive Lufbery Circle, each Japanese plane chasing the other one's tail."

The Japs circled for ten minutes, losing their bombers beneath the clouds. Finally realizing that they could not entice the two Navy flyers into the World War I circular trap, they broke their Lufbery forming into a tight formation and heading back for Manila. McCampbell called to his boys below, and joined by his five other fighters he climbed his Hellcats above the retreating Jap formation.

"For an hour or so we followed the formation of weaving Japanese fighters taking advantage of every opportunity to knock down those who attempted to climb up to our altitude, scissored outside of support from others, straggled or became too eager and came up at us singly."

During this single engagement Commander McCampbell

set a new aerial combat record by downing nine planes. This spectacular count included only those seen by himself or his wingman to explode or flame. There were numerous others seen with smoking engines as they dove away, and two were spinning toward the water.

The engagement was finally broken off when they ran low on fuel and ammunition. The Americans returned with only superficial damage to their airplanes caused by passing through the debris from exploding enemy aircraft.

In commenting on another of his victories, Commander McCampbell modestly related the circumstances involved in shooting down two Jap planes:

"We were attacking and I was sitting there over the target. Then I just happened to run into a single Jap plane, rolled over on him and made several passes. I kept hitting him but couldn't get him to burn. Finally he hit the water off the entrance to Manila Bay.

"Later on that same day our planes rendezvoused and ran into a couple of Zeros. I got on one's tail, made a couple of passes and got him."

In commenting on his acedom at that time (1944) he explained: "Actually I'm the air group commander on this ship and my real mission is directing others, not shooting down planes myself. It's all part of circumstance. All you have to do is see 'em first. I am fortunate in having a wingman (Roy Rushing) with eyes like an eagle. What I miss he gets."

For his services and his brilliant record in command of Air Group 15, Commander McCampbell was awarded the Congressional Medal of Honor, presented personally by the late President Franklin D. Roosevelt in ceremonies at the White House, 10 January 1945. He also holds the Distinguished Flying Cross, Gold Stars in lieu of a second and third Distinguished Flying Cross, the Navy Cross, the Legion of Merit, the Silver Star Medal and the Air Medal.

The second ranking Navy ace, Lieutenant Cecil E. Harris, a farm boy from Cresbard, South Dakota, fought both in the Mediterranean and Pacific, achieving acedom while serving with Fighting Squadron 18 and helping it gain the nickname "Two-a-Day Eighteen." In eighty-one days Cecil Harris shot down a total of twenty-four enemy aircraft, shooting down four Jap planes in one day on three separate occasions: once on 12 September 1944 over the central

Philippines, once on 12 October over Formosa, and once on 27 November when he picked off three Jap fighters in a morning sweep over Manila and destroyed another over the American task force during a Japanese daylight attack. In all his tours of combat, Lieutenant Cecil Harris' plane was never nicked by enemy fire.

Harris' record was followed closely by the third ranking Navy ace, Lieutenant Eugene A. Valencia of Alameda, California. Valencia returned from combat in early 1944 with seven Jap planes to his credit from attacks on Rabaul, Tarawa, the Marshalls, Truk, Saipan, Marcus and Wake. From his experience he became convinced of the extreme importance of close-combat teamwork. As a part of the experienced nucleus of a new air group being formed, Valencia was given command of a division—a four-plane fighting unit.

At Pasco, Washington, where the group was being readied for action, Valencia preached and practiced his convictions to his younger team mates: Lieutenants (jg) James E. French of Oakland, California; Clinton L. Smith, Jackson, Mississippi; and Harrie E. Mitchell, Richmond, Texas. The four men were together constantly and while others were resting and relaxing they were in the air practicing over and over unit maneuvers and dogfight techniques. Offensive tactics were devised and co-ordinated and often they would divide into two forces in simulated combat with each other. Valencia developed what he termed the "mowing machine," whereby they could remain constantly on the offensive with one Hellcat on the attack while the other covered from behind and above. When the first fighter completed his pass he would break to the rear and above the second, allowing the second to press in on attack, providing in effect a continuous attack with protection at all times. Valencia's experience began to rub off on the junior members and when they went into combat the four-man team became one of the deadliest divisions in the Pacific—tying the record of the Marine division headed by Marine air ace, Captain Joe Foss.

"We spent so much time in the air at Pasco that they began to check up on our gasoline consumption," laughed Valencia in recalling the occasion, "but it paid off. In all our missions we never had a single bullet hole in our planes."

Valencia's division got its baptism of battle in the carrier strike on Tokyo, 16 February 1945. Although few Jap planes were out to oppose the Hellcats, Valencia's division flamed six.

On 17 April in a strike at Kyushu the carrier tallyhoed thirty-eight Jap fighters including the newest type Japanese aircraft. Many of the Japs were Kamikaze suicide aircraft. The four men leaped into the fray and executing their smooth-working "mowing machine," Valencia shot down six Jap planes, French flamed four, Mitchell got three and Smith downed one for a very neat day's work.

Off Okinawa on 4 May they downed eleven more Japanese planes and on 11 May knocked ten enemy ships out of the sky.

During one dogfight Mitchell was chasing a fast Jap light bomber with Valencia providing tail cover. The faster Jap plane was slowly pulling away from Mitchell and was well out of range of Valencia, when Valencia pulled the nose of his Hellcat up in a steep climbing angle and fired several rounds, lobbing the bullets—like a long-range cannon—ahead of the fleeing bomber. Startled by the tracers, the Jap pilot turned his plane, inadvertently shortening the distance between his ship and that of the charging Mitchell, giving the Navy flyer an opportunity to make a quick pass at the bomber. In a flash the Hellcat was upon the Jap plane and Mitchell's blazing guns sent it down in flames. By the end of the war the four naval aviators had all become aces, bagging a total of forty-three Japanese planes; Valencia finished the tour, adding sixteen more kills to the seven from his earlier combat for a total of twenty-three kills, while French had a total of eleven, Mitchell ten and Smith six.

James French had taken up flying at eighteen under encouragement from his grandmother, Mrs. Dora C. Barber, who had taken her first airplane ride in a passenger liner across the country at the age of seventy. Lieutenant French's father had likewise instilled flying in James' blood, having served as an Army pilot in France in World War I.

Lieutenant Alexander Vraciu, from East Chicago, Indiana, was the fourth ranking ace of the naval air war. Shooting down nineteen enemy planes and destroying twenty-one more on the ground, Vraciu made six of his air-to-air kills in a record breaking eight-minute dogfight.

During the "Mariana Turkey Shoot"—the pilots' pet name for the Battle of Saipan which cost the Japanese four hundred planes—Lieutenant Vraciu along with the other pilots of the U. S. task force were aloft awaiting the expected enemy. They were not disappointed. As Vraciu described the action to a *New York Times* correspondent:

We went out at high altitude and from a far range we could see scattered groups of from twenty to fifty Jap planes each coming toward our carriers. They were all Judys [dive bombers]. As squadron leader I tallyhoed to the carrier and climbed to 25,000 feet, about 2,000 feet above the enemy planes.

For unknown reasons they were all massed together with the groups at various altitudes. It was a brilliantly clear day, about 10:30 A.M. and from my observations there were enough Japs around to satisfy everybody in my squadron.

They were thirty-five miles away when we started after them, and as they tried to separate from their groups I was able to apply the simple process of picking them off the edges. You might say it was comparable to riding herd in the sky.

Just as the first Jap approached, my belly tank ran dry and I shifted to an auxiliary and took that one [the Jap plane] out easily. In making the shift, a lot of oil got on my windshield and made the vision so poor I had to go within 150 yards of the next one before stopping it. The next two were knocked out on a run of about fifteen seconds.

Next in line were three heading for an American destroyer. I was able to get two of those, and must have hit the bomb of one of them, for he exploded, scattering plane parts through the air. The third was foolish enough to attack a battleship, which was the end of him.

During the course of the battle the fighters were returning to their carriers only long enough for more fuel and ammunition before renewing the battle. Vraciu, aside from shooting down six Japs that day, led his squadron to forty-one victories without losing a man.

In the following December in an air battle off Luzon in the Philippines, Lieutenant Vraciu caught a stray Jap bullet in his oil tank, and had to bail out over the enemy held island. Luck was with him: he had barely touched the ground when friendly guerrilla troops met him with a warm welcome and clothing. While in the Philippines, awaiting the arrival of the invasion forces, Vraciu continued his war, leading his own band of 160 guerrillas.

When MacArthur's invasion pushed back across the island, Vraciu walked into the startled American camp, grinning through an inch-long beard, with a Japanese pistol in one hand and a Japanese saber dangling from his shoulder. Still not done with fighting, he requested to be put back into the air to continue with the war.

As the war in the Pacific rolled westward the aerial victories became easier and easier. The quality of the Japanese pilot was becoming markedly poorer; their heavy losses and their Kamikaze suicide warfare was taking a dangerous toll of their able flyers. On the other hand, the American pilots were becoming more experienced, thus greatly altering the odds as they came up against the green, unskilled Nipponese pilots.

So in order to compare the later astonishing victories against seemingly superior numbers with those accomplished in the earlier years of the war, the vast difference between the enemy pilot proficiency level in the two periods must be taken into account.

"Total enemy losses in aerial combat as compared to our Navy planes shot down were 858 against our 266 in 1941–42—a ratio of 3.2 to one. In 1943, it was 1,239 enemy to our 233—a ratio of 5.3 to one. In 1945, it was 3,161 enemy to 146—a ratio of 21.6 to one. The total of 9,282 enemy planes shot down during the war as compared to our loss of 906 in aerial combat was a ratio of 10.2 to one, which is a fine testimonial to our airmen and their equipment." [*Aircraft Yearbook for 1946.*]

By the summer of 1945 the American forces had gained virtually complete domination of the Pacific air, including a certain surprising amount of freedom of action over the major islands of Japan. Artemus L. Gates, Assistant Secretary of the Navy for Air, reported on 30 June 1945:

By the early part of this year, we had complete domination of the air in all naval theaters of operation in the Pacific from our own West Coast and that of South

America to the East Indies, to China, and up to the very door of Japan. At this moment Navy search and patrol planes are operating over the South China Sea, East China Sea, Yellow Sea, Korea, the Sea of Japan, the Inland Sea, the southern approaches to the home islands, and over the Kuriles to the North. The battle for the control of the air over Japan itself is under way.

When the Japanese attacked Pearl Harbor the Navy had 5,999 flyers (5,225 officers, 774 enlisted men) and its Marine component had 659 flyers (610 officers, 49 enlisted men); at the signing of the Japanese surrender aboard the battleship *Missouri* the naval air arm had grown almost tenfold with a total of 49,950 Navy flyers (49,615 officers, 335 enlisted men) and 10,270 Marine flyers (10,224 officers, 46 enlisted men).

The Navy had engaged the enemy in every over-water campaign in the Atlantic and Mediterranean as well as across the island-studded Pacific, and the air arm had grown in the course of the war from the handy left hand to the powerful right fist. Sea power had become air power and the young men in the fast planes who had risen to battle from the rolling decks of U.S. carriers had led the way to the final triumph.

NAVY ACES LIST			15 March 1946
NAME	SER. NO.	SERVICE	NO. OF PLANES SHOT DOWN
McCampbell, David	072487	USN	34
Harris, Cecil E.	114286	USNR	24
Valencia, Eugene, A.	113030	USNR	23
Vraciu, Alexander	124731	USNR	19
Fleming, Patrick D.		USN	19
Kepford, Ira C.	145749	USNR	17
Stimpson, Charles R.	121639	USNR	17
Baker, Douglas			16 Missing
Nooy, Cornelius N.	177027	USNR	15
Hawkins, Arthur R.	240489	USNR	14
McCuskey, Elbert S.	081585	USNR	14
Wirth, John L.	146937	USN	14
Duncan, George C.	082484	USN	13½
Mehle, Roger W.	078670	USN	13⅓
Carmichael, Daniel A., Jr.	250521	USNR	13
Rushing, Roy W.	263563	USNR	13
Strane, John R.	106001	USNR	13
Twelves, Wendell V.	283102	USNR	13
Craig, Clement M.	086053	USNR	12

NAME	SER. NO.	SERVICE	NO. OF PLANES SHOT DOWN
Hedrick, Roger R.	077688	USN	12
Henry, William E.	084181	USNR	12
Masoner, William J., Jr.	082264	USNR	12
O'Hare, Edward H.	078672	USN	12
Shirley, James A.	112972	USNR	12
Carr, George R.	243216	USNR	11½
Bakutis, Fred E.	075028	USN	11
Blackburn, John T.	072292	USN	11
Dean, William A., Jr.	073624	USN	11
French, James B.	305948	USNR	11
Mallory, Charles, M.	251056	USNR	11
McWhorter, Hamilton, III	112968	USNR	11
Reber, James V., Jr.	354792	USNR	11
Rigg, James F.	079142	USN	11
Runyon, Donald E.	146644	USN	11
Stanbook, Richard E.	112421	USNR	11
Vejtasa, Stanley W.	081514	USN	11
Beebe, Marchall U.	077807	USN	10½
Reiserer, Russell L.	112294	USNR	10½
Murray, Robert E.	315070	USNR	10⅓
Elliott, Ralph E.	104741	USNR	10¼
Brown, Carl A., Jr.	114255	USNR	10
Coleman, Thaddeus T.	130401	USN	10
Mitchell, Harris E.	300998	USNR	10
Singer, Arthur, Jr.	263939	USNR	10
Swope, James S.	117177	USNR	10
Banks, John L.	263453	USNR	9½
Coats, Robert C.	084308	USNR	9⅓
Bassett, Edgar R.	085741	USNR	9 Missing
Berree, Norman R.	282924	USNR	9
Bright, Mark Kenneth	103989	USNR	9
Buie, Paul D.	072438	USN	9
Collins, William M., Jr.	073427	USN	9
Eastmond, Richard T.	114416	USNR	9
Feightner, Edward L.	116885	USNR	9
Franger, Marvin J.	114349	USNR	9
Harris, Leroy E.	082487	USN	9
Harris, Thomas S.	264207	USNR	9
Picken, Harvey P.	099854	USNR	9
Redmond, Eugene D.	250616	USNR	9
Rehm, Dan R., Jr.	263556	USNR	9
Stewart, James S.	097988	USNR	9
Van Haren, Arthur, Jr.	114841	USNR	9
Watts, Charles E.	250623	USNR	8¾
Chenoweth, Oscar I.	098540	USNR	8½
Dibb, Robert A. M.	104469	USN	8½ Dead
Foster, Carl C.	363333	USNR	8½
Hargreaves, Everett C.	250902	USNR	8½
Pigman, George W., Jr.	290832	USNR	8½
Plant, Claude W.	290758	USNR	8½ Missing
Self, Larry R.	329457	USN	8½
Gabriel, Franklin T.	263904	USNR	8¼
Gray, John Floyd	083440	USN	8¼
Bardshar, Frederic A.	181128	USN	8

NAME	SER. NO.	SERVICE	NO. OF PLANES SHOT DOWN
Barnard, Lloyd Glynn	104527	USNR	8
Bonneau, William Jerome	113024	USN	8
Burnett, Roy O., Jr.	098538	USNR	8
Doner, Landis E.	106392	USNR	8
Gile, Clement D.	099759	USNR	8
Griffin, Richard J.	099946	USNR	8
Hadden, Mayo A., Jr.	106401	USNR	8
Johnson, Byron M.	251379	USNR	8
Johnston, John M.	156453	USNR	8
Leonard, William N.	081229	USN	8
May, Earl	156739	USNR	8
Menard, Louis A.	114344	USNR	8
Miller, Johnnie G.	354770	USNR	8
Morris, Wayne		USNR	8
Mulcahy, Douglas W.	098456	USNR	8
Prater, Luther D., Jr.	264249	USNR	8
Reidy, T. H.	127691	USNR	8
Smith, Armistead B., Jr.	112214	USNR	8
Stanley, Gordon A.	301478	USNR	8
Winters, Theodore Hugh, Jr.	74935	USN	8
Burriss, Howard M.	130674	USNR	7½
Knight, William M.	112240	USNR	7½ Missing
Noble, Myrvin E.	157685	USNR	7½
O'Mara, Paul, Jr.	326348	USNR	7½
Symmes, John C. C.	125720	USNR	7½
Vorse, Albert C.	078768	USN	7½
Hibbard, Samuel B.	104017	USNR	7⅓
Pope, Albert J.	290833	USNR	7¼
Prichard, Melvin M.	145762	USNR	7¼
Brassfield, Arthur J.	079013	USN	7
Burley, Franklin N.	251231	USNR	7
Clark, Lawrence A.	346920	USNR	7
Clark, Robert A.	382541	USNR	7
Conroy, Thomas J.	326089	USNR	7
Cordray, Paul	130663	USNR	7
Cunningham, Daniel G.	145185	USNR	7
Dahms, Kenneth J.	354700	USNR	7
Davidson, George H.	158166	USNR	7
Dear, John W., Jr.	261375	USNR	7
Duncan, Fred L.	156381	USNR	7
Eckard, Bert	121599	USNR	7
Eder, Willard E.	083140	USN	7
Fecke, Alfred J.	114815	USNR	7
Fleming, Francis M.	125456	USNR	7
Franks, John M.	158077	USNR	7
Funk, Harold N.	077738	USN	7
Galvin, John R.	250594	USNR	7
Hill, Harry E.	106437	USNR	7
Jones, James M.	301462		7
Kirk, George N.	251145	USNR	7
Maxwell, W. R.	116459	USNR	7
Morris, Bert D., Jr.	109771	USNR	7
Ostrom, Charles H.	063351	USN	7
Register, Francis R.	106444	USNR	7

NAME	SER. NO.	SERVICE	NO. OF PLANES SHOT DOWN
Rennemo, Thomas J.	099967	USNR	7
Savage, Jimmie E.	104795	USNR	7
Silber, Sam L.	075313	USNR	7
Skon, Warren A.	263673	USNR	7
Thach, John S.	061281	USN	7
Troup, Franklin W.	337766	USNR	7
Traux, Myron M.	390909	USNR	7
Turner, Edward B.	098653	USNR	7
Voris, Roy M.	112299	USNR	7
Webb, Wilbur B.	285707	USN	7
Williams, Bruce W.	124247	USNR	7
Wolf, John T.	250624	USNR	7
Wordell, Malcolm T.	075121	USN	7
Kerr, Leslie H., Jr.	125501	USNR	6¾
Brewer, Charles W.	073306	USN	6½ Dead
Cozzens, Melvin	326302	USNR	6½
Davis, Robert H.	112818	USNR	6½
Fash, Robert P.	264199	USNR	6½
Flatley, James H., Jr.	062641	USN	6½
Fowler, Richard E., Jr.	283059	USNR	6½
Hardy, Willis E.	337890	USNR	6½
Haverland, Charles H., Jr.	325688		6½
Lundin, Walter A.	243199	USNR	6½
McGowan, Edward G.	124768	USNR	6½
Slack, Albert C.	282888	USNR	6½
Stokes, John D.	282895	USNR	6½
Taylor, Ray A., Jr.	278769	USNR	6½
Thelen, Robert H.	130592	USNR	6½
Turner, Charles H.	104555	USNR	6½
Bridges, Johnnie J.	124078	USNR	6½
Bare, James D.	173717	USNR	6
Barnes, James M.	354857	USNR	6
Batten, Hugh N.	326456	USNR	6
Beatley, Redman C.	263906	USNR	6
Blyth, Robert L.	320460	USNR	6
Brocato, Samuel J., Jr.	326457	USNR	6
Brunmier, Carland E.	084200	USNR	6
Burckhalter, William E.	125984	USNR	6 Missing
Bushner, Francis X.	112396	USNR	6
Byrnes, Matthew S., Jr.	114359	USNR	6
Carroll, Charles H.	157730	USNR	6
Coleman, William M.	073495	USN	6
Conants, Edwin S.	084084	USNR	6
Copeland, William E.	278187	USNR	6
Cowger, Richard D.	176494	USNR	6
Cronin, Donald F.	121885	USNR	6
Crosby, John T.	278158	USNR	6
Davenport, Murl W.	103966	USNR	6
DeCew, Leslie	106177	USNR	6
Denman, Anthony J.	086003	USNR	6
Drury, Paul E.	305837	USNR	6
Eberts, Byron A.	145229	USNR	6
Foltz, Frank E.	157740	USNR	6
Frendberg, Alfred L.	125331	USNR	6

NAME	SER. NO.	SERVICE	NO. OF PLANES SHOT DOWN
Gillespie, Roy F.	112583	USNR	6
Gordon, Donald	114378	USNR	6
Gustafson, Harlan I.	104705	USNR	6
Haas, Walter A.	083903	USNR	6
Hamilton, Robert M.	329438	USNR	6
Hanks, Eugene R.	125451	USNR	6
Heinzen, Lloyd P.	121192	USNR	6
Hoel, Ronald W.	081581	USNR	5
Huffman, Charles W., Jr.	301156	USNR	6
Hurst, Robert	158070	USNR	6
Kingston, William J., Jr.	363494	USNR	6
Lake, Kenneth B.	325679	USNR	6
Lamb, William E.	085330	USN	6
May, Richard H.	124819	USNR	6
Mencin, Adolph	098339	USNR	6
Mims, Robert	156707	USNR	6
Mitchell, Henry E.	315345	USNR	6
Montapert, John R.	283016	USNR	6
Moranville, Horace B.	291317	USNR	6
Moseley, William C.	112921	USNR	6
McClelland, Thomas G.	157644	USNR	6
McCormick, William A., Jr.	291312	USNR	6
Orth, John	346944	USNR	6
Poll, Tilman E.	326108	USNR	6
Paskoski, Joseph L.	116524	USNR	6
Pearce, James L.	122088	USN	6
Pound, Ralston M., Jr.	125670	USNR	6
Rosen, Ralph J.	350618	USNR	6
Rossi, Hermen J., Jr.	099730	USNR	6
Scales, Harrell H.	137104	USN	6
Seckel, Albert, Jr.	106945	USNR	6
Shands, Courtney	061256	USN	6
Smith, Clinton L.	320650	USNR	6
Smith, Nicholas J., III	299447	USNR	6
Starkes, Carlton B.	086060	USNR	6
Sturdevant, Harvey W.	176934	USNR	6
Tracey, F. W.	106261	USNR	6
Umphres, Donald E.	117178	USNR	6
Vineyard, Merriwell W.	243171	USNR	6
Wilson, Robert C.	176907	USNR	6
Yeremain, Harold	395905	USNR	6
Davis, Ralph H.	138203		5½
Dewing, Lawrence A.	315058	USNR	5½
Forrer, Samuel W.	105964	USN	5½
McLachlin, William W.	301090	USNR	5½
Revel, Glenn M.	106476	USNR	5½
Ross, Robert P.	084339	USNR	5½
Streig, Frederick J.	145269	USNR	5½
Winfield, Murray	325713	USNR	5½
Dunn, Bernard	326303	USNR	5⅓
Humphrey, Robert J.	347094	USNR	5⅓
Bryce, James A.	125187	USNR	5¼
Zaeske, Earling W.	281397	USNR	5¼
Amsden, Benjamin C.	351640	USNR	5

NAME	SER. NO.	SERVICE	NO. OF PLANES SHOT DOWN
Anderson, R. H.		USNR	5
Bailey, Oscar C.	112688	USNR	5
Barackman, Bruce MacD.	104144	USNR	5
Berkheimer, Jack S.	326660	USNR	5
Bertelson, Richard L.	347402	USNR	5
Billo, James D.	106892	USN	5
Bishop, Walter D.	263685	USNR	5
Blair, Foster J.	106266	USNR	5
Blair, William K.	106897	USNR	5
Blaydes, Richard B.	325662	USNR	5
Borley, Clarence A.	325881	USNR	5
Bruneau, Paul J.	084050	USNR	5
Buchanan, Robert L.	326183	USNR	5
Champion, Henry K.	315342	USNR	5
Clements, Robert E.	085181	USN	5
Cornell, Leland B.	130070	USNR	5
Denoff, Reuben H.	106046	USNR	5
Driscoll, Daniel B.	263457	USNR	5
Duffy, James E.	291305	USNR	5
Eccles, William G.	305706	USNR	5
Erickson, Lyle A.	299488	USNR	5
Evenson, Eric A.	223812	USNR	5
Farnsworth, Robert A., Jr.	325891	USNR	5
Flinn, Kenneth A.	291306	USNR	5
Foltz, Ralph E.	283003	USNR	5
Galt, Dwight B.	176558	USNR	5
Galler, Noel A. M.	074858	USN	5
Godson, Lindley W.	145537	USNR	5
Graham, Vernon E.	116962	USNR	5
Harman, Walter R.	114394	USNR	5
Hayde, Frank R.	240363	USNR	5
Hearrell, Frank C.	114495	USNR	5
Henderson, Paul M., Jr.	114325	USNR	5 Missing
Hippe, Kenneth G.	105984	USNR	5
Houck, Herbert N.	077679	USNR	5
Hudson, Howard R.	125741	USNR	5
Jensen, Hayden M.	081501	USN	5
Johnson, Wallace R.	291042	USNR	5
Kincaid, R. A.	095921	USNR	5
Kistik, William J.	354756	USNR	5
Lamoreaux, William E.	250604	USNR	5
Lillie, Hugh D.	301139	USNR	5
Mankin, Lee P.	188785	USN	5
March, Harry A., Jr.	100058	USNR	5
Martin, Albert E., Jr.	112868	USNR	5
Mazzocco, Michele A.	351599	USNR	5
Milton, Charles B.	130416	USNR	5
Mollenhauer, Arthur P.	320790	USNR	5
Munsen, Arthur H.	304159	USN	5
McCuddin, Leo B.	116827	USNR	5
McKinley, Donald J.	156549	USNR	5
McPherson, Donald M.	413937	USNR	5
Nelson, Robert J.	125212	USNR	5
Novak, Marvin R.	145198	USNR	5

NAME	SER. NO.	SERVICE	NO. OF PLANES SHOT DOWN
Olsen, Austin LeRoy	407089	USNR	5
Outlaw, Edward C.	075046	USN	5
Overton, Edward W., Jr.	095977	USNR	5
Owen, Edward M.	077583	USN	5
Phylips, David P.	351611	USNR	5
Phillips, Edward A.	305845	USNR	5
Reulet, Joseph E.	130655	USNR	5
Rhodes, Thomas W.	146501	USN	5
Rieger, Vincent A.	263671	USNR	5
Robinson, Leroy W.	315763	USNR	5
Robinson, Ross F.	306400	USNR	5
Schell, J. L.	130132		5
Shackford, Robert W.	250553	USNR	5
Shields, Charles A.	106544	USNR	5
Sipes, Lester H.	251385	USNR	5
Sistrunk, Frank	223752	USNR	5
Smith, Carl E.	326355	USNR	5
Smith, Kenneth D.	117174	USNR	5
Sonner, Irl V., Jr.	283035	USNR	5
Sutherland, James J.	077050	USN	5
Spitler, Clyde P.	176621	USNR	5
Stebbins, Edgar E.	075865	USN	5
Stone, Carl V.	315633	USNR	5
Strange, Johnnie C.	077670	USNR	5
Sutherland, John F.	081594	USNR	5
Taylor, Will W.	114461	USNR	5
Thomas, Robert F.	290853	USNR	5
Toaspern, Edward W.	325706	USNR	5
Topliff, John W.	145368	USNR	5
Torkelson, Ross E.	077797	USNR	5 Missing
Townsend, Eugene P.	223852	USNR	5
Van Der Linden, Peter, Jr.	250622	USNR	5
Van Dyke, R. D.	086105	USNR	5
Ward, Lyttleton T.	337770	USNR	5
Wesolowski, John M.	104291	USNR	5
West, Robert G.	106842	USNR	5
White, Henry S.	121251	USNR	5
Winston, Robert A.	075918	USN	5
Wooley, Millard, Jr.	106891	USN	5
Wrenn, George L.	112364	USNR	5
Zink, John A.	301158	USNR	5

7

MARINES—WORLD WAR II

MARINE AVIATION GREW slowly in the years between the two world wars and at the time of the Japanese attack on Pearl Harbor the entire United States Marine Corps had less than 250 planes. In June 1940 Congress had authorized 10,000 planes for the Navy, with 1,167 of these earmarked for the Marines. As the situation grew more serious in Europe the authorization was increased but only a small number of these had been delivered when the dark war clouds rolled up out of the East and rained fire upon the Pacific islands on that infamous Sunday morning. The swift Japanese attack destroyed all but one of the forty-eight available planes of the Marine Aviation Group 21 at Ewa Marine Air Station outside of Honolulu.

At Wake Island, 2000 miles away, the flyers of Marine Fighter Squadron 211 were proudly inspecting the twelve shiny Grumman Wildcats, which had arrived just three days before, and checking over their crisp new operating manuals, when the Japanese bombers poured destruction over the coral-white island. By the end of that day only five of the Wildcats were left. The Marine pilots bravely fought against overwhelming odds in the five remaining fighters, stopping a score of enemy aircraft and sinking two Jap destroyers. As a flying unit, VMF 211 (the "V" stands for heavier-than-air, "MF" for Marine fighter) stayed airborne for two weeks after the first attack; and when the last Wildcat had been destroyed the pilots fought as foot soldiers until Wake Island fell to the Japanese invaders.

Unrelenting, the Japanese gobbled up the Pacific, and by May 1942 the victorious Jap forces were reaching out for Midway Island, the last stronghold west of Hawaii. Available reinforcements were moved into Midway in a determined effort to halt the Japanese onslaught. A squadron of

AAF B-17 Flying Fortresses were flown in to help meet the brunt of the forthcoming assault. On 3 June 1942 a Japanese task force was sighted and in the early Pacific dawn, through the scattered cotton-puff clouds, the American airmen rose to meet the Jap Navy. Westward, behind the screen of the small task force, the big carriers were sending forth the bombers and fighters to devastate the island defenses. The Army Air Force, the Navy and the Marines, in a combined effort, hit the Japs with everything they had. In the ensuing Battle of Midway, the greatest encounter between air power and sea power, the young flyers stopped the Japanese and turned the tide of battle in the Pacific.

In the heat of the battle, one of the future Marine aces, Captain Marion Carl, while making a firing pass at a Japanese bomber, was jumped by three Zeros. Rolling over, Captain Carl dove toward the ocean to shake his pursuers. In his official report he stated that in the evasive dive he "firewalled" everything (his throttle to emergency war power, his propeller pitch control to full increase r.p.m. and his fuel mixture control to the full RICH position) for maximum speed and in so doing not only outdove the Zeros, but gained enough airspeed to zoom back up to make a pass on the three of them, shooting one down—the first of his 18½ kills.

Another future ace, Lieutenant Charles Kunz, who that same day shot down two Japanese bombers, returned in a very unhappy mood in regard to his aircraft. In a report to intelligence he made the following comparison between the combat capabilities of the Marine's Brewster Buffalo (F2A-3) and the Japanese Zero fighter: "The 00 fighter has been far underestimated [in previous intelligence reports]. As for the F2A-3, it should be in Miami as a trainer plane, rather than be used as a first-line fighter." But in spite of any misgivings, those were their only fighting machines and fight they did, running up an impressive tally against the Japanese. When the battle was over, the American flyers had struck a decisive blow across the knuckles of the greedy hand of aggression.

Eight months later, on the other side of the Pacific, as our forces moved into Guadalcanal, one of the most unusual adventures of the Marine's air war was unfolding. When the Navy had to withdraw its support from the landings on Guadalcanal, the Marines were up against overwhelming odds in the fight to hold their hard-won positions. At Henderson Field the order came down to put everything with wings into the air. Under this all-out effort, Major Jack Cram requested permission to take his Catalina PBY flying boat on a bombing mission. Permission was granted, and reveling in his one chance to get into the fighting end of the shooting war, he sought, found and twice torpedoed a Japanese transport vessel twelve miles out at sea. From overhead half a dozen Zeros flashed down after the lumbering, gangly Catalina flying boat. His torpedo attack successful, Major Cram, hugging the deck, hightailed it back to Henderson with the six Zeros making repeated stern sweeps, spraying the PBY with machine gun bullets. His situation seemed hopeless, so five of the Zeros slipped off to find more exciting sport, while one remained to finish the job. Grimly Cram droned on, with the Zero close behind pouring round after round into the PBY. By-passing Henderson Field, Cram skimmed over the treetops toward a fighter squadron auxiliary base with the Zero, almost in formation, shooting at him from behind.

Still unable to shake the Jap, Major Cram entered the traffic pattern at the fighter base. As he had hoped, a fighter (flown by Lieutenant Roger Haberman) was just entering the initial in the fighter overhead landing pattern. Haberman, seeing the strange sight, stretched his turn to become number three ship in the traffic pattern—directly behind the Zero. The strange procession rolled out on a long final approach and Haberman, without even bothering to pull up his gear, fired one burst into the Jap plane. The Zero burst into flames and crashed. Haberman continued his approach, landing behind the much-relieved Major Cram and his bullet-ripped PBY. The obliging Lieutenant Roger Haberman—a future Marine ace—was part of the "City Slickers" division of Captain Joe J. Foss' famed Flying Circus flight of VMF 121s.

Arriving in Guadalcanal in September 1942, Captain Joe Foss made history with his Flying Circus as he led his flight to seventy-two air-to-air victories, twenty-six of which he won himself. He had organized the two divisions of his flight into the Farm Boys and the City Slickers. Working together they became a team much feared by the Japanese aviators, and six of the eight men became aces. Their tally was impressive:

Farm Boys

Capt. Joseph J. Foss of Sioux Falls, S. D.	26
Lt. Greg Nash of Montrose, Calif.	8
Lt. William Freeman of Bonham, Tex.	6
Lt. Boot Furlow of Ogen, Arkansas	3
	43

City Slickers

Lt. Oscar Bates of Essex Fells, N.J.	4
Lt. Roger Haberman of Ellsworth, Wis.	7
Lt. Frank Presley of Encinitas, Calif.	6
Lt. W. P. Marontate of Seattle, Wash.	13
	30

"It's like football," the Marine ace said of his well co-ordinated team. "The ball carrier will end up eight yards behind the scrimmage line instead of two or more ahead if his team fails to co-operate and ward off the opposition. Whether you are going to shoot down any planes or even stay alive is determined by the boys you fly with."

Many of the stories about Joe Foss show that the man possessed a rare combination of fast reflexes, aggressiveness and luck. On one occasion Foss had dropped out of formation with one engine about to quit. Dropping down into a cloud deck above the mountains he intended to stay in the protective "soup" until Henderson Field was clear—at that time it was under bombardment. Looking up through the light hazy clouds above him he saw a Grumman screaming down with a Zero on his tail. At about the same time Foss' sick engine failed and he feathered it. The Grumman ducked into the cloud deck and the Zero swung over in front of Foss. Kicking his ship around he pasted the Zero and it fell from the sky. Joe continued, with one engine feathered, on back to Henderson.

The most unusual air adventure of the Flying Circus occurred in January 1943 when they held off an entire Japanese air armada without firing a shot. Over one hundred Jap Zeros and Bettys were reported headed for Henderson Field in one last all-out effort to destroy the American stronghold. Foss and his Flying Circus went up to meet them (it was felt at that time that the report of over a hundred approaching planes was greatly exaggerated). When the Japs began to arrive, it became obvious that the Japs really had sent the reported hundred planes, and Foss called for reinforcements. In the meantime he gave his own men a very strange order—considering his normal love of a dogfight. His order was to avoid combat and instead to continue a "thatching" pattern over the field. This gave the Japanese the impression of an American decoy, and they scanned the skies for what they feared to be great numbers waiting in the sun for them to strike the handful of P-38s. Puzzled, the Japs circled back and forth between Savo Island and Cape Esperance—between the American and Japanese territory. Occasionally three or four Zeros would make feints at the Flying Circus boys but they were ignored. Finally, unable to draw the Americans into a fight or to figure out what type of trap awaited them, they did the incredible. They turned tail and headed home, dropping their bombs harmlessly in the ocean. No bombs fell on Henderson Field that day, and Foss had accomplished one of the greatest aerial bluffs in history.

But not all battles had been easy and the boys were constantly in the air tangling with Japanese bombers, fighters, and once even a "Washing Machine Charlie" when they attempted a night interception of the Japanese nuisance raiders that were robbing the Marines of their sleep and keeping them holed up in malaria-ridden dugouts. That particular flight, Foss and Roger Haberman had a closer call from their own trigger-happy ack-ack people than from the enemy.

On 26 January, the commander on Guadalcanal decided that Joe and his boys had done enough and so the Flying Circus was sent back to Auckland, New Zealand, and on to the States for a welcomed rest.

Joe Foss is presently the Governor of South Dakota.

The big push back across the Pacific was gathering momentum and on Guadalcanal men and equipment poured in as the war in that area intensified. When, on 7th April 1944, the American radar warning system reported 160 Japanese planes headed toward the island, the Marines and Army

Air Force were able to send up over 60 fighters to meet the approaching air fleet. It was during this engagement that Lieutenant James E. Swett broke the six-kills-in-a-single-action record of the 5th AF's Colonel Neel Kearby. (Lieutenant Swett's record of seven kills in a single action was later tied by Captain William Shomo, also of the 5th AF, and near the end of the war was broken by top Navy ace Commander David McCampbell who shot down nine in a single action.)

Lieutenant Swett, called "Zeke" by his companions, had seen combat in air-ground support missions, but had never faced an enemy in the air. A little nervous, and very anxious for the opportunity, he took off with the other American flyers to meet the Japanese that April day. Leading a division he went in with the group as part of the first wave to intercept the Zeros and Aichi dive bombers as they came over the water to Guadalcanal. Peeling off at 15,000, Swett led his men into the attack. After the first pass and break-off Swett suddenly found himself behind six Aichi dive bombers with the rest of his men nowhere in sight. As he stated in his official mission report: "I got on the tail of the first one and gave it a squirt [burst of fire]. He jettisoned his bombs and burst into flame. . . . I skidded and mushed in behind No. 2 while my tracers laced him. He smoked and burned and went down. . . . I had trouble getting the third one boresighted. . . . As the Aichi (No. 3) nosed over in his bomb run, my first burst smoked him. When he pulled out, I was still on his tail. A few more bursts and he exploded. Just as I pulled away, one of our AA guns on Tulagi drew a bead [at his plane] and wrecked one of my port guns. They almost blew it out of my wing."

With his F4F wing crippled and a machine gun damaged, Swett turned for his base. On the way he spotted another flight of Aichis (nine of them) on their way home, flying low and fast in a follow-the-leader pattern. Swett poured the coal to his F4F and, diving on the planes, sent the rear one down in flames (No. 4); closing the gap he sent No. 5 and then No. 6 down in flames. With three of nine down, and six total, he was just getting warmed to his work. He caught up with the next one (No. 7) and shot it down in flames. With five to go, he closed the gap between the next dive bomber. By this time the Aichi's rear gunner was awake to what was happening and was waiting for the

American. They both fired at the same time, Swett with the last of his ammunition. Swett was wounded, the Aichi gunner was killed outright, and the Aichi (maybe No. 8) was last seen by Swett smoking as it headed for home. With his plane smoking badly, he headed back to Tulagi, but his fuel gave out two miles from shore, and he had to ditch the smoking plane in the channel. He was the twelfth man of both sides down in the drink that afternoon, so when the channel rescue boat pulled near his small escape kit raft, it approached cautiously, one sailor shouting, "Are you an American?"

"You're goddamn right I am!" shouted Swett.

The Navy man nodded. "Pick him up, it's okay. He's one of them loud-mouthed Marines."

For his work that afternoon, the 22-year-old Swett was credited with seven enemy planes and one probable, took a swim in the channel, suffered a broken nose, and received a Congressional Medal of Honor.

Actually the first Marine aces of World War II were not the dashing young lieutenants but two old throttle jockeys, Gregory Boyington and Edmund Overend, who had reached acedom (six Jap planes apiece) flying with Chennault's Flying Tigers before Pearl Harbor. After joining their basic military air arm, the Marine Corps, Overend added three more Jap planes to his total and "Pappy" Boyington racked up a grand total of twenty-eight enemy ships, and became the famed leader of one of the toughest Marine Fighter Squadrons in the Pacific.

Gregory Boyington—at the time a captain—left the Marine Corps in 1941 to fight with Chennault in China. When the Tigers were disbanded he returned to the Marines and served one tour of combat with VMF 121 in the Solomons campaign. At thirty-one, with the rank of major, Boyington was given a squadron command. A newly formed combat unit, the squadron nicknamed itself Boyington's Black Sheep because "Pappy" insisted on collecting the has-beens, what-nots, rejects, and misfits from all the other squadrons. He whipped his odd assortment into a hard combat unit, and they blazed new trails of aviation glory across the Pacific skies.

Pappy Boyington led by example, and on their first combat mission he shot down five Jap planes himself. At Kahili, the key Japanese air base in the Solomons, the Black Sheep were stumped but not stopped. The air base was a hold-out for hundreds of Jap fighters who were a menace to our forces in that area. The air base was protected by an elaborate ack-ack system, and attacking American flyers were suffering heavy losses while inflicting only minor damage upon the airfield.

In small groups Pappy and his Black Sheep flew high over Kahili and over the radio challenged the enemy, in hard, vulgar, insulting Japanese, to come out and fight. The young Jap pilots, full of spunk and fiery spirit, were goaded into a fight and took off after the Americans. The rest was easy; or as Pappy later remarked, "It was like shooting grouse; we got them on the rise."

This simple, but effective tactic cost the Japanese dearly, and in October 1943 Pappy and his Black Sheep were rotated out of the combat area for a well-earned leave.

Several months later, rested and back in business, the Black Sheep were chosen to lead a strike at Rabaul, to sweep away the fighter resistance so the bombers could go in and do their work. On the first fighter sweep against Rabaul the Japanese only nibbled at the bait that had been so effective at Kahili, so the total day's work amounted to six Japs down and two Americans down.

Back at the base, Boyington decided to switch tactics— if he couldn't go through center, he'd go around end. He drastically reduced the number of planes to be used in the sweep and switched to Chennault's highly effective two-man element operating in a small designated area. Again the Black Sheep led the strike at Rabaul and this time they shot thirty Jap planes out of the sky, with Pappy shooting down four of them himself, bringing his grand total up to twenty-four.

On 27 December, once more over Rabaul, he got No. 25 and missed three more. The press spotlight was on the colorful Pappy Boyington who was the first flyer in fifteen months to threaten the record of twenty-six held by Rickenbacker and Joe Foss.

On 3 January the Black Sheep struck Rabaul again, and on that afternoon Pappy sent down his twenty-sixth in a long, 400-yard burst at a Zero. He and his wingman, Captain George Achumun, then tore into two Jap fighters on the rise, each shooting one down (the twenty-seventh for Boyington) when Achumun was hit and rolled into a steep death dive. A number of Japs were attracted to the wounded ship and poured down on Achumun. Pappy joined the procession, diving on the Japs' tails and kicking his rudder back and forth, sprayed the Zeros with lead. (One went down—his twenty-eighth.) Just over the water, Pappy pulled out of his dive and his ship burst into flame. He rolled over and at 200 feet bailed out, taking part of the canopy with him and hitting the water almost as his chute opened. The Zeros were on him in an instant, covering the water with lead. When the attackers were gone he opened the life raft in the seat pack of his parachute and floated about waiting for Dumbo (American Air-Rescue) to pick him up. His own Black Sheep, learning of his trouble, circled above him. They remained with him until their fuel ran low, forcing them to return to their field. That night he disappeared, so it seemed, swallowed by the endless Pacific.

Although those that knew him had faith that he would return, he had not been heard from for over a year when the word finally leaked out that he was in a Japanese prison camp. Racing Dumbo to the rescue, a Japanese submarine had waited for nightfall to surface and take him to Omori, Japan, as a prize prisoner.

His Black Sheep completed that second tour five days later with a total of 94 planes shot down, 32 probables, 50 damaged, and 21 destroyed on the ground.

Another ace to make Marine history at Rabaul was First Lieutenant Robert M. Hanson, "Butcher Bob" of the VMF 215, the Marine's one-man airforce. He shot down twenty Japanese fighters over Rabaul in a period of seventeen days and won the Congressional Medal of Honor. Before coming to Boyington's stamping grounds, Hanson was already an ace. In his first battle over Rabaul "Butcher Bob" became a "double ace," shooting down five Zeros when his group attacked seventy Jap fighters attempting to stop B-25's on a ship bombing run at Simpson Harbor. This was his remarkable box score:

> 5 enemy aircraft destroyed in two tours at Bougainville

5	enemy	aircraft	destroyed	1st	flight	Rabaul
1	"	"	"	2nd	"	"
3	"	"	"	3rd	"	"
4	"	"	"	4th	"	"
3	"	"	"	5th	"	"
4	"	"	"	6th	"	"

Total: 25 enemy aircraft destroyed.

Twenty-year-old Hanson was killed by ground fire on a strafing run one morning just a few days before he was to complete his third tour. His record is so stupendous, so unbelievable and covered so few days that pressmen never had a chance to cover it. His Medal of Honor citation read: ". . . A Medal of Honor seems so great an award but yet so little that a nation can offer to its young men who gave their lives, deliberately, in their eagerness to serve their nation on the battlefield, far beyond the call of duty." Hanson could have gone home after completing his first tour but he stayed on, like so many other pilots who believed in the cause for which they fought and knew that on the second and third tours their combat experience made them far more valuable than a new man on his first tour.

Hanson, Aldrich and Spears of VMF 215 had a combined total of sixty planes shot down.

VMF 215, the first Marine squadron to receive the Navy Unit Commendation Award, had the following record:

137 Japanese planes shot down in 3 tours (18 weeks)
*106 Japanese planes shot down in 1 tour (6 weeks)
87 Japanese planes shot down in one month

10 Aces in the squadron

One very important development in Marine aviation to come out of the Pacific war was the progress with night fighter techniques. In the early winter of 1944 Lieutenant Colonel Frank Schwable, Commander of VMF (N) 531, first introduced radar techniques that he had learned from the British. The setup worked in a manner similar to present-day Ground Controlled Approach (GCA) landing systems. A land- or ship-based Ground Control Intercept (GCI) Station would pick up enemy aircraft on their large

* Later broken by the Death Rattler Squadron.

radar scanning scope and then the specially equipped Marine F4U's (Corsairs) were directed to within two miles of the "bogey" or enemy aircraft. The GCI unit gave the Corsair the speed, altitude and direction of the enemy, and a two-mile vector for contact. At two miles, the Corsair took over on its small scope and moved in for the kill. If the exhaust pattern on the small radar scope showed it to be an enemy aircraft and if no IFF (aircraft transmitting radar) was being transmitted, the enemy was fired at blind from 500 yards with continuous fire until the distance had been closed to 500 feet or the radar scope showed that the enemy plane was shot down. There were only six planes in Lieutenant Colonel Schwable's squadron and they paved the way for the modern Marine night fighters. He had four enemy planes shot down in seventy-two missions when he returned to the States. His successor, Lieutenant Colonel John Harshberger, also scored four victories.

While Lieutenant Colonel Schwable's new methods were being perfected and practiced, the other night fighter units were still depending upon good eyesight, fast triggers and seat-of-the-pants flying to do the job.

During the Leyte Island operation, Technical Sergeant John W. Andre, one of the few Marine enlisted pilots then still flying in the Pacific, scored five Jap planes one night for Lieutenant Colonel Peter D. Lambrecht's VMF (N) 541, the first Marine Corps squadron to land on Leyte. Andre that night pulled up behind two Japanese Jack bombers on their way home to Luzon after bombing Tacloban Field. As the Japs, unaware of Andre, turned on their final approach, they flipped on their landing lights. Andre got in the traffic pattern behind the two planes and as his speed narrowed the distance to fifty yards, he shot down the first plane. Closing to within a few hundred yards of the second plane he sent the next one down in flames with one long burst. Then he made several more passes over the field, this time strafing parked planes and buildings, destroying three more planes. (Although he destroyed five aircraft that mission, he was not rated as an ace since the Marines do not give official credit toward acedom for aircraft destroyed on the ground.)

It was not until near the end of the war that the Marine Corps got their first night-fighter ace. Captain Robert Baird won that honor when on 24 April 1945, with three kills already to his credit, he tangled with two Jap planes near the island of Ie in a brief but spectacular encounter. The 23-year-old captain was a member of Lieutenant Colonel Marion Magruder's "Black Mac's Killers" squadron whose mission was to make night interception of Japanese suicide planes. On that particular night Baird intercepted a Francis (a twin-engined night-fighter plane) and a Betty (a twin-engined medium bomber) both after the nearby naval force. In the black of night Captain Baird made two swift passes and the two Japanese planes flamed into the sea. Baird later shot down one more enemy ship to bring his final total up to six before the end of the war.

In the closing months of the war, a youthful unit, the Death Rattler Squadron commanded by 24-year-old Major George C. Axtell, Jr., broke all previous Marine records by shooting down 124½ enemy planes in less than two months in combat. "Big Axe," as the men called Major Axtell, had achieved earlier fame when in a single engagement and within a period of 15 minutes, he had shot down five Japanese planes. Leading his squadron to victory after victory, Big Axe not only shattered all existing records but his Death Rattlers did not lose a single man during their brilliant combat tour.

In one encounter on 22 April 1945 three Death Rattler men became aces the same day. Among these was Lieutenant Jeremiah J. O'Keefe, who led his seven-man patrol in an attack against thirty-nine Jap bombers. Shooting down four Jap planes, he turned to see a fifth Jap plane driving head-on in an attempt to ram his plane. O'Keefe poured lead into the Val and as it barely missed him he rolled over on his back to watch it crash into the ocean.

Then came the Big Bomb and the Japanese war machine crumbled. The signing of the surrender aboard the battleship *Missouri* silenced the chatter of the machine guns and the flaming terror in the Pacific skies.

The thousands of American prisoners of war were released from the Japanese camps, and many of the flyers who had been counted as lost showed up on the long lists of those being returned. Among these men was one of the Marine's most beloved heroes, Pappy Boyington. He came back in time to join his Black Sheep at a little bar in San Diego where they had all pledged to meet after the war. And there, reminiscing over their war adventures in a final farewell before turning to the bright future ahead, they sang perhaps for the last time a song that years before had echoed from the Quonset huts on lonely Pacific Islands (to the tune of the Yale Whiffenpoof Song):

To the one-arm joint at Munda,
To the foxholes where we dwelt,
To the pre-dawn take-offs that we loved so well,
Sing the Black Sheep all assembled,
With their canteens raised on high,
And the magic of their singing casts a spell.
Yes, the magic of their singing
And the songs we love so well,
Old Man Reilly, Mrs. Murphy and the rest,
We shall serenade our Gregory
While life and voice shall last . . .
Then we'll pass and be forgotten like the rest.

MARINE CORPS ACES IN WORLD WAR II

NAME	GRADE	E/A DESTROYED	
Boyington, Gregory (†)	Lt. Col.	28(*)	
Foss, Joseph J.(†)	Major	26	
Hanson, Robert M.(†)	1st Lt.	25	Deceased
Walsh, Kenneth A.(†)	Captain	21	
Aldrich, Donald N.	Captain	20	
Smith, John L.(†)	Lt. Col.	19	
Carl, Marion E.	Major	18½	
Thomas, Wilbur J.	Captain	18½	
Swett, James E.(†)	Major	16½	
Spears, Harold L.	Captain	15	Deceased
Donahue, Archie G.	Major	14	
Cupp, James N.	Major	13	
Galer, Robert E.(†)	Lt. Col.	13	
Marontate, William P.	1st Lt.	13	Deceased
Shaw, Edward O.	Captain	13	Deceased
Frazier, Kenneth D.	Captain	12½	
Everton, Loren D.	Major	12	
Segal, Harold E.	Captain	12	
Trowbridge, Eugene A.	Major	12	
Snider, William N.	Captain	11½	
DeLong, Philip C.	Captain	11 1/6	
Bauer, Harold W.(†)	Lt. Col.	11	Deceased
Sapp, Donald H.	Major	11	
Conger, Jack E.	Captain	10½	
Baldwin, Frank B.	Captain	10	
Long, Herbert H.	Major	10	
Mann, Thomas H., Jr.	Captain	10	
DeBlanc, Jefferson J.(†)	Captain	9	

(†) Received the Congressional Medal of Honor.
(*) Includes 6 planes shot down with the Flying Tigers in China.

NAME	GRADE	E/A DESTROYED	
Magee, Christopher L.	Captain	9	
Overend, Edmund F.	Major	9(*)	
Thomas, Franklin C., Jr.	Captain	9	
Loesch, Gregory K.	Captain	8½	Deceased
Morgan, John L., Jr.	Captain	8½	Deceased
Case, William N.	Captain	8	
Dobbin, John F.	Lt. Col.	8	
Gutt, Fred E.	Captain	8	
Herman, Edwin J., Jr.	Captain	8	
Hollowell, George L.	Captain	8	
Kunz, Charles M.	Major	8	
Narr, Joseph L.	2nd Lt.	8	
Nash, Gregory	Captain	8	
Post, Nathan T.	Lt. Col.	8	
Warner, Arthur T.	Major	8	
Yost, Donald K.	Lt. Col.	8	
Payne, Frederic R., Jr.	Lt. Col.	7½	
Baker, Robert M.	Major	7	
Brown, William P.	1st Lt.	7	
Caswell, Dean	2nd Lt.	7	
Crowe, William E.	Captain	7	
Haberman, Roger A.	Captain	7	
Hamilton, Henry B.	Warrant Off.	7	Deceased
Jensen, Alvin J.	1st Lt.	7	
McClurg, Robert W.	Captain	7	
O'Keefe, Jeremiah J.	1st Lt.	7	
Owens, Robert G., Jr.	Major	7	
Pittman, Jack, Jr.	1st Lt.	7	
Reinburg, Joseph H.	Major	7	
Rusham, John W.	1st Lt.	7	
Wade, Robert	1st Lt.	7	
Williams, Gerard M. H.	1st Lt.	7	
Mullen, Paul A.	Captain	6½	
Durnford, Dewey F.	2nd Lt.	6⅓	
Dillard, Joseph V.	1st Lt.	6⅓	
Terrill, Francis A.	1st Lt.	6⅓	
Axtell, George C., Jr.	Major	6	
Baird, Robert	Captain	6	
Bolt, John F., Jr.	Captain	6	
Chandler, Creighton	1st Lt.	6	
Conant, Roger W.	Captain	6	
Dillow, Eugene	Captain	6	Deceased
Dorroh, Jefferson D.	Major	6	
Drury, Frank C.	Major	6	
Fisher, Don H.	Captain	6	
Fraser, Robert B.	Major	6	Deceased
Freeman, William B.	1st Lt.	6	
Hall, Sheldon O.	Captain	6	
Hundley, John C.	Captain	6	
Jones, Charles D.	1st Lt.	6	
McManus, John	1st Lt.	6	
Percy, Gilbert	Captain	6	
Pierce, Francis E., Jr.	Major	6	

(*) Includes 6 planes shot down with the Flying Tigers in China.

NAME	GRADE	E/A DESTROYED	
Pond, Kenneth A.	2nd Lt.	6	Deceased
Presley, Frank H.	Captain	6	
Shuman, Perry L.	Major	6	
Stout, Robert F.	Major	6	Deceased
Valentine, Herbert J.	Captain	6	
Vedder, Milton N.	1st Lt.	6	Deceased
Hansen, Herman	Major	5½	
Hood, William L.	1st Lt.	5½	
Kirkpatrick, Floyd C.	1st Lt.	5½	
Lundin, William M.	Captain	5½	
Sigler, Wallace E.	Captain	5⅓	
Alley, Stuart C., Jr.	1st Lt.	5	
Braun, Richard L.	Captain	5	
Carlton, William A.	Major	5	
Davis, Leonard K.	Lt. Col.	5	
Dawkins, George E., Jr.	Captain	5	
Doyle, Cecil J.	2nd Lt.	5	Deceased
Drake, Charles W.	2nd Lt.	5	
Elwood, Hugh McJ.	Lt. Col.	5	
Farrell, William	1st Lt.	5	
Finn, Howard J.	Captain	5	
Fontana, Paul J.	Lt. Col.	5	
Ford, Kenneth M.	Captain	5	
Hacking, Albert C.	Captain	5	
Ireland, Julius W.	Major	5	
Kendrick, Charles	1st Lt.	5	
Laird, Wayne W.	1st Lt.	5	
McCartney, Henry A., Jr.	Captain	5	
McGinty, Selva E.	1st Lt.	5	
Olander, Edwin L.	Captain	5	
Phillips, Hyde	Major	5	
Poske, George H.	Major	5	
Powell, Ernest A.	Captain	5	Deceased
Ramlo, Orvin H.	Captain	5	
Scarborough, Hartwell V., Jr.	Captain	5	
Scherer, Raymond	Captain	5	
See, Robert B.	Captain	5	
Synar, Stanley	Captain	5	
Weissenberger, Gregory J.	Lt. Col.	5	
Wells, Albert P.	1st Lt.	5	
Yunck, Michael R.	Major	5	

8

FAR EAST THEATER IN WORLD WAR II

5TH, 7TH AND 13TH AIR FORCES

FIRST ESTABLISHED ON 1 November 1940, it was the Hawaiian Air Force which first felt the impact of the Japanese attack on Hickam Field next door to Pearl Harbor. Named the Seventh Air Force on 5 February 1942, the unit maintained a strictly defensive role in the early part of the war. When the Japanese tide was turned at Midway, there were no further serious enemy efforts made in the Central Pacific and the combat activities of the Seventh Air Force were slight. By late 1943, with growing naval strength and America gaining momentum in her Pacific offense, the Seventh Air Force became more active against the enemy, striking out over the broad expanses of the Pacific to lash at Japanese-held island bases. When the assault forces moved into the Marianas the Seventh's P-47's roared overhead to provide air support for the ground troops as they battled over the jungle-coated islands of Saipan, Guam, and Tinian. By the end of the war the Seventh Air Force had suffered sixty air-to-air losses against 110 Japanese planes destroyed and had been commanded by Major General Frederick L. Martin, Major General Clarence L. Tinker, Major General Howard C. Davidson, and Major General Willis H. Hale. After the war, the Seventh was merged into the Fifth Air Force under the present appellation, Far East Air Force. Because of the limited combat opportunities of this unit, only a few aces were generated. These men are listed at the end of this chapter with the Fifth Air Force compilation.

The Thirteenth Air Force was organized and established in January 1943 as the air support unit for the Solomon Islands and Bismarck Archipelago campaigns. As the American units moved into Guadalcanal the Thirteenth Air Force fought alongside the Navy, Marine and New Zealand air units, advancing with the ground forces through the central and upper Solomons as each new invasion provided new bases to launch the next attack—Russels, Rendova, New Georgia, Vella Lavella, Bougainville. Early in 1944 the Thirteenth took over the Rabaul area from the Fifth Air Force, and then on 15 June of that year the Thirteenth was joined with the Fifth Air Force under the command of General George C. Kenney in preparation for General Douglas MacArthur's return to the Philippines. Commanded by outstanding military aviation figures—Major General Nathan F. Twining and Major General Hubert R. Harmon—the Thirteenth Air Force generated twenty-nine aces of whom Lieutenant Colonel Robert B. Westbrook was the top ranking with twenty air-to-air kills.

From the record of the Thirteenth Air Force aces in aerial combat comes the story of one of the most extraordinary interceptions of the entire Pacific campaign. Naval intelligence in Washington had discovered that Admiral Isoroku Yamamoto, one of Japan's ablest military leaders and the director of the Japanese attack on Pearl Harbor, would be flying into the South Pacific on an inspection tour. Their information was detailed, and it revealed that Yamamoto, a man noted for his punctuality, would be flying in one of Japan's newest bombers over Ballale near Kahili in the Solomon Islands on 18 April 1943 at 0945. An order went out from the White House, issued by Frank Knox, the late Secretary of the Navy, that Yamamoto and his staff were to be destroyed.

Immediately, on Henderson Field, Guadalcanal, a plan was prepared. Eighteen P-38's were to make the strike against the Admiral's plane, which would be protected by a covey of Zero fighters. Four were designated as the attack section under Captain Thomas G. Lamphier, Jr. (an ace with six kills by the end of the war), with the remaining fourteen to provide cover under the overall command of Major John W. Mitchell (the leading ace in the Solomons area at that time).

The plans called for a 435-mile low-level over-water flight through enemy territory to arrive at Ballale at the appointed minute to meet the enemy admiral, who all his life had so obdurately demanded rigid punctuality. As Lamphier himself described the mission, "We had only eighteen Lightnings available for the mission and would look puny against the 100-odd fighters we anticipated would be milling about the Kahili skies to cover the Admiral's approach and landing. We had to find him, hit him and get out fast if we hoped to vote in the next election."

Using only a compass and airspeed indicator for navigation, Major Mitchell led his flight over the wave-skipping route to the appointed dot on the map just as the Admiral's entourage arrived on schedule. The carefully maintained radio silence was broken by a brief, "Bogey, ten o'clock high."

Instantly the flight split into two groups, Mitchell's group reached out for altitude as the powerful Lightnings began a steep climb for the cover position. Lamphier, leading his four-ship flight, moved in to attack, dropping belly tanks as they started skyward for the approaching formation. Flying in the third plane, Besbey Holmes couldn't eject his belly tanks and leveled off, kicking and yawing his Lightning to shake the tanks loose. Holmes' wingman, Raymond Hine, had to stick with him, leaving Lamphier and his wingman, Rex Barber, to press the attack.

Barber and I got to a point two miles to Yamamoto's right, and about a mile in front of him before his Zero cover saw us. They must have screamed the warning into their radios because we saw their belly tanks drop— a sign that they were clearing for action—and they nosed over in a group to dive on us, on Rex and me.

We closed in fast. Three Zeros which had been flying the seaward side of the Yamamoto formation came tearing down between it and us, trying to intercept us before we could reach Yamamoto's bomber.

Right behind them were the three Japanese Zeros from the inshore side of the formation.

Holmes and Hine were way off, down the beach, out of sight, and Mitch and his group were out of sight, too, climbing with throttles wide toward what they had every reason to believe would be the biggest fight of all, top Japanese cover from Kahili.

I was afraid we'd never get to the bomber that Admiral Yamamoto rode before the Zeros got us. I horsed

107

back on my wheel to get my guns to bear on the lead Zero diving toward me.

Buck fever started me firing before my Lightning's nose pointed in his direction. I saw the gray smoke from his wing guns and wondered with stupid detachment if the bullets would get me before I could work my guns into his face.

He was a worse shot than I was, and he died. My machine guns and cannon ripped one of his wings away. He twisted under me, all flame and smoke. His two wingmen hurtled past and I wasted a few bursts between them. Then I thought I'd better get my job done and go away before I got hurt.

I kicked my ship over on its back and looked down for the lead Japanese bomber. It had dived inland. As I hung in the sky I got an impression, off to the east, of a swirl of aircraft against the blue—a single Lightning silhouetted against the light in a swarm of Zeros. That was Barber, having himself a time.

Excitement in a fight works wonders with a man's vision. In the same brief second that I saw Rex on my right, and saw the Zeros I had just overshot, I spotted a shadow moving across the treetops. It was Yamamoto's bomber. It was skimming the jungle, headed for Kahili.

I dived toward him.

I realized on the way down that I had picked up too much speed, that I might overshoot him. I cut back on my throttles. I crossed my controls and went into a skid to brake my dive.

The two Zeros that had overshot me showed up again, diving toward Yamamoto's bomber from an angle slightly off to my right. They meant to get me before I got the bomber. It looked from where I sat as if the bomber, the Zeros and I might all get to the same place at the same time.

We very nearly did. The next three or four seconds spelled life or death. I remember suddenly getting very stubborn about making the most of the one good shot I had coming up. I fired a long steady burst across the bomber's course of flight from approximately right angles.

The bomber's right engine, then its right wing, burst into flame. I had accomplished my part of the mission. Once afire, no Japanese plane stopped burning, short of blowing up. The men aboard the bomber were too close to the ground to jump.

The two onrushing Zeros saw it, too. They screamed past overhead, unwilling to chance a jungle crash to get me. In that second I realized that my impetus would carry me directly behind the Mitsubishi's tail cannon.

My Lightning's belly was scraping the trees. I couldn't duck under the Mitsubishi and I hesitated to pull up over its line of fire, because I already was going so slow I almost hung in mid-air, near stalling speed. I expected those Zeros back, too.

Just as I moved into range of Yamamoto's bomber and its cannon, the bomber's wing tore off. The bomber plunged into the jungle. It exploded. That was the end of Admiral Isoroku Yamamoto.

Right around then, though, I got scared. I'd slowed so much to get my shots at Yamamoto's bomber that I was caught, so to speak, with my pants, and my heart, down around my ankles. My airspeed indicator coldly told me I was doing only 220 miles an hour, or less than cruising speed, and I had only ten feet of altitude.

For the first time on the mission, I pushed my mike button and called Mitchell. I asked him to send down anybody who wasn't busy. The two Japanese Zeros were diving at me again, almost at right angles, to my left.

I hugged the earth and the treetops while they made passes at me. I unwittingly led them smack across a corner of the Japanese fighter strip at Kahili, where Zeros were scrambling in the dust to take off. I made the harbor and headed east. With the Japanese on my tail I got into a speedy climb. At 20,000 I lost them. I was away with only two bullet holes in my rudder. Nothing more, except a year or two off my life.

The important and valuable missions of the Seventh and Thirteenth Air Forces notwithstanding, when the Far East theater is viewed as a whole with respect to the military aces, it was the combat of the Fifth Air Force which produced the top-scoring and greatest number (147) of Air Force aces in the theater. The top three aces of the Fifth Air Force shot down a total of 105 enemy planes and the four men who tied for fourth rank among that area's aces each shot down twenty-two Jap planes apiece. This is more clearly understood when it is pointed out that the Fifth Air Force contained the greatest number of fighter units in the Far East and was engaged in the greatest number of air battles. Thus, for the story of the aces in the Pacific war, it is necessarily from the Fifth Air Force that the story must come.

Originally established on 20 September 1941 as the Philippine Department Air Force, changed to the Far East Air Force the next month, it was finally dubbed the Fifth Air Force on 5 February 1942. While the unit was still under the name of Far East Air Force the Japanese impelled the unit into action by their bombardment of Pearl Harbor and almost simultaneous assaults against other American islands in the Pacific. On 11 December 1941, Lieutenant Boyd D. "Buzz" Wagner, one of the Fifth Air Force's early aces, took off from Clark Field in the Philippines on a reconnaissance mission—extremely hazardous one-man flights. After accomplishing his designated reconnaissance he roared down for a strafing run against the Japanese at Aparri. On his second pass over the field he glanced over his shoulder to find that he had been joined by five very hostile Zeros. A graduate aeronautical engineer, he knew he could get superior performance from his P-40 at sea level. Rolling over he split-S into a steep dive at the water. Two of the Zeros followed him down while three stayed overhead for cover. Wagner, barely getting enough speed to stay out of range of their guns,, couldn't shake the Zeros. Unable to outrun them, he decided to stop and fight. Easing off on the throttle he carefully slowed the P-40 down giving the Japs the impression that they were gradually overtaking him. When they had inched almost to within firing range, he abruptly chopped his throttle, and the startled Japs went sailing past. Buzz Wagner opened fire, kicking his rudder left and right, sending the astonished Jap pilots splintering into the water.

Remaining on the deck, he doubled back toward the Jap base at Aparri. Expecting the return of their own fighters, Buzz's P-40 took them by surprise. Coming in low over the water he poured lead into twelve parked Zeros, did a half-chandelle over the end of the field where he paused long enough to count five burning airplanes before he scooted for home. En route he ran into three more Zeros of which he flamed two. Then, as he stated in his report, ". . . my gas was running low so I returned home."

On 16 December 1941 in answer to an intelligence report that the Japs had twenty-five Zeros at Vigan Field, Buzz Wagner, leading a three-ship flight—Lieutenant Russell M. Church, Jr., and Lieutenant Allison W. Strauss—headed out on a reconnaissance, bombing and strafing mission. Using Chennault's tactics, Strauss took top cover while Wagner and Church went in on the bombing run. Wagner dropped his six 30-pound fragmentation bombs and was pulling up to join Strauss when Church was hit by anti-aircraft fire. His plane on fire, Church continued his run, dropping his bombs and machine gunning the remaining planes as the deadly anti-aircraft scored again and again on his crippled ship. Completing his run, Church struggled for altitude but his plane exploded and crashed to earth. Infuriated, Wagner dove down into the murderous fire, making five more strafing passes over the parked ships. One Jap plane tried to take off for battle with the fire-breathing P-40 and Wagner lost sight of him in the blind spot beneath his plane. Half-rolling his plane he took a quick look, then throttling back and rolling right side up, he let the Jap fly into his sights and with one short burst sent him crashing back down on the strip.

As the Americans were driven back by the Japanese victories in the Southwest Pacific and the East Indies, the airmen of the Fifth Air Force were regrouped in Australia as the nucleus for the air unit to be built up with reinforcements from the United States. Organized into a first-rate fighting Air Force, it was the Fifth that spearheaded MacArthur's drive along the New Guinea coast and, throughout 1943, the reduction of enemy air power on Rabaul. As the major objective in the Pacific war was "never to gain land masses or capture populous cities, but only to establish airfields (and fleet anchorages and bases) from which the next forward spring might be launched" the fighters of the Fifth advanced with the ground gains as the American forces marched back across the island-dotted Pacific—Woodlark, Kiriwina, Nassau Bay, Law, Nadzab, Finschhafen, Arawe and Saidor; Aitape and Hollandia; Wadke and Biak; Noemfoor and Sansapor. By mid-summer of 1944 the Fifth had helped place the American forces in a position to strike at the Philippines, which they

111

did with the combined air power of the Fifth and the Thirteenth Air Forces.

But perhaps the more important contribution to the final victory in the Pacific was not so much the blow against the Philippines, which the Fifth had helped make possible, but the contribution it had made to the metamorphosis in the Pacific air war. For two years the bitter jungle warfare, island hopping and constant aerial dogfighting had carried the Allies from Guadalcanal and Port Moresby to Guam and Sansapor—not only blunting the enemy's offensive air power but, more important, providing bases within B-29 bombing radius of Honshu. Now the strategic bombardment of Japan could begin: a new phase of the Pacific air war, hitherto unknown to the enemy, which ultimately resulted in the shattering of Japan's war industry and ended the conflict so victoriously and dramatically at Hiroshima and Nagasaki.

The Fifth Air Force was commanded by Lieutenant General Lewis H. Brereton, Lieutenant General George H. Brett and for the final victorious stages of World War II by General George C. Kenney.

The leading ace in the Fifth Air Force and America's all-time leading ace for all theaters and all wars was Major Richard I. Bong—the "ruler of the airwaves between New Guinea and the Philippines"—who destroyed forty enemy planes, and won every decoration the United States could give a combat flyer including the coveted Congressional Medal of Honor.

Born in Superior, Wisconsin, in 1920, Dick Bong attended the State Teachers College at Superior and in the June following Pearl Harbor he enlisted as an aviation cadet. He received his bars and wings in January 1942 and thereafter served as an instructor at Luke Field, Arizona, and Hamilton Field, California. Just outside of San Francisco, Hamilton Field offered some exciting temptations to the youthful Bong. It was when he fell victim to the pilot's greatest temptation that he caught the official eye of General George C. Kenney. The second lieutenant instructor was called before General Kenney on a serious buzzing charge, which included "looping the loop around the center span of the Golden Gate Bridge in a P-38 fighter plane and waving to the stenographic help in the office buildings as he flew along Market Street." General Kenney disciplined Bong but at the same time he was very much impressed with the flyer as a young man worth having in his command. Later when General Douglas MacArthur selected Kenney to head his Air Force in his drive back across the Pacific, Kenney called for fifty of his P-38 pilots of the Hamilton Fourth Air Force, and he personally saw to it that Richard I. Bong was included in that fighter group.

Dick Bong rose quickly and was soon a flight leader in the Flying Knights Squadron, where he helped lead his squadron to victories at the impressive rate of ten to one. Bong himself flew 146 missions, totaling 365 hours of combat flying during which time he flamed twenty-eight Japanese airplanes. When he had topped Rickenbacker's old record—twenty-six—by a comfortable margin, Bong was pulled out of combat and sent back to the United States to pass on his valuable experience to green cadets at gunnery school.

Although glad to make available his deadly techniques, Dick Bong was not content to sit in the States while there was still some more shooting to be done. Eight months later he managed to talk his way back to the Pacific, but they restricted him to a noncombatant job as an advanced gunnery instructor. Nevertheless, as a noncombatant gunnery instructor he managed to shoot down twelve more planes, commenting on his new kills: ". . . demonstration is a pretty good way of teaching. Anyway I had to get my flight pay." On 4 January 1945, by an order out of General H. H. Arnold's office, Bong was again pulled out of combat and sent back to the United States. Bong had served in the Pacific in combat with the Fifth Air Force for two years, and it was the desire of the top brass to preserve his remarkable abilities for the future of the Air Force.

In a letter for a Fifth Air Force survey intended to accumulate the valuable advice of the aces, Dick Bong wrote:

From the experience I have gained in individual combat in this theater against a number of different types of Japanese fighters and bombers these facts stand out.

Defense against Jap fighters is resolved around the superior speed of our fighters. If you are jumped from above, dive to pick up an indicated speed of at least 350 miles per hour, then level out and start a shallow climb at high airspeed. Generally speaking, a Jap fighter will not follow you in a high-speed dive, but occasionally one does and if such happens, a turn to the right for 90° will throw the Jap behind. The controls stiffen up to excess in high-speed dives, and he cannot follow a sharp-diving turn. A turn into the Jap is always effective because they have a healthy respect for the firepower of our planes. An indicated airspeed never less than 250 miles per hour in combat is good life insurance.

Offensive measures go according to the number of the enemy, but they are always hit-and-run because the Jap can out-maneuver us about two to one. Any number of Nips can be safely attacked from above. Dive on the group, pick a definite plane as your target, and concentrate on him. Pull up in a shallow high-speed climb and come back for another pass. Single enemy planes or small groups can be surprised from the rear and slightly below a large percentage of the time. He seems to be blind, or he does not look directly behind him enough to spot you, and your first pass should knock him down. Against bombers, it is quite safe to drive right up on the tail of any of them with two exceptions—the Betty and the Helen. These two planes have 20-mm. cannon which cover a 30° arc to the rear, and a beam attack broken off before you reach this one is the best attack.

After dashing forty planes to the earth, Bong was back in the quiet setting of Burbank, California, whetting his aerial appetite in the Air Corps' newest thinking in fighter ships—the jet. It was the beginning of a new era in aviation and Bong was part of the exciting new revolution in air power. The new Shooting Star—P-80—was the hottest thing with wings and he eagerly applied his combat knowledge in testing the tactical-operational potentialities of this winged blowtorch. On 6 August 1945, only nine days before the final victory to which he had so gloriously contributed, Major Richard I. Bong, at 24, was killed when his jet crashed during an emergency landing. A new Air Force Base in Wisconsin has been named in honor of this brave airman.

Major Thomas B. McGuire, Jr., a veteran Fifth Air Force fighter pilot, shot down thirty-eight enemy planes in aerial combat and was the second leading ace in the Far East theater.

Thomas McGuire was born in Ridgewood, New Jersey, 1 August 1920. His family later moved to Sebring, Florida, where he completed high school. After attending Georgia Institute of Technology he enlisted as an aviation cadet, graduating with wings and bars in February 1942. He served in the U. S. and Alaska and in March 1943 went to the South Pacific as a pilot with the 49th Fighter Group of the Fifth Air Force. (He later served with the 475th Fighter Group.)

On Christmas Day, 1944, McGuire volunteered to lead a squadron of fifteen planes to provide protection for heavy bombers attacking Mabalaent Airdrome. As the formation crossed Luzon, it was jumped by twenty angry Jap fighters. In the battle that followed McGuire shot down three Japanese planes.

The following day he volunteered to lead a squadron to Clark Field. Over the target area one of the bombers was hit by flak. As the bomber left the formation it was rushed by Japanese fighters. McGuire entered the fight and purposely exposed himself to attack to enable the crippled bomber to escape. He shot down one and went after the other three. He destroyed two of the remaining three before leaving the fight and rejoining the formation. On the way out of the target area, McGuire shot down another Jap, his fourth of the day, bringing his total to thirty-eight.

On 7 January 1945 he led a flight of four P-38's over a Jap-held airstrip on Los Negros Island. A single Jap Zero jumped them from out of the clouds. When the attack started the formation was flying at 2,000 feet in hopes of catching Jap planes taking off. McGuire led his squadron into a tight Lufbery Circle snaring the Zero inside. The Jap made a sharp turn to get out of the trap but the P-38's stayed with him all the way down to two hundred feet. There the formation scattered and the enemy plane maneuvered into position on the tail of one of the Lightnings. The pilot called for help and McGuire tried to respond.

Realizing the seriousness of his fellow pilot's plight and knowing that it might prove fatal to himself, McGuire willfully violated three rules he constantly preached to his pilots:

(1) Never attempt combat at low altitude.

(2) Never let your airspeed fall below three hundred miles per hour in combat (P-38 Lightnings).

(3) Never keep your wing tanks in a fight.

McGuire was flying at 180 m.p.h. at two hundred feet and his wing tanks had not been released. In a tight maneuver McGuire's plane stalled, fell off on a wing and crashed.

The next day Lieutenant General Kenney sent Mrs. McGuire a personal letter bearing the unhappy news saying: "I felt that he would make a name for the command as well as for leadership and great personal courage. The accident which left him vulnerable on January 7 and in which he met his death was sheer chance as Major McGuire was one of the most capable fighter pilots I have known."

Shortly before his death Major McGuire tried to help the young pilots by writing out his ideas of combat tactics in response to a Fifth Air Force survey conducted among their aces:

To completely cover fighter tactics in a letter would be impossible but I would like to give a résumé of my views on combat tactics, both individual and squadron, based on my personal combat experience.

On individual combat tactics, aggressiveness is the keynote of success. A fighter pilot must be aggressive. The enemy on the defensive gives you the advantage, as he is trying to evade you, and not to shoot you down. Never break your formation into less than two-ship elements. Stay in pairs. A man by himself is a liability, a two-ship team an asset. If you are separated, join up immediately with other friendly airplanes. On the defensive, keep up your speed. A shallow, high-speed dive or climb is your best evasive action against a stern attack. You must never reverse your turn; that is asking for it. Try to make the Jap commit himself, then turn into his attack. If forced to turn, go to the right if possible.

Go in close, and then when you think you are too close, go on in closer.

At minimum range your shots count and there is less chance of missing your target. On deflection shots, pull your sight through the Nip. Most shots in deflection are missed by being over or under rather than by incorrect

116

lead. Never turn with a Nip past the point where you can't hold your lead. Don't let the Nip trick you into pulling up or turning until you lose your speed. Always clear yourself before and during an attack. It is always the one you don't see that gets you. On long-range missions especially don't chase a single out of the fight; he is probably trying to lure you away from the scrap. Your job is to provide cover for the bombers and you reduce the effectiveness of your squadron if you get sucked out of the fight.

Squadron formation multiplies your problem. You not only have to think of yourself, but also of fifteen men behind you. The squadron commander's responsibility lies not only to his own formation, but also to the bombers he is covering. Radio control by the squadron commander can be had only if the men in the formation keep their radio conversation to an absolute minimum. I like the squadron to drop from escort formation to string formation as soon as the enemy is sighted. We use a string of flights made up of four ship components. Each man should be back six to ten ship lengths with an interval about double that between flights. In a fight, outside of the first pass, the flights are independent in picking their targets, staying of course in the same general area. No flight should chase enemy aircraft out of the fight unless the enemy has been split up and is leaving the vicinity.

For his conspicuous gallantry in action over Luzon on 25 December and 26 December 1944, Major McGuire was posthumously awarded the Congressional Medal of Honor.

Other comments in the survey by a few of the other top theater aces throw further light on the tactics and problems in that theater during the fury of island fighting.

Colonel Charles H. MacDonald, third ranking Fifth Air Force and Far East Theater ace, with twenty-seven kills, and at the time Commanding Officer of the 475th Fighter Group, had this to say:

The formation we fly is what we call out here the standard U. S. Formation. It is a four-ship flight with

117

the elements staggered and flexible. It is simple and easy to fly, yet the leader has visual and positive control. The disposition of the squadrons depends on the type of mission.

When we get over the target the flights fall into the fighting formation. That is, each flight forms itself into a loose string. These strings are mutually supporting and when they are weaving and criss-crossing present an extremely difficult nut to crack.

If I were to pick out the most valuable personal traits of a fighter pilot, aggressiveness would rate high on the list. Time and again, I have seen aggressive action, even from a disadvantageous position, completely rout a powerful Nip formation. And conversely, have seen flights lose their advantage through hesitation. Obviously, aggression can be carried to the point of foolhardiness. However, this sort of action is never so foolish as poking around looking for an ideal setup and ending up by being jumped yourself.

Lieutenant Colonel Gerald R. Johnson, fourth ranking ace with twenty-two kills and Commanding Officer of the 49th Fighter Group, wrote:

During my experiences in operating against the Japanese Air Force there have been evident certain characteristics and traits peculiar to the Japanese as airmen. A knowledge and an understanding of these characteristics is necessary in order to effectively combat the Jap.

First, the quality of the pilots encountered has decreased. It appears that the Jap Air Force consolidates a group of experienced pilots into a few "hot" outfits instead of spreading these men (and their experience) evenly throughout all its units. One example was the "Cherry Blossom Hiko-Sentai" which covered the Bismarck Sea Convoy in March 1943. Recently, we have engaged a few Japanese fighter pilots who have shown exceptional skill and aggressiveness. The Jap fighter planes have all been very maneuverable and when flown by an experienced pilot become a most difficult target to destroy. Fortunately, however, the majority of Japanese pilots encountered are not of this calibre. They are excellent stick-and-rudder men, but their weakness is that all their maneuvers are evenly co-ordinated. They make use of sharp turns and aerobatic maneuvers, seldom using skids, slips, or violent un-coordinated maneuvers in their evasive tactics. Another characteristic of the younger pilots is their definite lack of alertness. In many instances we have engaged enemy fighters and they made no effort to evade our initial attack, evidently because they didn't see us.

In order to effectively attack the Jap, *you must see him first.* If he has an altitude advantage, it is desirable to either climb up to his level or get above him before attacking. You cannot wait to decide what he is going to do; you must plan your attack as you go into action. If your attack is sudden and aggressive, the enemy will be at a disadvantage regardless of his numbers and position. Do not wait; attack immediately and pick your targets with the intent to destroy.

We attack as a squadron, but fight in elements of two. The wingman and his element are inseparable and form a most flexible combat team. No matter how the fight progresses all friendly fighters must remain in the same relative area in order to give each other mutual protection. If a fighter becomes separated from his element, he must join another fighter immediately.

When attacking a superior formation of enemy fighters, we approach at high speed, either on the same level or from above. Our intent is to destroy two or three in the initial attack and scatter their formation. When the enemy formation has been broken, it is possible to pick them off individually. Every effort must be made to reduce the angle of deflection while within firing range. Most kills are made on enemy fighters when the attack is made with less than twenty degrees deflection. Upon meeting a force superior in numbers, it is necessary that everyone attack together. Hit and run is still a most effective tactic if you hit fast and hard.

When attacking an inferior force we use only the strength necessary and always maintain a flight or an element as top cover. If we see a single Jap plane and suspect a decoy, we send in an element to make the kill, while the remainder of the flight or flights wait for the fighters to dive out of the clouds.

Colonel Neel Kearby, one of the four tied for fourth-place ranking ace in the Fifth Air Force and the Far East theater, was a great practicer of the "aggressive tactics" sermons that the theater aces preached. He constantly sought combat although it was not required as part of his official duties. Tallying twenty-two Jap kills by the end of the war, Colonel Kearby was also a recipient of the Congressional Medal of Honor for his gallantry while engaged in combat near Wewak, New Guinea, on 11 October 1943 where he shot down six enemy planes in one engagement.

The medal was presented to him personally by General Douglas MacArthur who cited him thus:

Colonel Kearby volunteered to lead a flight of four fighters [two two-ship elements] to reconnoiter the strongly defended enemy base at Wewak. Having observed enemy installations and reinforcements at four airfields and securing important tactical information, he saw an enemy below him, made a diving attack and shot it down in flames.

The second formation then sighted about twelve bombers escorted by thirty-six fighters. Although his mission had been completed and his fuel was running low and the numerical odds were twelve to one, he gave the signal to attack. Diving into the midst of the enemy airplanes he shot down two enemy aircraft.

The enemy broke off in large numbers to make a multiple attack on his airplane, but despite his peril, he made one more pass before seeking cloud protection. Coming into the clear he called his flight together and led them to a friendly base. Colonel Kearby brought down six enemy planes in this action, undertaken with superb daring after his mission was completed.

Colonel Kearby's six-planes-in-a-single-action record (top Air Corps record in FEAF) was topped on 11 January 1945 by Captain William A. Shomo, who flamed seven Jap ships out of the sky in a dogfight over Luzon in the Philippine Islands. General Kenney tells the story:

On 11 January a couple of youngsters from the 82nd Tactical Reconnaissance Squadron took off from Mindoro in the P-51 (Mustang) fighters to look over the Jap airdromes in the northern part of Luzon and see whether or not they were occupied.

The leader was the squadron commander, Captain William A. Shomo. His wingman was Second Lieutenant Paul M. Lipscomb. Flying at 200 feet altitude, just southwest of Baguio, they suddenly saw about 2,000 feet above them a twin-engined Jap bomber, escorted by twelve of the latest-type Jap fighters. They told me afterward they figured it must be some very important general or admiral being evacuated back to Japan—it might even be Yamashita himself. Neither of them had ever been in combat in their lives, but they figured you had to start sometime and here was a wonderful opportunity.

Shomo, with Lipscomb hugging his wing, climbed to the attack and opened fire. Either the Nips didn't see them before the shooting started or they mistook the P-51's for some of their own aircraft. It was probably the first time they had seen the Mustang, as it had arrived in the theater only a week or so before.

Shomo promptly shot down the bomber while Lipscomb destroyed a fighter. The fight was now on. The Nips had broken formation and now tried to get reformed and do something about the two hornets that seemed to be swarming all over them, but they just weren't good enough. In addition to the bomber, Shomo got six fighters, while Lipscomb shot down four fighters. The remaining two Japs left at high speed for the north and a quiet place to land in Formosa. The kids flew around taking pictures of the eleven wrecked and smoking Jap planes on the ground and then headed back home.

I asked them, when they landed, why they let the other two Nips get away.

"To tell the truth, General," said the cocky, blond Shomo, "we ran out of bullets." Tall, lanky, drawling Lipscomb grinned and nodded confirmation.

I made Shomo a major and put in a recommendation to MacArthur for a Congressional Medal of Honor. Lipscomb I recommended for a Distinguished Service Cross and promoted to the grade of first lieutenant. Their awards came through a few days later. The record score in a single air combat for all time had been established.

Seven victories in one combat, and particularly in the first combat, is still an astounding score.

An interesting angle to the story came that evening when I was chatting with the two youngsters. I asked them what they did for a living before they got in the Air Force. Lipscomb was a Texas cowboy. Shomo—believe it or not—was a licensed embalmer. Poor Nips.

Another little sidelight to this story that the general did not mention was their return to the home field. It was the custom for victorious airmen to do a Victory Roll over the home field for every enemy aircraft destroyed. As the two planes roared back over the field all eyes turned skyward for that colorful symbol of conquest. Shomo made his roll and all nodded approvingly, for this had been Shomo's first combat. Then he rolled again, then a third roll and a fourth. The men began to cheer. His fifth and sixth brought out the brass, and his seventh roll sent the surprised commanders angrily to their jeeps to meet the cocky young upstart who had dared violate the sacred symbol reserved only for the victorious. There was no place for exhibition acrobatics in the traffic pattern.

Lipscomb was the first to land, and in between the furious bellowing of the brass, he was able to explain that Shomo really had shot down seven Japs. "And not only did he get seven," drawled the Texan, "but Ah got four."

"Then why didn't you make your four victory rolls," he was later asked.

"Well, sir," the words rolled out slowly, "Ah just got checked out in this plane, and Ah ain't sure Ah know how."

Major William D. Dunham, with fifteen kills, was the commanding officer of the newly formed 460th Fighter Squadron (P-47's) when he led his Black Rams on their heroic strike against Nip transports attempting to reinforce Ormoc. In answer to the query by the survey he stated:

I feel it a privilege to write you about my experience in fighter tactics in the Southwest Pacific, and I hope that my comments, along with those of other pilots who have had similar experience in this theater, will prove helpful in better preparing new Thunderbolt pilots for their part in our work.

In this theater, the best individual defensive tactic is a hard and fast offensive, regardless of the odds. This tactic used in defense takes full advantage of the superior speed and diving ability of the P-47. It permits a pass at the enemy and a fast dive away with little danger of being shot down.

If you are attacked from above while you are at cruising speed, and the attacking planes have excessive speed, the best defensive maneuver is a sharp aileron roll to the right and down, diving out 180° from the direction of the attack. *This maneuver cannot be started too soon,* but must be executed just before the attacking plane is within range. The slow aileron action of the Japanese fighters at high speeds makes it impossible for them to pull through far enough to get the proper lead, and by the time he can change direction you should have enough speed to easily outdistance him.

Brigadier General Paul B. Wurtsmith, who commanded the 5th Fighter Command, summarized the matter very neatly:

"Credit for their success is shared in a large part by the men working on the line and in the various departments who are a major part of any flying team. It has been found by experience in this theater that three rules must be followed by all fighter pilots who wish to be successful: (1) Never be surprised; (2) Always fight aggressively in pairs; (3) Never circle combat."

But the American surveys can never speak as highly of American tactics in the Pacific war as do the reports from the Japanese top air operation personnel themselves. They respected most the American fighters' bomber-escort techniques, especially "scissoring" or "thatch weaving"—the unit maneuver employed by the fighters as they wove back and forth in a protective net over the lumbering bombers and developed by the Navy's brilliant aerial strategist, Lieutenant Commander John S. Thach. American fighter pilots in the Far East theater had one unbreakable rule when flying bomber escort which the Japanese felt made our bombers less vulnerable: "Stay in formation, regardless, and protect the bombers." Any pilot who broke off from escort to dogfight with an enemy plane or planes received disciplinary action when arriving at his home base

123

even if he shot down the enemy planes. (This was a policy that was not always followed in the air fights over Europe.)

The U. S. Strategic Bombing Survey revealed that the Japanese pilot thought his odds were best with head-on attacks at the American bombers and six o'clock (dead astern) attacks on the fighters except in the case of Corsairs, Hellcats or Warhawks because the Japanese fighters could never catch them at low altitudes. The Japanese considered the F4U Corsair the top U. S. fighter plane at any altitude, the P-38 Lightning the best at high altitude and the P-40 Warhawk best at low altitude.

In all instances the Japanese pilot had the greatest respect for the prowess of the American airmen. In the early stages of the war the Japanese enjoyed superiority in numbers. This edge was whittled down by the destructiveness of our flyers and the productive ability of the nation's aircraft industry. Nevertheless, regardless of which side the advantage of numbers favored, the American airmen displayed consistently superior flying skill, gradually winning the vicious war that was waged in the Pacific for air supremacy.

(GENERAL ORDERS)   5 September 1945
No............148

OFFICIAL CREDIT FOR DESTRUCTION OF ENEMY AIRCRAFT BY FIGHTER PILOTS

1. *Personal Records.* 1. As of 1 July 1945, the following individual standing for the destruction of enemy aircraft has been compiled and published from all existing records:

	NAME	RANK	CREDITS
1.	Bong, Richard I.	Major	40
2.	McGuire, Thomas B., Jr.	Major	38
3.	MacDonald, Charles H.	Colonel	27
4.	Johnson, Gerald R.	Lt. Col.	22
5.	Mahurin, Walker M.	Lt. Col.	22*
6.	Kearby, Neel E.	Colonel	22
7.	Robbins, Jay T.	Major	22
8.	Lynch, Thomas J.	Lt. Col.	20
9.	Welch, George S.	Major	16
10.	Cragg, Edward	Major	15
11.	Dunham, William D.	Major	15
12.	Homer, Cyril F.	Major	15
13.	De Haven, Robert M.	Captain	14
14.	Roberts, Daniel T., Jr.	Major	14
15.	Eastham, David B.	Captain	12
16.	Ladd, Kenneth G.	Captain	12
17.	Watkins, James A.	Captain	12
18.	West, Richard L.	Captain	12
19.	Lent, Francis J.	1st Lt.	11
20.	Loisel, John S.	Lt. Col.	11
21.	Smith, Cornelius M., Jr.	Captain	11
22.	Sparks, Kenneth C.	1st Lt.	11
23.	Aschenbrener, Robert W.	Major	10
24.	Giroux, William K.	Captain	10
25.	Harris, Ernest A.	Captain	10
26.	Reynolds, Andrew J.	Captain	10
27.	Stanch, Paul M.	Captain	10
28.	Summer, Elliot	Major	10
29.	Bank, William M.	Lt. Col.	9
30.	Champlin, Fredric F.	Captain	9
31.	Curdes, Louis E.	1st Lt.	9**
32.	Dahl, Perry J.	Captain	9
33.	Fawning, Grover E.	Captain	9
34.	Forester, Joseph M.	Captain	9
35.	Hill, Allen E.	Major	9
36.	Kiser, George E.	Major	9
37.	Paris, Joel B., III	Captain	9
38.	Smith, Meryl M.	Lt. Col.	9
39.	White, Robert H.	1st Lt.	9
40.	Allen, David W.	1st Lt.	8
41.	Benz, Walter G., Jr.	Major	8
42.	Damstrom, Feruley H.	1st Lt.	8
43.	Gardner, William A.	Captain	8

* Credited with the destruction of 21 Aircraft in ETO.
** Destroyed 8 of these in ETO.

125

	NAME	RANK	CREDITS
44.	Harris, Frederick A.	Captain	8
45.	Hart, Kenneth F.	1st Lt.	8
46.	Jones, John L.	Captain	8
47.	O'Neill, John G.	Captain	8
48.	Roddy, Edward F.	Captain	8
49.	Rowland, Robert R.	Colonel	8
50.	Shomo, William A.	Major	8
51.	Stanton, Arland	Major	8
52.	Wagner, Boyd D.	Lt. Col.	8
53.	Adams, Burnell W.	Captain	8
54.	Blair, Samuel V.	Captain	8
55.	Davis, George A., Jr.	Captain	7
56.	Dean, Zach W.	1st Lt.	7
57.	Dunaway, John S.	1st Lt.	7
58.	Elliott, Vincent T.	1st Lt.	7
59.	Fisk, Jack A.	Captain	7
60.	Grant, Marvin E.	1st Lt.	7
61.	Grosshuesch, Leroy V.	Captain	7
62.	Hennon, William J.	Captain	7
63.	Jett, Verl E.	Captain	7
64.	Lewis, Warren R.	Major	7
65.	Moore, John T.	Major	7
66.	Morehead, James B.	Captain	7
67.	Pierce, Sammy A.	1st Lt.	7
68.	Purdy, John E.	1st Lt.	7
69.	Smith, Carroll C.	Major	7
70.	Smith, Richard E.	1st Lt.	7
71.	Strand, William	Captain	7
72.	Wire, Calvin C.	1st Lt.	7
73.	Andrews, Stanley O.	1st Lt.	6
74.	Baker, Ellis C., Jr.	2nd Lt.	6
75.	Brown, Meade M.	Captain	6
76.	Czarnecki, Edward J.	1st Lt.	6
77.	Dent, Elliott E., Jr.	Captain	6
78.	Degraffenreid, Edwin L.	2nd Lt.	6
79.	Drier, William C.	Captain	6
80.	Eason, Hoyt A.	1st Lt.	6
81.	Everhart, Lee R.	Captain	6
82.	Fleischer, Richard H.	Captain	6
83.	Foulis, William B., Jr.	Captain	6
84.	Gallup, Charles S.	Major	6
85.	Gresham, Billy M.	1st Lt.	6
86.	Hagerstrom, James P.	1st Lt.	6
87.	Howard, Robert L.	1st Lt.	6
88.	Ince, James C.	1st Lt.	6
89.	Jordan, Wallace R.	Major	6
90.	Landers, John D.	1st Lt.	6
91.	Lane, John H.	1st Lt.	6
92.	Lucas, Paul W.	Captain	6
93.	Meuten, Donald	1st Lt.	6
94.	Mugavero, James D.	1st Lt.	6
95.	Murphey, Paul C., Jr.	Captain	6
96.	Pietz, John, Jr.	1st Lt.	6
97.	Smith, John C.	1st Lt.	6

NAME	RANK	CREDITS
98. Wandrey, Ralph H.	Captain	6
99. Wenige, Arthur E.	1st Lt.	6
100. Witt, Lynn E., Jr.	Captain	6
101. Wright, Ellis Wm., Jr.	Captain	6
102. Adams, Robert H.	1st Lt.	5
103. Ambort, Ernest J.	2nd Lt.	5
104. Brown, Harry W.	Captain	5
105. Castle, Neil K.	2nd Lt.	5
106. Cloud, Vivian A.	Captain	5
107. Cowdon, Harry L.	Captain	5
108. Curton, Warren D.	1st Lt.	5
109. Day, William C., Jr.	Captain	5
110. Della, George	2nd Lt.	5
111. Dick, Frederick E.	1st Lt.	5
112. Dikovitsky, Michael	1st Lt.	5
113. Donaldson, I. B. Jack	1st Lt.	5
114. Dubisher, Francis E.	Major	5
115. Felts, Marion C.	1st Lt.	5
116. Flack, Nelson D., Jr.	Captain	5
117. Gholson, Grover D.	1st Lt.	5
118. Gibb, Robert D.	1st Lt.	5
119. Gupton, Gheatham W.	1st Lt.	5
120. Hnatio, Myron M.	1st Lt.	5
121. Hunter, Alvaro J.	Captain	5
122. Jones, Curran L.	Captain	5
123. King, Charles W.	Major	5
124. Kirby, Marion F.	1st Lt.	5
125. Knapp, Robert H.	Captain	5
126. Lutton, Lowell C.	1st Lt.	5
127. McDowough, William F.	Major	5
128. McGee, Donald C.	Captain	5
129. McKeon, Joseph T.	Captain	5
130. Mankin, Jack C.	Captain	5
131. Mathre, Milden E.	2nd Lt.	5
132. Monk, Franklin H.	1st Lt.	5
133. Morriss, Paul V.	Captain	5
134. Myers, Jennings L.	1st Lt.	5
135. Nichols, Franklin A.	Major	5
136. O'Neill, Lawrence F.	1st Lt.	5
137. Pool, Kenneth R.	1st Lt.	5
138. Popek, Edward S.	1st Lt.	5
139. Porter, Philip B.	1st Lt.	5
140. Ray, C. B.	1st Lt.	5
141. Suehr, Richard C.	Captain	5
142. Sullivan, Charles P.	Captain	5
143. Sutcliffe, Robert C.	1st Lt.	5
144. Tilley, John A.	1st Lt.	5
145. Troxell, Clifton H.	Major	5
146. Vaught, Robert H.	Captain	5
147. Yaeger, Robert R., Jr.	Captain	5

13TH AIR FORCE ACES
(Including crew members)

	NAME	RANK	CREDITS
1.	Westbrook, Robert B.	Lt. Col.	20
2.	Harris, Bill	Lt. Col.	16
3.	Shubin, Murray	1st Lt.	12
4.	LeSicka, Joseph J.	Captain	9
5.	Head, Coatsworth	Captain	8
6.	Mitchell, John	Major	8
7.	Shuler, Lucien	Captain	7
8.	Gaunt, Frank	Captain	7
9.	Wheadon, Elmer	Captain	7
10.	Holmes, Besbey	1st Lt.	6
11.	Lanphier, Thomas, Jr.	Captain	6
12.	Adair, Oliver L.	1st Lt.	5
13.	Bade, Jack	Captain	5
14.	Baird, Raphael F.	2nd Lt.	5
15.	Barber, Rex	1st Lt.	5
16.	Byrnes, Robert	Captain	5
17.	Cross, John O.	2nd Lt.	5
18.	Fiedler, William	1st Lt.	5
19.	Gladen, Cerns	1st Lt.	5
20.	Stehle, Raymond D.	1st Lt.	5
21.	Agnew, John W.	S/Sgt.	5
22.	Bowen, Wilbur L.	T/Sgt.	5
23.	Cielinski, Joseph J.	S/Sgt.	5
24.	Held, Charles F., Jr.	S/Sgt.	5
25.	Lee, Harold K.	S/Sgt.	5
26.	O'Brien, Frank, Jr.	T/Sgt.	5
27.	Stefanski, Edward J.	Sgt.	5

128

9

CHINA-BURMA-INDIA

10TH AND 14TH AIR FORCES

THE 10TH AIR Force was established on 12 February 1942 to comprise the only U. S. air unit in the entire China-Burma-India theater. Although the stakes were high, the prospect of striking a decisive blow did not seem bright enough for the Allies to throw heavy forces into this area. Also there was the problem of supply, which was probably greater in the China-Burma-India area than in any other zone of combat. The distances from the United States or from Great Britain to India were great and within the theater itself the supply lines stretched for thousands of miles with completely inadequate transportation facilities. Virtually all war materials destined for China had to be air lifted under the most severe natural and military hazards.

In a letter to General H. H. Arnold, Major General Clayton Bissell in October 1942 graphically explained the transportation difficulties:

From the base port of Karachi to the combat units in China is a distance greater than from San Francisco to New York. From Karachi, supplies go by broad-gauge railroad a distance about as far as from San Francisco to Kansas City. They are then transshipped to meter gauge and to narrow gauge and go a distance by rail as far as from Kansas City to St. Louis. They are then transshipped to water and go down the Ganges and up the Brahmaputra, a distance about equivalent to that from St. Louis to Pittsburgh. They are then loaded on transports of the Ferrying Command in the Dinjan Area and flown to Kunming—a distance greater than from Pittsburgh to Boston. From Kunming, aviation supplies go by air, truck, rail, bullock cart, coolie and river to operating airdromes—a distance about equivalent from Boston to Newfoundland. With interruption of this communications system due to sabotage incident to the internal political situation in India, you can readily appreciate that regular supply presents difficulties.

America's major aim in that part of the Far East was to keep China in the war, which they accomplished for the most part by providing lend-lease and technical assistance. For strategy purposes China, Burma and India were all linked together into one theater of operations under the command of Lieutenant General Joseph W. Stilwell. Taking command in February, 1942, with his limited resources and meager equipment, General Stilwell could fight at best only a stop-gap war in which he was confined primarily to the air operations of his 10th Air Force.

By the end of spring 1942, Singapore had fallen and the yellow tide had poured over Burma, swallowed up Rangoon, engulfed Myitkyina, and driven a giant wedge into Allied holdings virtually sealing off China from her sources of supply. The only route left was across the ragged Himalayas with peaks scratching the top of the sky at altitudes up to 18,000 feet—an uncertain and dangerous route. Although the 10th Air Force had been too inadequate (air personnel in CBI numbered 3,000 men) to materially aid in the defense of Burma or substantially assist the British in the defense of India, they had the entire chore of protecting the vital "Hump" and in keeping open the one remaining link with the otherwise besieged China. This task they successfully carried out throughout the rest of the hostilities.

Lieutenant General Lewis H. Brereton was the first 10th Air Force Commander, followed by Major General Clayton L. Bissell and later Major General Howard C. Davidson. During the bulk of the 10th's operations from April 1942 to March 1944 the flyers destroyed 210 enemy aircraft to their own losses of 75.

As commander of the China Air Task Force attached to the 10th Air Force, Brigadier General Claire Chennault continued to head the air units in China. Finally, under the urgings of Generalissimo Chiang Kai-shek, these units were created into a separate United States Air Force—the

14th Air Force—on 10 March 1943. Still under General Chennault's guiding genius, the 14th Air Force covered Southeast and Central China, the South China Sea, Hainan, Formosa, North Burma and Thailand, assisting the 10th Air Force in guarding the Hump route, aiding the Chinese ground operations and attacking Japanese air forces and shipping in accordance with their primary mission of preserving Chinese territory as a base for possible future attacks on Japan itself. In the traditions of the earlier Flying Tigers, Chennault's men inflicted damages on the Japanese completely out of proportion to the small American and Chinese forces involved. From February 1943 to March 1944 the American score was 477 enemy aircraft destroyed to 126 U. S. losses.

The air war in the China-Burma-India area was perhaps more trying than in most of the other theaters: supplies, equipment and living conditions being as much of an enemy as the formidable Jap. As Captain Albert J. Baumler described his early days with Chennault's units shortly after the United States' entry into the war: "Often Chennault was down to a bomber force of five B-25's and maybe twenty P-40's. Just enough fuel and ammunition came over the Hump to keep us fighting. We got nothing else. Most of us had the clothes on our backs; a guy with two pairs of socks had a wardrobe. We couldn't get winter uniforms, coveralls, gloves or shoes. Not that we needed fancy uniforms; there was no place to go. We just sat around, off duty, playing old cracked jazz records and talking about home, home, home."

But in spite of the unfavorable conditions the men stuck grimly to the difficult task before them. The fortunes of war were not favorable as the Japanese war machine pushed farther and farther into China. Still the Americans stayed on the offensive, as limited as it might be. In carrying their small air war against the enemy, the principal American unit concerned with air-to-air combat was the 23rd Fighter Group. Under the original Air Force plans the American Volunteer Group in China was to be transferred "on paper" automatically into the 23rd Fighter Group. However, when it became apparent that very few of the Flying Tiger people could be retained, new men had to be trained to replace the experienced AVG personnel

131

returning to America. At the time of the official transfer, in July, it was common knowledge among the Japanese as well as Americans that most of the Flying Tigers were going home, and the Japs anxiously awaited the departure of their unloved enemy and the arrival in combat of green, inexperienced fighter pilots.

On 4 July the Jap force winged in over Kweilin in their new twin-engined fighters, the I-45's, expecting to meet the young American pilots and anticipating, at long last, a field day. They were sadly disappointed. General Chennault had anticipated their actions and had talked two squadrons of his old Flying Tigers into staying behind for two extra weeks to disillusion the Japs and to help the newly formed 23rd Fighter Group. On this particular occasion the old troopers were waiting in the sun for the Jap formation and in a very few minutes thirteen Jap fighters were twisted wreckage in the Chinese mountains.

In stepping up to his new leadership of the entire China Air Task Force, General Chennault placed the command of the fighter group in the capable hands of Colonel Robert L. Scott, who led his 23rd Fighter Group in the victorious reduction of the Japanese air machines in China, and in so doing shot down thirteen Japanese planes himself and destroyed one on the ground for a total of fourteen kills. General Chennault wrote of Colonel Scott:

Colonel Robert L. Scott, Jr., served under my command from July 1, 1942, to January 9, 1943, as Commander of my fighter force. The only criticism of his actions as Group Commander was that he consistently scheduled himself as a pilot on all possible missions. He led all types of combat missions but specialized in the most dangerous, such as long-range fights to strafe from minimum altitudes Jap airdromes, motor vehicles, and shipping deep in enemy territory. It was often necessary for me to forbid his participation in combat missions in order to enable him to discharge the many other duties of a Group Commander. . . . Colonel Scott's group of fighters always operated against greatly superior numbers of the enemy. Often the odds were five to one against them. Their planes and equipment were usually battered by hard usage and supplies were extremely limited. Both

Scott and his handful of pilots had one resource in unlimited quantities—courage.

On 2 September 1942 Colonel Scott was leading a flight on a raid on Jap gunboats at Sintze-Hukow Strait. After successfully sinking or seriously damaging all the boats Colonel Scott called for his ships to re-form. At the last minute he saw something and circled back to take a look while his seven P-40's went speeding off to the rendezvous point.

When he pulled up again to catch his flyers they were already little specks on the horizon, too far ahead for him to catch up. So he pulled back his power to cruise and settled down to flying along behind them at their homeward altitude of slightly more than a thousand feet. Suddenly out of the sun darted several Zeros. Their guns blazing, they pounced upon the almost helpless ship (at low altitude and at slow speed). Instinctively, Colonel Scott did the one thing that could save him: he turned directly toward the Japs, pushing his aircraft's nose down for speed. If he had tried to turn away, their crossfire would have made short work of him.

As it was, I surprised them and went underneath them very fast and into the sun. Thus, when they looked around, I had the sun in my favor, and from that time on I was using it. But as I pulled up firing, I held the trigger down and "froze." I heard the cannon of the Zero—I felt the recoil of my six guns—I felt things hit "Old Exterminator"—and then I saw a cloud of black smoke in front of my nose. I shut my eyes involuntarily and dove again.

Something hit my ship with the same sound you get when you suddenly fly into heavy rain. I opened my eyes and everything was dark. I smelled the smoke and cordite and gasoline and thought I was on fire. Just then I realized I was still firing. I reached up, grabbed the handle, rolled the canopy open—and saw light. I rolled it shut again and realized that the blackness had been caused mostly by oil on my windshield. The speed of my dive had blown most of that off now, and though I couldn't see very well, I could make out the horizon. . . .

I think I was halfway home before I fully realized that I had shot it down and hadn't run into it.

On 23 October 1942 Colonel Scott was again leading his fighters, this time on a bomber-escort mission. It was the China Air Task Force's first big bomber raid deep into Japanese territory. Their target was the shipyards and harbor between Kowloon and Hongkong, which was reported to be filled with heavy shipping on its way to the Solomons and Saigon. As the B-25's finished their bombing run they were jumped by fast climbing Zeros and Colonel Scott and his fighter boys flashed to the attack. The colonel described his own particular part in this air battle:

I was diving now, aiming for the lead Zero, turning my gunsight on and off, a little nervously checking again and again to see that the gun switch was at "on." I jerked the belly-tank release and felt the underslung fifty-gallon bamboo tank drop off. We rolled to our backs to gain speed for the attack and went hell-bent for the Zeros. I kept the first Zero right in the lighted sight and began to fire from over a thousand yards, for he was too close to the bombers. Orange tracers were coming from the B-25's too, as the turret gunners went to work.

Five hundred yards before I got to the Zero, I saw another P-40 bearing the number 151 speed in and take it. That was Tex Hill. He followed the Zero as it tried to turn sharply into the bombers and shot it down. Tex spun from his tight turn as the Jap burst into flames. I took the next Zero—they seemed to be all over the sky now. I went so close that I could see the pilot's head through the glass canopy and the little tail wheel that was not retracted, and I knew it was a Navy Zero—the little wheel was built for the arresting gear of a carrier. My tracers entered the cockpit and smoke poured back, hiding the canopy, and I went by.

As I turned to take another ship below me, I saw four airplanes falling in flames toward the waters of Victoria Harbor. I half-rolled again and skidded in my dive to shake any Zero that might be on my tail. I saw another P-40 shooting at a Jap, but there was a Zero right on his tail. I dove for this one. He grew in my sights, and as my tracers crossed in front of him he turned into me.

I shot him down as his ship seemed to stand still in the vertical bank. The ship was three or four hundred yards from me, and it fell toward the water for a time that seemed ages. An explosion came, and there was only black smoke; then I could see the ship again, falling, turning in a slow spin, down—down—down.

I shot at everything I saw. Sometimes it was just a short burst as the Jap went in for our bombers. Sometimes I fired at one that was turning, and as I'd keep reefing back on my stick, my ship would spin, and I'd recover far below. I shot down another ship that didn't see me. I got it with one short burst from directly astern, a no-deflection shot. In this attack I could see the Japanese ship vibrate as my burst of six fifty-caliber guns hit it. First it just shook, then one wing went up. I saw the canopy shot completely off; then I went across it. Turning back in a dive to keep my speed, I watched the enemy ship, as it dove straight down, stream flames for a distance the length of the airplane behind.

As I looked around now the bombers were gone, but climbing up from the South I saw four twin-engine ships that I thought were I-45's; later we decided they were Japanese Messerschmitts. I had plenty of altitude on the leader, and started shooting at him from long range, concentrating on his right engine. He turned to dive, and I followed him straight for the water. I remember grinning, for he had made the usual mistake of diving instead of climbing. . . . I came up to within fifty yards and fired into him until he burned.

In that day's action Colonel Robert Scott had shot down four enemy aircraft.

While his action and leadership in that theater was exceptionally outstanding, outstanding ability was the rule rather than the exception in his 23rd Fighter Group. For, while all the men certainly didn't become aces, they all flew with the "ace attitude" which accounts to a great extent for their high margin of victories in spite of their shortage of equipment and manpower. Colonel Scott explained this attitude:

When men went out of the door to get into their ships and take off there was no handing to friends on the

135

ground of last letters to take care of, no entrusting of rings and watches to roommates. For fighter pilots don't think of not coming back. They are invincible, or think they are, and they have to be that way. Down in our hearts we may figure that some accident will get us some day, when we are old and gray, when our beards get in the way of the controls, or we get to where we don't see well or react fast—but we know that no enemy fighter is good enough to shoot us down. If that happens it's just an accident.

These thoughts are the "chips" that we carry on our shoulders, and they have to be there—arrogant, egotistical chips mellowed by flying technique and experience and fortified by the motto, "Attack!" Never be on the defensive. Shoot the enemy down before he can shoot you down. You are better than he is, but don't give him a chance. He may get in a lucky shot but you're invincible. Move toward any dot in the sky that remotely resembles an airplane. Move to attack, with switches on and the sight ready. If it's not a ship or if it's a friendly one you'll be ready anyway, and your arrogant luck will last longer.

An outstanding example of this type of pilot was Major Albert J. (Ajax) Baumler, who, when he arrived in China to fight with the Flying Tiger group shortly after Pearl Harbor, was already an air ace, having shot down seven enemy ships (Messerschmitts and Fiats) while flying and fighting for the Loyalists in the Spanish Civil War. Baumler, a true soldier of fortune and a flyer who loved to fight, achieved double acedom, adding to his air victories, by shooting down five Jap planes with the 14th Air Force.

When he first arrived in China, Baumler was amazed at the organization and skill of the ragged, dirty men he met. Commented Baumler:

"On my first day, I watched the Tigers shoot down nine Japs over our field, losing one of their own. I thought I'd learned something about combat flying in Spain, but these guys were simply terrific. Chennault had taught them the tactics he couldn't get our brass hats to adopt. They were up against odds of five to one, twenty to one, anything. Flying as co-ordinated teams, avoiding combat until they were set just right, they tore in and slaughtered the Japs. They did it so well that it looked easy."

But it didn't take Ajax Baumler long to become a valuable and important part of the organization. In the battle of Hengyang, Baumler performed a feat that caused Colonel Scott to later describe it in his book, *God Is My Copilot*, as one of the "nerviest" things he had ever seen accomplished:

We had a few ships that had been strafed badly on the ground; some of them had been shot to pieces, and in others the engines or hydraulic systems had been damaged. In most cases these same ships couldn't be got off the ground when the Japs came over; sometimes they were caught three or four times by Zeros, and consequently they were in a continual state of repair.

One of these was old Number 104, the ship that Ajax had been flying. The ground crew had worked on it for days, but whenever they'd have it just about ready to be taken back to the factory at Kunming for overhaul, the Japs would catch it again. Finally one morning Ajax must have said, "The hell with it." For when the "Jinbao" came he went and got into the crippled fighter to take off before the Japs could get there to strafe it again. He told me later that he was tired of seeing it sitting on the ground as a target; whether it would fly or not, he was going to get it taxiing as fast as it would go and at least make it harder to hit than it had been in the revetment. Well, Ajax did better than taxi—he got off. But the story of it all reached me later on.

I was on the ground that day, and didn't see it. But I heard Ajax talking on the radio, and I heard his six guns when he caught one of the Zeros. Just a little later I saw the trail of black smoke that marked the enemy ship going down. I was glad to hear Ajax talking that morning; for a minute I'd thought that smoke might be he, going down in that luckless Number 104. All the time he'd been flying the ship he'd been having to pump the landing-gear up manually, for the hydraulic system had been shot up by the Jap strafer days before. Added to this, an exertion which is no pleasant task at fighting altitudes, was a more painful experience. The cards were

137

stacked even more heavily against Ajax in this jinx ship, for his electrical system was shorting out.

On his take-off from Hengyang, as he gave the ship the gun, Baumler had felt a terrible electrical shock through his sweaty hand on the stick control. He couldn't turn the stick loose or the ship would have crashed in the take-off run; so he grimly held on. Take hold of the spark plug of your car some time while the engine is running, and you'll feel just about what Ajax felt. But he kept holding it until he was at an altitude where it was safe to turn the stick loose, get out his handkerchief, and wrap it around the stick.

Even after he had been through the fight and came in to land at Ling-Ling he had to take some more of the shock cure, for by that time the handkerchief was damp and the electricity was jumping through it. He couldn't stay long on this last field, for the Japs were on the way back in waves; so he reserviced and taxied out to take off. Though the engine was now missing badly, Ajax couldn't wait—the Japs would be there in a matter of minutes.

He tried a take-off with the current going through his arms again and the engine spitting and sputtering—and at the end of the runway he still hadn't enough speed to get in the air. He would swerve the ship about and try the other direction. Finally after three runs he got the fighter plane in the air, pumped the wheels up by hand and continued doing it for five hundred miles—and so flew back to Kunming. He told me later it didn't matter what he did now; when he got in jail they'd never be able to electrocute him in the chair if old P-40 Number 104 had failed to do it that August morning.

Thus the Curtiss-Wright P-40, the vaunted queen of American fighters, was the primary flying tool for the U. S. air war in China. They also used a few P-43's and P-38's while the bomber boys utilized the medium Mitchell B-25 bomber and later some heavy Liberator B-24 bombers, but primarily it was the P-40 that carried the war to the enemy and brought the American flyers back home to fight another day. The 14th Air Force ace Major William N. Reed, in commenting on the relative merits of the American fighter stated:

"The Jap Zeros are hot planes and much more maneuverable than the Tomahawk I was flying, but, believe me these American planes can take punishment. The Zero, far lighter, is a cinch for machine-gun bursts, but the Japs have learned that American planes can be shot full of holes and still fly."

Still, in spite of the impressive tallies of victory after victory, the pattern of the air conflict was not always so one-sided for the American airmen, as, for example, the air battle on 20 August 1943 when the Japanese turned the tables on the 14th Air Force fighters. Taking advantage of clearing weather the Japanese climbed to altitudes greatly in excess of the lower ceiling of the P-40. Avoiding the new high-flying American P-38's at Ling-Ling they jumped the P-40's at Hengyang and Kweilin. Using Chennault's own tactics, they maintained their extreme altitude until the time was perfect, then the Japs dived at the Americans, making one pass and climbing back to the safety of their superior altitude. That day the 14th Air Force felled two Japs but paid for this with three American ships.

The P-40 was admittedly becoming obsolete, but new planes were a long way from the Chinese theater, leaving the American units to fight with the machines they had.

From the beginning, the war in this theater had been spotty with the American forces at no time well enough equipped to devote their full attention to any one objective for any length of time or with any substantial amount of equipment.

In January, 1943, Colonel Robert L. Scott, Jr., was ordered back to the United States to contribute his valuable knowledge of the superior tactics his unit, under Chennault, had used so successfully to the young pilots then going through the highly accelerated flying schools. As his replacement General Chennault selected a man who, like Scott, was piling up impressive victories and was later to become one of the 14th Air Force's top aces with thirteen air-to-air kills, Bruce K. Holloway.

Earlier in the Chinese air war Colonel Holloway, then a major and Colonel Scott's executive officer, was shot down while leading a strike against truck columns near Chefang. Barely crossing the river which divided the Chinese and Japanese lines he crash-landed in a soft paddy field. His trip back across the primitive Chinese countryside involved the most unique survival story in the sagas of those aviators who had to "walk back." Although only an hour by plane from the base at Kunming, his trip by sedan chair, donkey and water buffalo, in addition to the overabundance of hospitality from the grateful peasants of the remote villages, took three weeks and won for him the pet name of "Lochinvar of the Salween." As Colonel Holloway recalled later, the Chinese had "almost killed me with hospitality. . . . What with the wine I drank, I was careful to pick the broadest horse available to ride away on."

By the autumn of 1943 the CBI had produced the highest scoring noncommissioned ace of the war, Technical Sergeant Arthur P. Benko of Bisbee, Arizona, a bomber gunner who destroyed a total of eighteen Jap planes. During a scrap on 2 October 1943 he received several bullet nicks and in return shot down seven Jap Zeros during a single engagement over Haiphong.

"I never worked that turret so fast before," he told a reporter shortly after the battle. "They tell me the scrap lasted about forty minutes, but it seemed like a minute to me. You have to be on the alert every second. My guns jammed twice. I had to clear them in a hurry.

"The Japs are using those new Zeros, which certainly are fast and come in close. They've got lots of guns, those boys. But our P-40's gave us great protection; they never left us, staying right along close. It also helps to have your own crew. You just feel right at home when you have your own gang along."

Sergeant Benko, a quiet, slightly graying outdoors man, ascribed his remarkable record to luck and to his love of guns. He had been brought up with firearms and had been hunting and shooting all his life in the open country of his home in the West. Prior to entering the service he had been the champion rifle shot of Arizona, and had always liked "ink shooting"—throwing cans or eggs into the air and shooting them in flight without using the gun sights. It was undoubtedly this early training and his experienced eye that enabled him to take such a heavy toll of Japanese aircraft.

The CBI's top scoring air-to-air victor was Major John C. Herbst, who won the respect of all who knew him for his expert flying ability. Colonel David Lee (Tex) Hill, one of the old time Flying Tigers and leader with the 14th Air Force, after giving consideration to his wide acquaintance among combat pilots, stated that Herbst "ranks with the best combat pilots I have known." He also won the nickname "Pappy" for his advanced years (thirty-five at that time) as a combat fighter pilot.

Before the war John Herbst had been a tax advisor with a west coast oil corporation; but his big weakness was airplanes. As the rumblings of war grew louder, he realized that he was too old to get a combat pilot's commission in the United States Army so in May 1941 he joined the Royal Canadian Air Force. Shipped to England he flew everything the British had: Spitfires, Hurricanes, Beaufighters, Hudsons, Venturas, Blenheims and Mosquitos. The next May he transferred to the U. S. Air Force and unhappily found himself flying a swivel chair in an unabsorbing ground job.

Unable to stand his land anchor, he helped himself to an airplane one early Sunday morning and dashed aloft for a spin. He wrung the aircraft out, not knowing that the assumedly deserted beach over which he buzzed was occupied by Colonel David L. Hill and his wife who were out for an early morning walk. Colonel Hill, who recognized good flying when he saw it, knew that a highly skilled pilot was at the controls even though Herbst was expertly breaking every rule in the books.

A year later when Herbst turned up in China unannounced, Tex Hill remembered the brilliance of his illegal flying and grabbed him for his fighter unit. Within six weeks Colonel Hill had put Pappy Herbst at the command of a fighter squadron, and Pappy's courage, good judgment and quiet personality built his squadron into one of the Group's finest fighting units.

In May 1943 Premier Hideki Tojo had declared: "The Imperial Japanese Army and Navy have occupied and secured all strategic areas in Greater East Asia and their power and prestige command vast areas in the Pacific and in the Indian Oceans. We are now in readiness to deal a thorough and crushing blow at the enemy's armed power. I wish to give expression to the conviction of Japan that she will so effectively crush America and Britain that they will not be able again to extend their baneful tentacles into East Asia."

But someone had forgotten to inform the hard-pressed flyers in the China-Burma-India theater. By the middle of 1944 the 10th Air Force had, with the British air units, gained undisputed control of the sky over Burma and had never ceased the difficult and arduous chore of aerial supply over the Hump. By the middle of 1944 the 14th Air Force was facing a showdown battle with the Japanese forces in China. In the following year, the Japanese giant began to shrink and, although neither the 10th nor the 14th Air Force ever received sufficient reinforcements to extend greatly the scope of their limited operations, they were slowly pushing the Japs back to their island home as larger American forces swept back across the Pacific to the final victory.

CHINA-BURMA-INDIA THEATER AIR FORCE ACES, WORLD WAR II

NAME	RANK	HOME	DESTROYED AIR	DESTROYED GROUND	TOTAL
Chapman, Philip G. (KIA)	Major	Unknown	7	16	23
Herbst, John C.	Colonel	Pala, Calif.	21	2	23
Benko, Arthur J.*	S/Sgt.	Bisbee, Ariz.	9	9	18
Hampshire, John F. (KIA)	Captain	Grants Pass, Ore.	17	.	17
McComas, Edward O.	Lt. Col.	Winfield, Kans.	14	3	17
Scott, Robert L.	Colonel	Macon, Ga.	13	1	14
Holloway, Bruce K.	Colonel	Knoxville, Tenn.	13	.	13
Paxton, Heyward A., Jr.	1st Lt.	New Smyrna Beach, Fla.	6½	5	11½
England, James J.	Major	Jackson, Tenn.	10	1	11
Older, Charles H.	Lt. Col.	Beverly Hills, Calif.	7	4	11
Richardson, Elmer W.	Captain	San Antonio, Tex.	8	3	11
Turner, William L.	Major	Idalon, Tex.	6½	4	10½
Alison, John R.	Lt. Col.	Daytona Beach, Fla.	10	.	10
Grosvenor, William, Jr.	Captain	Newport, R.I.	5	5	10
Mahon, Keith	Captain	Oklahoma City, Okla.	6	4	10
Reeves, Leonard R.	1st Lt.	Lancaster, Tex.	8	2	10
Stewart, John S.	Captain	Worland, Wyo.	5	5	10
Westermark, Robert V.	1st Lt.	Cut Bank, Mont.	6	4	10
Bolyard, John W.	1st Lt.	Unknown	9	.	9
Cruikshank, Arthur W.	Major	Ruston, La.	8	.	8
Gordon, Matthew M., Jr.	1st Lt.	Pueblo, Colo.	8	.	8
Lombard, John D.	1st Lt.	Unknown	8	.	8
Liles, Robert L.	Captain	St. Louis, Mo.	7	1	8
Little, James W.	1st Lt.	Fincastle, Ky.	7	1	8
Reed, William N.	Major	Marion, Iowa	7	1	8
Williams, James M.	Captain	Huntsville, Tex.	7	.	7
Arasmith, Lester L.	1st Lt.	Unknown	6	1	7
Colman, Philip E.	1st Lt.	Roanoke, Va.	7	1	7
Clinger, Dallas A.	2nd Lt.	Laramie, Wyo.	6	.	6

CHINA-BURMA-INDIA THEATER AIR FORCE ACES, WORLD WAR II (continued)

NAME	RANK	HOME	DESTROYED AIR	GROUND	TOTAL
Goss, Edmond R.	Major	Tampa, Fla.	6	..	6
Lubner, Martin M.	Captain	Montgomery, Ala.	6	..	6
Marks, Mortimer D.	Major	Bayonne, N. J.	6	..	6
Mulhollom, Robert F.	1st Lt.	Chicago, Ill.	6	..	6
Parham, Forrest F.	Captain	Kensington, Minn.	6	..	6
Smith, Robert E.	Captain	Cincinnati, Ohio	6	..	6
Vincent, Clinton D.	Brig. Gen.	San Antonio, Tex.	6	..	6
Baumler, Albert J.	Major	Trenton, N. J.	5	..	5
Bonner, Stephen J., Jr.	Captain	Guymon, Okla.	5	..	5
Bearden, Aaron L.	1st Lt.	Houston, Tex.	5	..	5
Callaway, Raymond L.	Major	Grove City, Minn.	5	..	5
DuBois, Charles H.	1st Lt.	Richmond Heights, Mo.	5	..	5
Duke, Walter F.	Captain	Leonardtown, Md.	5	..	5
Gouldthrite, George W.	T/Sgt.	Spokane, Wash.	5	..	5
Hammer, Samuel E.	1st Lt.	Neal, Kans.	5	..	5
Jones, Lynn F.	Captain	Mercedes, Tex.	5	..	5
Kimball, Melville B.	1st Lt.	Greystone, R. I.	5	..	5
Hollmeyer, Edward M.	Captain	Everett, Wash.	5	..	5
Pryor, Roger C.	Major	Starkville, Miss.	5	..	5
Quigley, Donald L.	Major	Marion, Ohio	5	..	5
Schultz, Robert P.	Captain	Sandusky, Ohio	5	..	5
Webb, Willard J.	Major	Alton, Ill.	5	..	5

144

* Gunners are not normally considered aces, but is here listed because he was so designated by his Command.

CHINA-BURMA-INDIA THEATER CONFIRMED VICTORIES

In the CBI Theater air-to-ground kills as well as air-to-air kills were credited. The following is a list of those CBI flyers who received credit for five or more victories including grounds kills.

NAME	RANK	HOME	DESTROYED		TOTAL
			AIR	GROUND	
Reynolds, Thomas A.	Major	Stephens, Ark.	3	38½	41½
Moore, James T.	Captain	Plant City, Fla.	..	17	17
Reed, Robert E.	1st Lt.	Lima, Ohio	2	14	16
Brown, Robert E.	Captain	Unknown	2	13	15
Terry, Wade H., Jr.	1st Lt.	Unknown	2	13	15
Finberg, Floyd	Major	Duluth, Minn.	3	11	14
Binkley, Ira A.	1st Lt.	Unknown	1	11	12
Anderson, Louis W., Jr.	1st Lt.	Unknown	3	8	11
Pearson, Wesley D.	2nd Lt.	Fairfield, Idaho	2	9	11
Swetland, Paul H.	1st Lt.	Unknown	2	9	11
Muenster, Lester E.	1st Lt.	Unknown	1	9	10
Wells, Robert D.	1st Lt.	Wyalusing, Pa.	1	9	10
Field, Warren E.	Unknown	Unknown	4	5½	9½
Conn, John C.	1st Lt.	Unknown	4	5	9
Howard, Lauren A.	Captain	Unknown	..	9	9
Brink, Thomas U., Jr.	1st Lt.	Lansdowne, Pa.	3	5	8
Branz, John R.	Captain	Unknown	1	7	8
Denney, Chester N.	Captain	Bidwell, Ohio	3	5	8
Mahoney, Grant	Major	Valleio, Calif.	3	5	8
Rector, Edward F.	Major	Marshall, N. D.	3	5	8
Dowis, Kendal B.	1st Lt.	Detroit, Mich.	4	3	7
Harrison, James B.	2nd Lt.	Unknown	..	7	7
Kosa, Silven E.	1st Lt.	Unknown	..	7	7
Lindell, Keith G.	Major	Albuquerque, New Mex.	3	4	7
Cole, Heston C.	1st Lt.	Unknown	1	5	6
Copenbarger, Charles	1st Lt.	Blue Mound, Ill.	..	6	6

CHINA-BURMA-INDIA THEATER CONFIRMED VICTORIES (continued)

NAME	RANK	HOME	AIR	GROUND	TOTAL
Folmar, James F.	Captain	Pensacola, Fla.	2	4	6
Granger, Kenneth G.	Unknown	Unknown	2	4	6
Honeycutt, John W.	2nd Lt.	Charlotte, N. C.	1	5	6
Long, Nimrod W. E.	1st Lt.	Unknown	:	6	6
Loose, Hubert	1st Lt.	Auburn, Ala.	1	5	6
Niemeier, Norman F., Jr. (KIA)	1st Lt.	Unknown	3	3	6
Hill, David L.	Colonel	Victoria, Tex.	4½	1	5½
Koran, George T.	1st Lt.	Unknown	1½	4	5½
Cousins, Wallace D.	Captain	Washington, D. C.	3	2	5
Cook, Charles E., Jr.	1st Lt.	Unknown	2	3	5
Colleps, Carl H.	1st Lt.	Unknown	:	5	5
DiStefano, William E.	1st Lt.	Syracuse, N. Y.	: 3	2	5
Dunning, John A.	Lt. Col.	San Antonio, Tex.	2	3	5
Everest, Frank K., Jr.	Captain	Fairmont, W. Va.	:	5	5
Glenn, Maxwell H.	Major	Winnfield, La.	: 2	3	5
Klump, Frank D.	Captain	Robinson, Ill.	1	4	5
Miller, John B.	1st Lt.	El Paso, Tex.	:	5	5
McMillan, George B.	Lt. Col.	Winter Garden, Fla.	: 4	1	5
McKinney, William H.	1st Lt.	Unknown	1	4	5
Opsvig, John T.	1st Lt.	Minot, N. Dak.	1	4	5
Perelka, Charles W.	1st Lt.	Staten Island, N. Y.	:	5	5
Ray, J. Edgar	2nd Lt.	Norwood, Ohio	:	5	5
Reynolds, Oliver	Unknown	Miami, Fla.	: 1	4	5
Slocumb, Clyde B., Jr.	Major	Doerun, Ga.	2	3	5
Spann, Bobby J.	1st Lt.	San Antonio, Tex.	:	5	5
Van Ausdell, Robert L.	Major	Eaton, Ohio	: 2	3	5

146

10

NORTH AFRICA AND
MEDITERRANEAN—WORLD WAR II

9TH, 12TH, 15TH AND NORTHWEST AFRICAN AIR FORCES

DURING THOSE FATEFUL years when England stood alone against the Nazi war machine, the U. S. was throwing her fullest support, short of open war, behind the efforts of the brave British. The Lend-Lease Act, passed in 1941, made it possible for the United States to pass much-needed equipment and weapons to those critical battle areas across the Atlantic. Curtiss P-40 Tomahawks began to trickle into the lean British arsenals in the dusty African desert. Following the airplanes came a handful of officers and enlisted men to aid in the operation and maintenance of the American built fighters. But the demand was always greater than the supply as the Axis forces of Marshal Erwin Rommel rolled victoriously across the barren land.

The successes of the Germans and Italians in the Mediterranean and Middle East area spurred the U. S. to increase the lend-lease assistance of personnel and equipment. By summer of 1941 it had become evident that an administrative agency would be necessary to handle the increasing flow of military traffic into that section, so by the end of September the War Department had created the United States Military North African Mission under the charge of Brigadier General Russell L. Maxwell. However, before he could get his organization into a real operation the Japanese struck Pearl Harbor and the following day the United States was at war with Germany and Italy as well as the Empire of Japan. Immediately the mission became the military arm in aid of an actual rather than a potential ally.

Quickly the War Department began creating a U. S. Air

Force in that war theater and in June 1942 Major General Lewis H. Brereton was dispatched from his command in the China-India-Burma Theater to take command of the U. S. Army Middle East Air Force under the ground units of General Maxwell. The Middle East Air Force was designated the 9th Air Force in the following November and remained in Africa until the final defeat of Rommel's Afrika Korps. The 9th also participated in the Sicily invasion of the Italian campaign.

On 1 October 1943 the 9th Air Force was moved to England to lend suport to the 8th Air Force's strategic bombardment of Europe. When the 9th Air Force was transferred to England it had run up a 3 to 1 margin of victory over the enemy destroying 610 enemy aircraft in air-to-air combat as compared to 227 losses of its own planes.

The 12th Air Force was formed on 20 August 1942 to provide the bomber-fighter air arm and fighter cover for the pending Anglo-American invasion of North Africa. The British, with their backs to the Suez Canal (Alexandria), turned the tide and drove the Desert Fox westward out of Egypt across the desert, breaking his grip at El Alamein. Meanwhile the Americans accomplished their invasion and drove southward and eastward until they had joined hands with their victorious Allies. When the campaign in Africa was over in the summer of 1943, the operations of the 12th Air Force were moved to Italy as the squeeze was put upon Germany's once arrogant war machine. The commanders of the 12th Air Force were Major General James H. Doolittle, Lieutenant General Carl Spaatz, and Major General John K. Cannon. From November 1942 to 1 March 1944 the 12th Air Force had a record of 2,959 enemy aircraft destroyed in the air to its own losses of 1,473 planes. This 12th Air Force record includes the operations of the 15th Air Force from 1 November 1943 when the 15th Air Force was formed as the strategic bombardment element of the Northwest African Air Force. The 15th Air Force was formed initially under the command of General Doolittle with personnel and equipment from the 12th Bomber Command including one P-47 and three P-38 fighter groups which were attached to the three bomber wings to serve as fighter escorts for the strategic bombardment missions against the soft underbelly of

Hitler's Germany. Later in the war, the fighters were diverted to tactical missions for fighter sweeps across Europe and close support for ground units.

In the first days of the war American aircraft continued to trickle into Africa and the Middle East and it was not until the summer of 1942 that an entire fighter group was dispatched en masse to the desert war. Under top-secret orders the P-40 Warhawks and pilots of the 33rd Fighter Group under the command of Lieutenant Colonel (now Brigadier General) William W. Momyer were loaded aboard the British auxiliary carriers *Chunango* and *Archer;* their destination—Africa. Silently the *Archer* sliced through the blue Atlantic, while on board in charge of thirty-five P-40's Major Phil Cochran, a squadron commander under Lieutenant Colonel Momyer, excitedly awaited the fighting and action he craved.

On 1 November 1942 the *Archer* had steamed to within 100 miles of North Africa. Topside the Warhawks were readied. Then at a signal from the bridge the "advanced attrition" fighters of the 33rd Fighter Group were catapulted from the pitching deck. They dipped down over the bow, hugged tight to the water as they gained precious airspeed, then rose skyward as they climbed out toward the Dark Continent beyond the misty horizon to land at Port Lyautey. Across the top of Africa they winged, stopping at Allied airfields along the way until they had finally arrived at their new home at Muqeibile, Palestine.

Although the deployment of land-based fighter planes from an aircraft carrier by catapult was a remarkable feat in aerial history, Major Cochran and his boys were very unhappy with the arrangements they found at their new base. They had come to the Middle East for combat and there seemed to be very little around. Cochran decided to lead his squadron back west where the fighting was going on; so he led his men to Rabat, Morocco, for what he termed "further training." The brass of the 12th Air Force, when they got wind of the outfit's activities, ordered them dispersed, and Cochran was ordered to Tunisia with seven of his pilots. Reaching Oudjda in eastern Morocco their P-40's were taken from them and they were grounded. Cochran, however, didn't approve of this idea, got back in his plane and continued his flight eastward into Tunisia. There Cochran ran into a situation much to his liking. He found himself on a small American airfield where a disorganized P-40 squadron was doing little or nothing in what he felt was a potentially crucial area. As the highest-ranking officer in the squadron he assumed command, receiving no objections from anyone—there being no one in the outfit with a very clear idea of their purpose in southern Tunisia.

The small group—Americans and French—soon began to come alive under Cochran's leadership. Using superb aerial-guerrilla tactics he was able to outguess and outbluff the German and Italian forces at almost every turn. His unorthodox unit was soon dubbed the Red Scarf Guerrillas. The job that Cochran sliced out for his men was the destruction of enemy supplies, tanks, vehicles, weapons and ammunition dumps. He was also interested in the destruction of enemy aircraft, but because his unit was numerically inferior to that of the enemy he preferred not to have his planes engaged in combat with the foe unless necessary, lest he lose ships and seriously hinder what he considered the most important function of his small P-40 squadron.

Soon after Cochran's arrival the reputation of the Red Scarf Guerrillas began to grow. As Phil Cochran explained it:

. . . the French began to call us up and tell us about tanks and trucks they saw on different roads. We'd go out and look for them—sometimes we didn't find them. Gradually we became big operators.

I remember one of those operations in particular. One day Captain Levi Chase, my operations officer, went out by himself and destroyed eighty-four guns and a few trucks. Altogether we must have destroyed about three hundred trucks—we became so damn efficient in this type of work that the Jerries and Eyeties weren't able to move a truck anywhere in Tunisia by daylight.

After we had done that for a while, we got to know the country pretty well ourselves and began to cook up other things to do. For instance, we knew that the enemy had only about a dozen locomotives on all their little lines down there, so we got to blasting them—for sheer diversion, we went after their oil and munitions dumps. Chase, my "One-Man Wave of Terror," was the best man I've ever seen in spotting those things from the air. One time he strafed a lot of haystacks and they all exploded, proving that he was right—the enemy had hidden ammunition under them.

We used to hunt light tanks all over southern Tunisia, and when we found them we would strafe them with our fifty-calibers. They would play dead, and then at night the crews would run them into Arab courtyards or dry gulleys and camouflage them. So we'd track them down and shoot more holes into them before they could be repaired. We didn't have armament to blast them, but our "fifties" kept them out of action. Often we would observe troop movements, report them to the French and then go back and strafe them, and the French would occupy one or more towns.

Finally, the people back at headquarters saw what a job we were doing and sent us a squadron of bombers to fool around with—we had plenty of fun thinking up bombing missions and then escorting the jokers.

But Cochran's preference for low-level attack did not keep them entirely out of dogfights for in one five-day period alone his unit destroyed thirty-four German planes, and the squadron's Captain Levi Chase became the top-scoring ace in the Northwest Africa Air Forces.

Phil Cochran's success in the early desert war was due primarily to his limitless ingenuity. On one occasion one of the Guerrillas' younger pilots became lost while chasing and shooting down a Nazi bomber at night.

Just then I heard one of the kids over the radio saying he was lost; he was asking for directions. The lost pilot was Lieutenant Thomas (Tom A. Thomas), that baby-faced youngster who tried so hard to grow heavy whiskers to look the part of a guerrilla fighter. Thomas had jumped on the third Heinie and had chased it out into the night fifty miles before he'd caught up with it and nailed it. But as he pulled up from his strike, Thomas realized he was lost. You can't blame him—he was green and hadn't had time to familiarize himself with the surrounding countryside.

Well, I tried to keep his spirits up by insulting him— you see, at first I thought he was somebody else. Anyway, I'd say to him, "I don't mind losing you, you stupid lug, but we can't afford to lose another P-40. Try and see the lights on my ship and steer a thirty course." The kid would answer politely: "I don't see your lights, sir." He never forgot to say "sir," but he was plenty confused.

Of course he couldn't see the light of the smokecans there on the field. But I got an idea: I called down to the control room to tell the ack-ack batteries to fire—first the one at the west end of the field, then the one to the east, and so on to give us an outline of the field. And as a finale, I asked that all of the batteries fire in unison. I stayed up there with my lights on, and as the guns began to fire, the kid saw the field all right and got his directions, and we both came down. When you tell about it, it sounds just like a movie.

When the Germans had initiated the close-support tactics of their fighters, they had operated with telling effect in the rapid advances of the Nazi *Blitzkrieg*. But in Africa the top British air officer, Air Chief Marshal Sir Arthur Tedder, was violently opposed to the direct control of the air units by ground commanders. The American flying organizations working with and under the British in Africa were fully behind Marshal Tedder's arguments. The Marshal reasoned that with each ground unit directly controlling the air units the planes would be tied down to ground formations in "penny packets" and would thus often be wasted on "fleeting and unsuitable targets" instead of being "available for concentrated blows" as they would be under a centralized authority. He won his fight and with centralized control of the Allied air units he employed them in concentrated strikes against the enemy. In May 1942 Rommel wheeled his armor into attack on Field Marshal Bernard Montgomery's British 8th Army position at Gazala. Tedder's air force struck, and the concentrated power of the British air might stopped Rommel and turned back the attack.

From that day forward no further argument for the centralization of air power was needed. Rommel had, in general, been reluctant to attach any importance to air support and had considered the airplane only another fighting tool of the ground forces, assigning his own air units in part to outlying army units. Consequently, he did not have enough planes at his immediate command to stand off the violent onslaught from the African skies, although in total the Germans had a superior number of aircraft in the African theater at that time. After the British victory at Gazala Marshal Tedder stated: "Any lingering idea that the RAF was simply a useful adjunct of the land forces ... was finally swept away."

The unexpectedly rapid fall of Rommel at El Alamein greatly tempered the American invasion of North Africa. U. S. forces stormed ashore at Algiers, Oran, and Casablanca, while overhead the 12th Air Force had only a minor role to play in the drama as the RAF and Royal Naval Air Force covered the one-day-long invasion at Algiers, while at Oran and Casablanca Navy carrier-based planes winged over the invading forces. Nevertheless, the units of the 12th Air Force got their awaited baptism of battle and during the course of the hard African fighting Lieutenant W. J. Sloan of Richmond, Virginia, flew and fought his P-38 Lightning to twelve air-to-air victories to become the top 12th Air Force ace.

Then came the abandonment of the famed Afrika Korps by Hitler and the surrender of the Nazi forces in the Middle East and North Africa. Turning northward the victorious Allies continued their preparations for the big push on the Continent. Sicily was invaded with 9th Air Force support and the Italian campaign was well under way. The 9th Air Force was then transferred to England and there joined with the 8th Air Force in the strategic bombardment of Europe. It was while involved in those operations that Lieutenant Glenn T. Eagleston became the leading ace of the 9th Air Force.

Born in Farmington, Utah, and graduated from pilot training on 29 September 1942, Lieutenant Eagleston was officially credited with eighteen and one-fourth enemy aircraft shot down in World War II, which total he increased by two MIGs in Korea.

In September 1944, Lieutenant Eagleston was leading the 354th Fighter Group on a dive bombing mission deep into the heart of Nazi Germany. As Eagleston, now a colonel, described the action:

Our assigned task was to dive-bomb and strafe three separate German airdromes that were known to have many fighter aircraft and copious quantities of flak, making it a lucrative target for military purposes but an unlucrative target for fighter pilots' dive-bombing purposes. The Luftwaffe came to our rescue, however, and "bounced" my Group of some forty-eight airplanes with a hundred-plus Messerschmitt 109's, shortly after we had crossed the Rhine River. We were forced to salvo our bombs near a little town of which I do not recall the name. However, by some astute maneuvering, skill and cunning, plus gross quantities of luck, I managed to turn their "bounce" into a very fine advantage to the Group and in the resulting scrap we destroyed twenty-three German aircraft and damaged several others while losing only one aircraft and pilot. This was about my most interesting "dogfight" as it ranged from about 25,000 feet down to the deck and lasted for about half an hour. It seemed to me that throughout this scrap I had been getting absolute maximum performance from my trusty Mustang and was terrifically impressed with my own flying ability and astounded to find that my wingman had stayed with me all through these combat maneuvers. The wind was thoroughly taken from my sails when after the fight was over I discovered that my wingman, Lieutenant Fred Couch, still had his two 500 pound bombs attached to the airplane. Incidentally, I shot down three 109's that day, because of his fine performance.

One of the old hands at aerial combat in the 9th Air Force was thirty-year-old Major James H. Howard, who had already achieved acedom with Chennault's Flying Tigers.

On 11 January 1944 Major Howard led a group of Mustangs to cover a bomber formation destined for Oschersleben and Halbeitstadt. During the ensuing air battle Howard singlehandedly fought off thirty to forty enemy planes which were attacking the bombers. He successfully shot down three German ships and possibly destroyed six more. In the action that day a gaping hole was shot in his left wing and for his gallantry Howard was awarded the Congressional Medal of Honor and promoted to lieutenant colonel.

His action is best described in his citation:

On that day Colonel Howard was the leader of a group of P-51 aircraft providing support for a heavy bomber formation on a long-range mission deep in enemy territory. As Colonel Howard's group met the bombers in the target area the bomber force was attacked by numerous enemy fighters. Colonel Howard, with his group, at once engaged the enemy and himself destroyed a German ME 110. As a result of this attack Colonel Howard lost contact with his group and at once returned to the level of the bomber formation. He then saw that the bombers were being heavily attacked by enemy airplanes and that no other friendly fighters were at hand. While Colonel Howard could have waited to attempt to assemble his group before engaging the enemy, he chose instead to attack singlehanded a formation of more than 30 German airplanes. With utter disregard for his own safety he immediately pressed home determined attacks for some 30 minutes, during which time he destroyed three enemy airplanes and probably destroyed and damaged others. Toward the end of this engagement three of his guns went out of action and his fuel supply was becoming dangerously low. Despite these handicaps and the almost insuperable odds against him, Colonel Howard continued his aggressive action in an attempt to protect the bombers from the numerous fighters.

While unquestionably a superior pilot, he was considered by his men more valuable as an air commander. As one of Howard's men described his abilities: "He flies into enemy territory, waits until enemy aircraft come to attack the bombers, looks the situation over and then dispatches flights from his group where they will do the most good."

By the summer of 1944 the 9th Air Force was producing a new kind of ace as American pilots began engaging the robot "buzz bombs" in strange one-sided dogfights. James B. Dalglish, a twelve-victory ace, destroyed three of the jet-propelled bombs as part of his impressive tally.

As the Allied noose drew tighter around the German neck the "buzz" bombardment of England was launched. From June until August 1944, when the launching sites were captured, the V-1 rockets were fired against London and Southern England at the rate of almost a hundred a day. The bombs traveled between 2,000 and 2,500 feet in altitude and created a high-pitched squeal from the pulsating jet engine which propelled them. The scream of the V-1 was audible to all, as was the silence caused by the fuel shut-off which sent all who heard it scurrying for cover as the bomb began a steep glide to its target.

Relentlessly the American fighters pounded the rocket sites and shot from the skies those they could. The rocket's minimum airspeed of 450 miles per hour gave the Allied pilots little time to spare. The first technique employed to shoot down the V-1's was the ninety-degree deflection shots. This only allowed one pass at the bomb and required a great deal of accuracy. The later and more successful technique developed by the flyers was to fly alongside the bomb in a tight formation, tuck a wing under the bomb's wing and, applying a little opposite aileron, roll the buzz bomb, tumbling its gyros and causing it to crash short of its target.

As Captain John J. Voll, top-scoring ace of the 15th Air Force, climbed wearily from his plane after his fifty-seventh and last combat mission he remarked, "It was a helluva battle." This was on 16 November 1944 and during his preceding five months in combat he had flamed seventeen German ships. On this last mission he downed four more in the toughest battle of his fighting career, bringing his final total to twenty-one enemy aircraft destroyed.

With his radio shot away Captain Voll was returning early from a bomber escort mission in Germany. Alone over Northern Italy he spotted a Junkers 88 and winged over after it. It led him on a merry chase across the Adriatic to a German air base and a hornet's nest of enemy aircraft. Out of the sun seven Focke-Wulfs pounced Voll's plane, while five Messerschmitts came in from another direction for what appeared to be an easy kill. Quickly closing on the Junkers he blasted it out of the sky and wheeled around to take on the remaining twelve Germans. In the ensuing dogfight he shot down two of the attacking FW 190's and one of the ME 109's and gave the rest of the pack a good working over, getting two more probables and damaging two more. "Then I got a break and scrammed, eluding the other five."

In one of his earlier dogfights Captain Voll had downed three Germans without firing a shot. Attacked by the enemy he maneuvered two so that they collided and crashed and then lured the third German into a screaming dive at the ground in which Voll but not the German recovered.

Captain Voll, a 22-year-old farm boy from Goshen, Ohio, was the top ace in the entire Mediterranean theater as well as in his own 15th Air Force.

In a raging dogfight over the Baltic another 15th Air Force ace, Second Lieutenant Jack Lenox, Jr., in his P-38 Lightning had already flamed one German ship and was pouring lead into another when he noticed that the German pilot was trying to bail out. Fascinated, Lieutenant Lenox ceased firing his guns and flipped on his gun camera to record on film the bail-out. His eyes glued on the disembarking German he failed to look around and in a flash he was bounced by a diving ME-109.

The next thing I knew [he recounted], my canopy was shattered on the left, my engine was burning and I was in a tight spin. My first reaction was to recover from the spin and my P-38 responded beautifully. Acting almost automatically, I went right into my fire-feather procedures on the burning engine. My spinal column must have been doing all my thinking for me, for the next thing I realized was that the fire was out and the ship seemed to be doing all right, so I took off for home.

After I had gotten settled down on course I began to take inventory of the cockpit and myself. The canopy was shattered and the metal behind the throttle quadrant was twisted. My left sleeve had been torn and to my horror I saw blood oozing out. I checked my arm feeling for broken bones and wiggling my fingers. So far I had felt no pain. But as I tried to raise my arm I suddenly realized that I was paralyzed—my arm would not move. Figuring that I was in shock and suddenly scared that I might lose my left arm, I broke open the first-aid kit strapped to my chest and took out the morphine hypodermic. Giving myself the needle was the hardest thing I ever did; but I realized that when I came out of shock my shattered arm would be in extreme pain, and I still had to land my crippled Lightning.

I was nearing the field and figuring my procedures for making a one-armed landing when to my relief, surprise and embarrassment I discovered that all this time I had had my jacket sleeve caught on the throttle lock. I waved my arm around the cockpit in joy.

On the ground I found that my oozing blood had come from the smallest scratch, and I unhappily realized that the dreaded hypodermic needle had been for naught. Needless to say, I was greatly relieved, but so embarrassed that it was some time later before I could bring myself to mention my folly to the boys.

From the west, from the south and east the Allied armies squeezed the perimeter tighter and tighter around the Nazi fortress. In the air the pace quickened as around the clock the heavies and the mediums blackened the German skies. The Fatherland shuddered beneath the deadly shower of steel and fire that left the once-formidable war machine smoking rubble and twisted steel. The shattered *Luftwaffe* was driven from the sky and fighters, unmolested from the air, roared at treetop level across the hostile soil sweeping all before them. The Third Reich faltered as day after day American airmen smashed at will the last remnants of the crumbling Nazi fortress.

9TH AIR FORCE ACES

(Accredited by "Confirmation of Victory Credits Board")
Includes Middle East (North Africa) Operations

NAME	RANK	HOME	VICTORIES
Eagleston, Glenn T.[1]	1st Lt.	Alhambra, Calif.	18½
Beerbower, Don M.	Captain	Hill City, Minn.	15½
Bradley, Jack T.	Major	Brownwood, Texas.	15
Carr, Bruce W.[2]	1st Lt.	Wallace, Wisc.	14
Dahlberg, Kenneth H.	Captain	Unknown	14
Emmer, Wallace N.	Captain	St. Louis, Mo.	14
Hoefker, John H.	Captain	Ft. Mitchell, Ky.	13
Stephens, Robert W.	Captain	St. Louis, Mo.	13
East, Clyde B.	1st Lt.	Chatham, Va.	13
Brueland, Lowell K.	Captain	Calendar, Iowa	12½
Dalglish, James B.[3]		Unknown	12

[1] Total victories 23½ including aircraft destroyed on the ground.
[2] Total victories 25½ including aircraft destroyed on the ground.
[3] Includes 3 V-1 bombs.

NAME	RANK	HOME	VICTORIES
Turner, Richard E.[4]	Captain	Bartlesville, Okla.	12
Frantz, Carl M.	1st Lt.	Brownville, Pa.	11
O'Conner, Frank Q.	1st Lt.	San Francisco, Calif.	10½
Coffey, Robert L., Jr.	Lt. Col.	Johnstown, Pa.	10
Overfield, Lloyd J.	2nd Lt.	Leavenworth, Kans.	9
McDowell, Don	1st Lt.	Los Angeles, Calif.	8½
Culberston, Omer W.	1st Lt.	Minneapolis, Minn.	8
Goodnight, Robert E.	1st Lt.	Portland, Ore.	7½
Hunt, Edward E.	2nd Lt.	Los Angeles, Calif.	7½
Lasko, Charles W.	Captain	Nemacolin, Pa.	7½
Lamb, George M.		Unknown	7½
Fisher, Edwin O.		Unknown	7
Douglas, Paul P., Jr.	Lt. Col.	Paragould, Ark.	7
Anderson, William Y.		Unknown	7
Rogers, Felix M.		Unknown	7
Whittaker, R. E.		Unknown	7
Koenig, Charles W.		Unknown	6½
Welden, Robert D.		Unknown	6¼
Blumer, Lawrence E.	Captain	Walcott, N. Dak.	6
Gray, Rockford V.	Major	Cincinnati, Ohio	6
Larson, Leland A.	1st Lt.	Bay City, Mich.	6
Mobbs, George D.	Captain	Wooster, Ark.	6
Shoup, Robert L.	1st Lt.	Port Arthur, Texas	6
Simmons, William J.	2nd Lt.	Los Angeles, Calif.	6
Emmerson, Warren S.		Unknown	6
Milliken, Robert C.	2nd Lt.	Hadna, Wyo.	6
Howard, James H.		Unknown	6
Gumm, Charles F.		Unknown	6
Reynolds, Robert		Unknown	6
Byrne, J. R.		Unknown	6
Bickel, Carl G.[8]		Unknown	5½
King, William B.		Unknown	5½
Long, Maurice G.		Unknown	5½
Edwards, E. B., Jr.		Unknown	5½
Miller, Thomas F.		Unknown	5¼
Campbell, W. B.		Unknown	5¼
Axtell, Eugene D.	1st Lt.	Excelsior, Minn.	5
Byrne, Robert L.	1st Lt.	St. Louis, Mo.	5
Cleaveland, Arthur B.	1st Lt.	Springfield, Ohio	5
Duffy, Richard E.	2nd Lt.	Walled Lake, Mich.	5
Ernst, Herman E.	1st Lt.	Ringgold, Ga.	5
Graham, Robert F.	2nd Lt.	Beresford, S. Dak.	5
Gross, Clayton K.	1st Lt.	Spokane, Wash.	5
Hendricks, Randall W.	Major	Youngstown, Ohio	5
King, David L.	1st Lt.	Jonesville, Calif.	5
Kopsel, Edward H.	2nd Lt.	Chicago, Ill.	5
Magoffin, Morton D.	Colonel	Deerwood, Minn.	5
Overcash, Robert J.	1st Lt.	Mooresville, N. C.	5
Powers, MacArthur	2nd Lt.	Inwood, L. I., N. Y.	5
Schilke, James F.	Captain	Milwaukee, Wisc.	5
Smith, Paul A.[4]	1st Lt.	Billings, Mont.	5

[4] Includes 1 V-1 bomb.

NAME	RANK	HOME	VICTORIES
Tierney, Robert E.[4]	2nd Lt.	Kansas City, Mo.	5
Fisk, Harry E.		Unknown	5
Matte, Joseph Z.		Unknown	5
Rudolph, Henry S.		Unknown	5
Rose, Franklin		Unknown	5
Ritchey, Andrew J.		Unknown	5
Duncan, D. D. A.		Unknown	5
Burns, Robert G.		Unknown	5
Paisley, Melvyn R.		Unknown	5

FIFTEENTH AIR FORCE ACES

NAME	RANK	HOME	CREDITS
Voll, John J	1st Lt.	Goshen, Ohio	21
Green, Herschel H.	Major	Mayfield, Ky.	18
Varnell, James H.	Captain	Charleston, Tenn.	17
Brown, Samuel J.	Captain	Tulsa, Okla.	15
Brooks, James L.	2nd Lt.	Roanoke, Va.	13
Parker, Harry A.	Captain	Milford, N. H.	13
Skogstad, Norman C.	1st Lt.	Barron, Wisc.	12
Brezas, Michael	Captain	Bloomfield, N. J.	12
Goebel, Robert J.	2nd Lt.	Racine, Wisc.	11
McCorkle, Charles M.	Colonel	Newton, N. C.	11
Riddle, Robert H.	2nd Lt.	Chicago, Ill.	11
Leverette, William L.	Lt. Col.	Lykesland, S. C.	11
Goehausen, Walter J., Jr.	2nd Lt.	Webster Grove, Mo.	10
Molland, Leland P.	1st Lt.	So. Fargo, N. D.	10
Lowry, Wayne L.	1st Lt.	Mason City, Neb.	10
Dorsch, Frederick J., Jr.	Captain	Pittsburgh, Pa.	8
Warford, Victor E.	Major	Chiakasha, Okla.	8
Brown, Samuel J.	2nd Lt.	Dover, Mass.	8
Collins, Frank J.	Major	Breckenridge, Texas	8
Fiedler, Arthur C., Jr.	1st Lt.	Oak Park, Ill.	8
Sangermano, Philip	Flt. Off.	Peterborough, N. H.	8
Curdes, Louis E.	2nd Lt.		8
Carroll, Walter J., Jr.	1st Lt.	New York, N. Y.	7
Ainlay, John M.	1st Lt.	Santa Monica, Calif.	7
McLaughlin, Murray D.	1st Lt.	Basin, Wyo.	7
Dunkin, Richard W.	1st Lt.	Huntington, Ind.	7
Emmons, Eugene H.	1st Lt.	Lawrenceville, Ill.	7
Simmons, John M.	Captain	Gadsden, Ala.	7
Maloney, Thomas E.	1st Lt.	Cushing, Okla.	7
Adams, Charles E., Jr.	2nd Lt.	Denver, Colo.	6
Buck, George T., Jr.	Captain	Accomac, Va.	6
Dillard, William J.	Captain	Grand Saline, Texas	6
Hurd, Richard F.	1st Lt.	Dobbs Ferry, N. Y.	6
Harmeyer, Raymond F.	1st Lt.	Montgomery, Ala.	6
Shipman, Ernest	2nd Lt.	Long Island, N. Y.	6
Franklin, Dwaine R.	Captain	Deming, N. Y.	6

[4] Includes 1 V-1 bomb.

NAME	RANK	HOME	CREDITS
Johnson, Arthur G., Jr.	2nd Lt.	Litchfield, Minn.	6
Davis, Barrie S.	1st Lt.	Zebulon, N. C.	6
Emmert, Benjamin H., Jr.	1st Lt.	Erwin, Tenn.	6
McDaniel, Gordon H.	1st Lt.	Sweetwater, Tenn.	6
Ford, Claude E.	Captain	Oildale, Calif.	5
Griffith, Robert C.	2nd Lt.	Austin, Tex.	5
Gardner, Warner F.	Major	Casenovia, N. Y.	5
Holloway, James D.	2nd Lt.	Columbus, N. C.	5
McGuffin, Sammy E.	1st Lt.	Manhattan Beach, Calif.	5
Daniel, William A.	Colonel	Birmingham, Ala.	5
Dorris, Harry W.	Major	Harrisburg, Ill.	5
Faxon, Richard D.	1st Lt.	Great Barrington, Mass.	5
Loving, George G., Jr.	1st Lt.	Lynchburg, Va.	5
Smith, Jack R.	1st Lt.	San Simon, Ariz.	5
Trafton, Frederick O., Jr.	1st Lt.	So. Berwick, Me.	5
Thompson, Robert D.	2nd Lt.		5
Wilhelm, David C.	1st Lt.	Chicago, Ill.	5
Benne, Louis	2nd Lt.	Somerset, Pa.	5
Jones, Warren L.	2nd Lt.	Live Oak, Calif.	5
Lenox, Jack, Jr.	2nd Lt.	Enid, Okla.	5
McGuyrt, John W.	1st Lt.	Canton, Ohio	5
Seidman, Robert K.	1st Lt.	Pittsburgh, Pa.	5
Taylor, Oliver B.	Colonel	Palto Alto, Calif.	5
Wright, Max J.	Captain	Chappell, Neb.	5
Curtis, Robert C.	Major	Washington, D. C.	5
Lawler, John B.	1st Lt.	Baltimore, Md.	5
Aron, William E.	1st Lt.	Oaklyn, N. J.	5
Novotny, George P.	1st Lt.	Toledo, Ohio	5
Kienholz, Donald D.	1st Lt.	Bayard, N. Mex.	5
Lathrope, Franklin C.	2nd Lt.	Blue Island, Ill.	5
Hatch, Herbert B.*	1st Lt.		5
Miller, Armour C.	Captain	Claverlock, N. Y.	5

* 5 FW-190's in one day.

ACES—HEADQUARTERS, TWELFTH AIR FORCE

NAME	RANK	HOME	VICTORIES
Sloan, William J.	2nd Lt.	Richmond, Va.	12
Hurlbut, Frank D.	Flt. Off.	Salt Lake City, Utah	9
Momyer, William W.	Lt. Col.	Seattle, Wash.	8
Baseler, Robert L.	Major	Ardmore, Pa.	7
Kinsey, Claude R.	2nd Lt.	Aurora, Ill.	7
Brunner, Robert M.	T/Sgt.	Dixon, Calif.	6
Campbell, Richard A.	1st Lt.	Ferriday, La.	6
Guerard, Jack D.	S/Sgt.	Beaufort, S. C.	6
Payne, Carl W.	1st Lt.	Columbus, Ohio	6
Rounds, Gerald L.	2nd Lt.	Fenton, Mich.	6
Schildt, William J.	2nd Lt.	Hamlin, N. Y.	6
Taylor, Ralph G.	Captain	Durham, N. C.	6

NAME	RANK	HOME	VICTORIES
Thyng, Harrison R.	Major	Barnstead, N. H.	6
Vaughn, Harley C.	Major	Sapulpa, Okla.	6
White, Thomas A.	2nd Lt.	Kelso, Wash.	6
Zubarik, Charles J.	1st Lt.	West Allis, Wisc.	6
Bowker, Fred E.	Sergeant	Oak Park, Ill.	5
Bradley, John L.	Captain	Dallas, Texas	5
Cochran, Paul R.	2nd Lt.	Hutchinson, Kans.	5
Hanna, Harry T.*	2nd Lt.	Westfield, Ill.	5
Johnson, Clarence O.	2nd Lt.	Ada, Minn.	5
Knott, Carroll S.	1st Lt.	Bakersfield, Calif.	5
Myshall, Joseph R.	S/Sgt.	Millinocket, Me.	5
McArthur, Paul G.		Reform, Ala.	5
McArthur, T. H.	Captain	Caradan, Texas	5
Osher, Ernest K.	Captain	Esterville, Iowa	5
Owens, Joel A.	Captain	Skintook, Okla.	5
Smith, Virgil H.	1st Lt.	McAllen, Texas	5
Vinson, Arnold E.	Captain	Monticello, Mass.	5
Visscher, Herman W.	2nd Lt.	Kalamazoo, Mich.	5
Walker, Walter B., Jr.		Stamford, Conn.	5
Weatherford, Sidney W.	1st Lt.	San Marcos, Texas	5
Wolford, John L.	1st Lt.	Cumberland, Md.	5

* 5 in one day.

TWELFTH BOMBER COMMAND ACES, WORLD WAR II

NAME	RANK	HOME	CREDITS
Warmer, Benjamin F.*	S/Sgt.	San Francisco, Calif	9

* 7 in one day. Gunners are not normally considered aces, but is so here listed because he was so designated by his Command.

NORTHWEST AFRICAN AIR FORCE ACES, WORLD WAR II

NAME	RANK	HOME	CREDITS
Chase, Levi R.	Major	Cortland, N. Y.	12
Feld, Sylvan	1st Lt.	Lynn, Mass.	9
Hill, Frank A.	Major	Hillsdale, N. J.	9
Collinsworth, J. D.	1st Lt.	Berger, Texas	8
Crawford, Ray	2nd Lt.	Alhambra, Calif.	6
McDonald, Norman L.	Captain	Framingham, Mass.	6
Sears, Meldrum L.	Captain	Paris, Ill.	6
Fischette, Charles R.	2nd Lt.	Clyde, N. Y.	5
Jorda, Joseph W.	1st Lt.	New Orleans, La.	5
White, John H.	1st Lt.	Kensett, Ark.	5

NORTHWEST AFRICA STRATEGIC AIR FORCE ACES, WORLD WAR II

NAME	RANK	HOME	CREDITS
Kuentzal, Ward A.	2nd Lt.	Delano, Calif.	7
Liebers, Lawrence P.	2nd Lt.	Glendale, Calif.	6
Mackay, John A.	1st Lt.	St. Albans, Vt.	5
Waters, Edward T.	2nd Lt.	Highland Park, Mich.	5

11

BRITAIN AND EUROPE—8TH AIR FORCE

THE 8TH AIR Force comprised some hundred or so bases scattered throughout the United Kingdom, and its story is that proud chronicle of the mastery of the European skies and the aerial destruction of the German war machine. The major part of the 8th Air Force record concerns strategic bombardment . . . the amazing accounts of a "dozen Fortresses pioneering daylight bombing on August 17, 1942, through the long uphill fight of 1943; the bombing of rubber production; the shock of losing 60 bombers in the attack on the Shweinfurt ball-bearing works; the fight against weather as the *Luftwaffe* grew in potency in 1943; the development of long-range fighters that could give us escort all the way; the fine days in February, 1944, which permitted our all-out offensive against the German air force; the assault on V-weapon sites months before the first buzz bomb hit London; the pounding of airfields and transportation along the 'invasion coast'; the opening of the strategic oil campaign on April 5, 1944, from Italy and on April 11 from England; D-Day on June 6, the sealing off of the battlefield on the Seine-Loire triangle; carpet bombing for the breakthrough at St. Lô on July 25, the sweep across France, the Ardennes, the Rhineland; Operation Clarion; the Ruhr; and finally, Germany prostrate under nearly a million and a half tons of bombs." (*The Army Air Forces in World War II,* University of Chicago.)

Interwoven in this fabric of aerial victory is the vital role played by the fighter pilots of the 8th Air Force in sweeping the *Luftwaffe* from the skies and gaining and maintaining Allied air supremacy. The 8th Air Force's Fighter Command was composed of three fighter wings—

each wing composed of five fighter groups and each fighter group of three fighter squadrons—and together the fighter pilots of these three wings destroyed over nine thousand German airplanes.

In the early stages of the 8th Air Force's air war in Europe the American airmen met and gradually began to wear down the enemy's air strength. With the perfection of daylight bombardment and the stepped-up day-and-night attacks against German industry the *Luftwaffe* began to noticeably weaken. By January 1944, it was becoming obvious that German air chief, Hermann Goering, would no longer send his planes up unless the advantages were his and the odds right. With the German planes no longer coming up to meet them, the Allied forces had no choice but to go down and get them. Thus the 8th Air Force entered into another phase of air war in the many-pronged drive to destroy German air power—strafing.

Strafing had been first practiced by the Germans thirty years before, and it was they who gave the technique its name from the German verb *strafe,* meaning "to punish." It had its early start with the Fokkers and Junkers of World War I in attacks against ground troops in the trenches. When the Allies adopted the technique—using Nieuports and Sopwiths—they also adopted the verb, and "strafe" became a permanent part of the airman's vocabulary.

Actually strafing is one of the most dangerous maneuvers in the fighter pilot's repertoire and was responsible for the loss of many of the top aces in the 8th and 9th Fighter Commands. But the strafe attack was the only recourse against the reluctant German air arm.

Getting down to ten feet or less above the runways and hardstands on German airfields, the American airmen flew through heavy flak and dodged towers and power lines to machine gun and bomb the parked enemy aircraft. Mustangs (P-51), Thunderbolts (P-47) and Lightnings (P-38) would return from strafing missions on the Continent with the tips of their propellers folded back from chewing into the ground or into the paved runways of *Luftwaffe* airdromes. Chunks of high-tension wires were found in airscoops or wrapped around bomb racks. One P-51 ace came back with a turnip in his scoop.

It was generally felt that in that theater the danger and difficulty involved in destroying an airplane on the ground was far greater than that involved in an air-to-air victory, so that planes destroyed on the ground were credited to the fighter pilots and included in the score of enemy kills.

When V-E Day rang down the final curtain on the European conflict the three fighter wings of the 8th Air Force had run up an impresive tally of 9,275 enemy aircraft destroyed and produced more aces than any other numbered air force. The final tally by fighter groups is shown on p. 166.

The top ace in the 8th Air Force was Colonel John C. Meyer who destroyed twenty-four German planes in the air and thirteen on the ground during his two years with the 8th Air Force in Europe.

Born in Brooklyn, N. Y., 3 April 1919, he had completed two years at Dartmouth College in Hanover, N. H., when he enlisted in the aviation cadet program in November 1939. Graduating in July 1940, he served in the United States and Iceland until January 1943, when he was directed to organize and activate the 487th Fighter Squadron at Westover Field, Mass. The following July he took his squadron to Europe as part of the 352nd Fighter Group of the 8th Air Force.

He shot down his first German plane in late October 1943.

FINAL TALLY IN EUROPE
15 FIGHTER GROUPS OF 8TH AIR FORCE

Fighter Victory Credits Board Results

(1st mission flown on 13 April 43
Base Horsham St. Faith, England)

GROUP	TOTAL EA DESTROYED	TOTAL OPER. LOSSES	RATIO OF LOSSES TO EA DESTROYED
	65th Fighter Wing		
4th	1006½	241	1 to 4½
56th	1006	128	1 to 8
355th	860	175	1 to 4½
361st	351½	81	1 to 4
479th	433	69	1 to 6⅓

166

66th Fighter Wing

55th	577½	181	1 to 3¼
78th	684	167	1 to 4
339th	689	97	1 to 7
353rd	724	137	1 to 5¼
357th	688½	128	1 to 5½

67th Fighter Wing

20th	435	132	1 to 3⅓
352nd	776	118	1 to 6½
356th	271	122	1 to 2¼
359th	360	106	1 to 3½
364th	463	134	1 to 3½

Total   9275

On 8 May 1944 he led a flight of eight fighters in an attack against a much larger force trying to intercept an American bomber formation. The enemy flight was dispersed but during the engagement Colonel Meyer and his wingman became separated from their flight and lost considerable altitude. While regaining it, they saw another flight of fifteen or more enemy fighters flying toward the bombers. The two pilots attacked, breaking up the formation with Colonel Meyer shooting down three German fighters.

Six months later over Kassel, Germany, he singlehandedly attacked a flight of twenty to twenty-five Focke-Wulfs and Messerschmitts destroying four of them.

In November 1944, he became Deputy Commander of the 352nd Fighter Group and during the following two months destroyed eleven aircraft in nineteen missions.

Colonel Meyer became the leading European ace on Christmas Day 1944, when he shot down two more German fighters, bringing his total air and ground kills to thirty-two.

A week later, on New Year's Day, he and the 487th Fighter Squadron met the enemy under very unfavorable conditions. Just as he and the twelve ships he was leading were taking off, the field was attacked by fifty German fighters. Undaunted, he continued the take-offs and personally engaged the German leader just as his own aircraft became airborne. Without combat airspeed Colonel Meyer nevertheless maneuvered with the German and shot him down. The squadron followed his fighting example, and during the course of the battle shot down twenty-three of the enemy fighters and broke up the attack on the airdrome without a single loss to themselves.

On a later occasion, while leading a group of Mustangs (P-51), he discovered twenty planes parked at an airdrome between Mannheim and Würzburg and destroyed them all, getting five himself. "It was a perfect set-up," he said later. "I kept two of the squadrons as top cover and led my own down to strafe. First we knocked out the flak emplacements, then made ten passes over the field. It was like a merry-go-round."

Colonel Meyer returned to combat in the Korean War and added two jet victories to his impressive tally.

A trio of the aces in the 56th Fighter Group, Hubert Zemke, David Schilling and Francis S. Gabreski, gave the Germans a great deal of trouble and caused the Germans to nickname them "The Terrible Three."

Lieutenant Colonel Francis Gabreski was the leading fighter ace in the 8th Air Force for air-to-air kills, and the third ranking ace in total enemy aircraft destroyed, with a record of thirty-one air-to-air kills and two and one-half destroyed on the ground.

Born 28 June 1919, at Oil City, Pennsylvania, he was the son of natives of Warsaw who immigrated to the United States from Poland. He attended the University of Notre Dame at South Bend, Indiana, for two years and left the premedical course there to enlist as an aviation cadet in July 1940. He graduated from the flying cadets in March 1941, and was stationed at Wheeler Field, Hawaii, at the time the Japanese attacked Pearl Harbor. Gabreski returned to the U. S. in October 1942 and then went to England where he was assigned to the 315th Polish Spitfire Squadron of the Royal Air Force for training tactics and flying Spitfires. While flying with this squadron, he put in thirteen combat missions over German-occupied territory.

Gabreski was awarded the Polish Cross of Valor by General Sikoski, Commander in Chief of the Polish Forces, for courage in action while temporarily attached to the Polish Air Force.

In February 1943 he was transferred to the 8th Air Force and assigned to the 56th Fighter Group.

In November 1943 Colonel Francis Gabreski was leading his squadron on a bomber escort mission near Oldenburg, Germany, when a large number of Messerschmitt 110's, protected by a top cover of single-engine fighters, fell into a formation to fire rockets into the bomber formation. It was a deadly attack on the bomber formation and the Thunderbolts screamed into battle. Singling out the leading ME 110, Gabreski opened fire from dead astern and closed in. Smoke poured from the German plane and parts of the ship were torn off as Colonel Gabreski opened fire in short, effective bursts. But he was closing so rapidly that he was soon flying through debris and had to dive to avoid a collision. Smoke and burnt fragments of the ME 110 entered his cockpit through the heater vent and the enemy ship itself skimmed the top of his canopy before it went down. The leading edge of his P-47's right wing was crushed and his left wing torn, but nevertheless he climbed back up to continue guarding the bombers. Spotting another ME 110 trying to get into attack position he dived on it sending a second German plane plummeting to the earth. Through his leadership that day his outnumbered flight was able to disperse the enemy rocket-launching planes and for his action he was awarded the Distinguished Service Cross.

Colonel Gabreski refused to use tracer bullets, as most of the fighter pilots did, because, as he stated: "Sometimes you miss with the first bullets and the tracers give you away." He also preferred to go into combat with half the ammunition normally carried, contending that a full load made the wings too heavy to turn conveniently inside a Messerschmitt. He also believed in getting in close. His idea: "Wait until you get 'em right in the sights, then short bursts. There's no use melting your guns."

Fifteen days later, almost a year after his first victory, Gabreski went on what was to be his final mission before coming home. Leading his squadron on a strafing mission against a German airfield near Coblenz, he suddenly felt his plane lurch as the propeller touched a slight mound in the field. With the propeller bent he was unable to climb directly above the airfield for sufficient altitude to bail out and even had he been able, he would have only been inviting a murderous barrage from the anti-aircraft gunners on the field. With no alternative, he crash landed, setting his plane down on the edge of the field and fleeing. "The flak was so heavy that rather than take a chance of getting hit, I ran the plane into the ground at well over 200 m.p.h, kicked the right rudder which gives the wings the shock and climbed out without a scratch."

He was captured five days later by German farmers. When he was brought before a German interrogation officer the Nazi happily crowed, "Hello, Gabby, we have been waiting for you for a long time."

He was liberated from Stalag-Luft #1 near Barth just after V-E Day and returned to the United States for assignment to Wright Patterson AFB, Dayton, Ohio, as a test pilot. While there he was promoted from lieutenant colonel to colonel and in September 1946 was relieved from active duty. He joined Douglas Aircraft Corporation as a foreign sales representative. However, in April 1947 he returned to active duty and became Commander of the 55th Fighter Squadron at Shaw AFB, Sumter, South Carolina. In September 1947 he entered Columbia University to begin a four-year Russian course from which he graduated. His record as an ace was reopened for more entries in the Korean conflict when he added jets to his enemy kills.

Colonel David C. Schilling, the fourth ranking ace in the 8th Air Force, destroyed twenty-two and one half German planes in the air and ten and one half on the ground. He was born at Leavenworth, Kansas, 15 December 1918, and later moved to Kansas City, Missouri. In June 1939, he graduated from Dartmouth College at Hanover, New Hampshire, with a Bachelor of Arts degree in geology. Three months later he joined the Air Force and in May 1940 graduated from flying school. In June 1940 he joined the 56th Pursuit Group at Charlotte Air Base, North Carolina. Two and a half years later he went to England as a squadron commander with the 56th Pursuit Group (later renamed the 56th Fighter Group), under the command of Colonel Hubert Zemke. Subsequently he was appointed executive officer of the group and in August 1944 became its commander.

While leading the 56th on a mission over Arnheim, Germany, on 23 December 1944, his group ran into 250 German fighters flying 1500 feet below them. Attacking the formation they shot down thirty-seven planes, with only one loss to themselves, and Colonel Schilling made the jackpot five-in-one-day.

On 21 January 1945 Colonel David Schilling noted that the "turnover among American fighter pilots because of combat losses and completion of tours of duty has resulted in a decline in experience and leadership ability in recent months." The veteran 56th Fighter Group "had had twenty-two aces a year ago and now one was left. The others had been shot down or had rotated to the United States. [Of those shot down all but one were victims of flak.] At the same time the German air force has suffered much more serious permanent losses in leaders. German fighters now fly in large groups with only one experienced pilot leading them."

Colonel Zemke, the third man of the "terrible trio" in number of enemy kills, was the leader of the three, as Commander of the 56th Fighter Group. Zemke's record of twenty-five kills included almost every type of German aircraft, including partial credit for a shared victory with Lieutenant Norman Benolt of Furnace, Massachusetts, for the air-to-air destruction of a Nazi jet plane. Known as the "fightingest" commander in Europe, Zemke always preferred to personally lead his group on their combat strikes.

Zemke attended and graduated from the University of Montana (forestry major). He later enlisted in flight school and was commissioned in the Army Air Corps in June 1936. He went on active duty two years later and visited England and Russia as an observer and to demonstrate the Tomahawk fighter (P-40). He was in Russia in 1941 when the Japanese attacked Pearl Harbor. Returning to the United States, he received command of the 56th Fighter Group, one of the first American fighter groups sent to Britain.

Zemke arrived at acedom on 20 October 1943. On a patrol over Emden, Germany, he spotted a ME 109 below and radioed to his wingman, "Let's go down."

I turned right and started down; I closed fast on the ME 109, opening fire from dead center and a little above, giving him three short bursts. The first burst must have killed the pilot because he took no evasive action. My shots were hitting just at his wing roots. I moved in closer to about 200 yards and fired again. Still there was no evasive action as I watched more strikes on his wings and fuselage. I closed to about 150 yards and gave him a final burst. His wheels came down and he started smoking and the plane dove slowly over on its back going through a cloud bank out of control. I broke for the sun and joined the other Thunderbolts out over the water. That's how #5 went.

In the fall of 1943 Zemke's flyers had decided to shoot for a new record: 100 enemy planes destroyed by Christmas. However, they exceeded all expectations arriving at the 100 figure by 6 November to become the first fighter group in the European theater of operations to destroy 100 planes. In regard to this accomplishment Major General William Kepner said in a message to the group: "For each of them an untold number of our bombers were saved. You have brought great credit to yourselves, the 8th Fighter Command and the Armed Forces of your country."

On Friday, 26 November 1943, fighter planes of the 8th Air Force had their biggest day up to that time, destroying thirty-six German fighter planes with a loss of only four of their own. P-47's and P-38's went to Paris early in the day with heavy bombers and destroyed three German planes and later in the day took Forts and Liberators to Bremen and knocked down thirty-three enemy interceptors. At the same time, the Zemke group destroyed twenty-six enemy planes.

Combat began immediately after they rendezvoused with the bombers, as forty to forty-five German planes were initiating an attack on the bombers at almost the same time. Captain Walter Mahurin, who became the first 8th Fighter Command double ace, described the action:

We went in around the bombers and found a bunch of ME 110's strung out behind the Forts. At first we thought they were stragglers, but as we came in closer we identified them as Messerschmitts and came in shooting. All three of the planes I destroyed caught fire, but none of them exploded. Two of the pilots bailed out;

the third was struggling in his cockpit and seemed to be caught there.

This action was in contrast to that time in May during an Antwerp mission. I made a bounce on five 190's. Inasmuch as I'd never seen a Jerry before, I was scared to death and messed up generally. The Jerries knocked my ammunition bay door open, and there was my ammunition dangling out in the breeze. I did a skid which is hard to shoot at, but the Jerries shot at me and they were good and I was scared to death.

On 20, 21 and 22 February 1944 the 56th shot down forty-three without a loss. On 8 March 1944, Zemke's group had almost three hundred enemy aircraft destroyed before they lost an ace. Men had gone down—fifty altogether—but it always seemed to be younger, inexperienced pilots. A strange combination of luck with flak, good crew chiefs, and skill always seemed to get the aces back as represented by the return from a dogfight of First Lieutenant Ralph A. Johnson. Although badly shot up Johnson managed to get his P-47 back to Engalnd. When he attempted to lower his landing gear one became stuck up and the other down. Zemke, who had already landed, immediately took off again and flew alongside the troubled Johnson. The Radio Control Room recorded the following conversation:

Z—Have you tried to shake it down?

J—Yes.

Z—Get way up and try again. If you can't shake it down, you'll have to jump—be careful. Go over to the lake straight ahead. Put your landing gear handle in the down position, do a bank on the left wing and snap it over to the right. Let me get a little ahead.

J—Okay.

Z—That hasn't done it. Do some violent weaving back and forth.

J—Sir, my landing gear handle is stuck.

Z—Is it stuck down?

J—Yes, sir.

Z—Let's go upstairs. Follow me. (Pause) Do you want to try one wheel?

J—I certainly do, sir.

Z—Let me take a good look at you. You do not have any flaps and will need plenty of field.

J—Whatever you say, sir.

Z—Better bail out. How much gas have you got?

J—About thirty gallons. (Pause) That fellow didn't do a very good job of gunning me.

Z—I'm afraid of a landing.

J—You aren't half as scared as I am, sir.

Z—It's not so bad. (To station) His plane is in bad shape. I'm going to have him bail out NE of Margate. (To Johnson) We'll go up to 10,000 ft. Did you come back alone?

J—No, sir. One of the boys came back with me.

Z—Be sure to hold your legs together when you go over, and count ten. Try shaking it once more.

J—Yes, sir.

Z—You don't have to "sir" me up here. Head her out to sea.

J—Yes, sir. Is it okay now?

Z—Open up the canopy.

J—It is open, sir. It's been open for a long time.

Z—Okay, mighty fine. The crate is heading out to sea.

Colonel Zemke didn't have to talk to him after that. Johnson turned his plane over, dumped himself out and left the Thunderbolt roaring out toward the open water by itself. The plane hit harmlessly and Lieutenant Johnson parachuted to safety in the water below.

Colonel Zemke not only commanded a fighter group, but whenever he was flying he led the pack. Once they got forty-three parked aircraft while following him across an airfield and damaged another twenty-three. Another time he led them into combat with fifty Germans and got two himself while his pilots were bagging twenty-seven more.

At the end of his tour Colonel Zemke was rotated home, much against his will, for a much-needed rest. On 13 August 1944 Zemke had talked his way back overseas, this time commanding the 479th Fighter Group.

On 30 October 1944 Colonel Zemke led his unit on a mission over the Continent; that evening Hubert Zemke was reported missing in action. "We were flying at about 28,000 feet," said Lieutenant Richard D. Creighton (later to become a jet ace in Korea), "escorting bombers to Hamburg when Zemke appeared to be having trouble. The weather was very bad. The last I saw of him he was going down through an overcast."

Colonel Hubert Zemke returned to the U. S. after his release from a prisoner of war camp at the end of the hostilities.

The two top fighter groups in the 8th Air Force, the 56th Fighter Group and the 4th Fighter Group, were both led by brilliant and gifted air leaders. Colonel Zemke's counterpart in the 4th was Colonel Donald J. Blakeslee of Fairport Harbor, Ohio, who flew more missions and stayed in continuous active combat longer than any other American aviator—flying between 400 and 500 combat missions and well over 1,000 combat hours.

Blakeslee replaced Colonel Chesley Peterson as the commander of the 4th Fighter Group when Peterson was rotated back to the States, and he continued as the group leader through many aircraft changes—Spitfires, Thunderbolts, Mustangs—and many history-making air battles from Dieppe to Berlin. Blakeslee's great value to his unit at Debden, England, was not his flying ability, but—like Zemke with the 56th—his matchless ability as an air commander. In battle he ruled the sky from his cockpit keeping control over 40 to 50 planes as they zoomed and roared, twisted and dove across the heavens, and he played his ships like men in a chess game, fighting them in the most effective manner against the fury of the *Luftwaffe*, while at the same time he was himself flaming fifteen Germans from the sky and destroying two on the ground.

On one mission over Berlin, Blakeslee was selected to direct the combat operations of the entire 8th Air Force Fighter Command, which meant the active control from his small cockpit of almost eight hundred fighter planes. And considering the rapidity with which the fighter units became separated in a dogfight, it was a large job that was entrusted to the 4th's famed commander. Blakeslee handled that job as he had all the others, with "decisiveness, boldness, personal magnetism and zest for battle."

Blakeslee had great physical stamina and for his entire three and a half years as a combat leader he personally led his group into combat with an inexhaustible zest and a natural animal cunning for seeking and destroying the enemy. He loved aerial combat and his unit at Debden with the same fierce spirit as Brooklynites loved baseball and their Dodgers.

As the two top fighter groups in the 8th Air Force, the 4th and the 56th maintained a constant rivalry and while the 56th "Wolfpack" was for a long time the top scoring group, toward the end of the war the 4th finally caught up, evened the score, and at the very last eased into first place by a one-half victory margin.

The fighting spirit of Blakeslee's group produced many aces, tops among whom were the team of Captain Don S. Gentile and Captain John T. Godfrey, who were referred to by Prime Minister Winston Churchill as the Damon and Pythias of the twentieth century.

Don Gentile destroyed twenty-three German planes in the air and seven on the ground during three years' service with both the RAF and the USAAF in Europe. Born at Piqua, Ohio, in 1920 he learned to fly in high school and had a total of 300 hours' flying time when he was "rejected" by the Air Corps. Disappointed, he turned to the Royal Air Force and by December, 1941, he was appointed an RAF Pilot Officer and flew with various RAF squadrons out of England until June 1942 when he joined the famed Eagle Squadron.

On the 19 August 1942, Dieppe Raid, Gentile destroyed his first enemy craft, an FW-190 and a JU-88, within ten minutes of each other, for which he was awarded the British DFC.

The next month he was commissioned a second lieutenant in the USAAF and assigned to the 4th Fighter Group of the 8th Air Force in Europe. At the same time Captain John T. Godfrey transferred from the RAF and was assigned to the 4th Fighter Group. He became Gentile's wingman and the two formed a combat team which General H. H. Arnold termed the "greatest of any war."

On a mission in the Paris area, Gentile, this time without his able companion, came close to being a victim of the enemy's guns, surviving only because of his superb flying skill. Captain Grover C. Hall, Jr., in his history of the 4th Fighter Group, *1000 Destroyed,* described the action:

Gentile bagged one FW and was pumping away at a second. He roared earthward at about 650 m.p.h., guns flaming. The Hun dived straight into the ground with an orange spray flash and his slipstream almost sucked Gentile into the ground after him. Gentile put the stick in his belly to climb back up to the rest of his squadron.

He had concentrated on his shooting in the dive, serene in the belief that his wingman was screening his tail. As his plane groaned out of the powerful, leaden Thunderbolt dive, Gentile heard the muffled thump of FW 190 cannon fire and saw what is called "corruption" fly over his port wing. Gentile's earphones flapped with the urgent cry of another pilot:

"Break, Gentile, break! Break, Gentile, you damfool!" *Gentile* was Gentile's nickname.

Miles away over the channel, Major General Kepner was cruising about following the combat over his radio. To General Kepner the shout sounded like:

"Break, *General*, you damfool!"

General Kepner couldn't imagine who could be flying in combat with enough rank to address him as damfool, but just the same, he told Gentile later, he reefed his Thunderbolt around and broke like mad to port.

Gentile went into a tight turn with the Hun. Not many pilots could turn in a Thunderbolt on the deck with an FW 190, but Gentile had the skill and was too frightened to worry about spinning out. The Hun had his No. 2 glued on his wing and he soon showed Gentile he was a tough adversary. Gentile went shuddering and shaking over the tree-tops with the two Germans. He was cold with fright, the same as he had been in his green RAF days when he escaped a German assailant with violent black-out turns and pull-outs, thus winning the bet that his body could stand more black-outs than the Germans.

On some reverse turns Gentile squirted what little ammunition he had left after downing the other two Jerries. Now he found himself without ammunition and with two determined, accomplished killers on his tail. In the head-on attacks the German discerned that the Thunderbolt's wings were not firing; this made him press the attack that much more resolutely. The Hun peppered Gentile with some 30° deflection shots. Gentile pulled away and flicked down.

One of the Germans had been lost in the maneuvering

and Gentile found himself going around in circles over the trees, rawhided by the German. Gentile was defenseless without ammunition; his one chance of surviving the vendetta was to evade the German fire until his ammunition was also exhausted. The German kept pressing for the one brief opportunity of lining the Thunderbolt up in his sights. Gentile's hand got clammy on the throttle.

"Help! Help! I'm being clobbered!" Gentile screamed in near-panic.

Somewhere above in the clouds the rest of his squadron was flying about. Until this day Gentile remembers the imperturbable drawl of Willard Millikan answering:

"Now, if you will tell me your call sign and approximate position we'll send help."

Gentile shot back, "I'm down here by a railroad track with a 190!"

But Millikan couldn't find Gentile. The duel—cannon vs. flying skill—went on down below. Characteristically, Gentile began talking to himself: ". . . Keep calm, Gentile . . . don't panic."

Gentile still managed to keep one jump ahead of the German, but his desperation mounted. The Hun was lathered and remorseless, having seen the American clobber the two 190 pilots, his acquaintances and perhaps his friends. He knew by now that the American with the "Donnie Boy" insignia was a superlative pilot; this was a chance to blast an American ace out of the sky without risk. He kept firing, but the American always climbed or banked just inside his line of fire.

Gentile felt like giving up; he was going to be shot down anyway; it would be better to get some altitude and bail out. But he had some last words:

"Horseback, Horseback! If I don't get back—tell 'em I got two 190's!"

The two fighters were flat-out on the deck, down by the railroad track, the German on the American's tail firing. The German began to close the gap. Gentile suddenly honked his ship up and stood it on his prop until it quivered and was ready to stall out. For the first time Gentile had gotten above the Hun and could have swooped down on him for a kill had his ammunition not been exhausted.

. Gentile had preserved himself. He had made the Hun fire all his ammunition without hitting him. The German suddenly peeled off and sulked for home, his two FW *kameraden* unavenged.

However, being on the defensive was a very unusual situation for Gentile, who, with his teammate Godfrey, constantly pressed the enemy. Unlike the normal wingman, Godfrey alternated with Gentile as leader and they took turns shooting down planes and protecting each other. Their teamwork was so effective that Hermann Goering once remarked that he would gladly give two of his best squadrons for the capture of Gentile and Godfrey.

Canadian-born Captain John T. Godfrey is officially credited by the Air Force with eighteen enemy planes in the air and eighteen on the ground; five probables; twelve damaged; plus the destruction of fifteen locomotives during 150 combat hours in the ETO.

Born in Montreal, Canada, in 1923, his parents brought him to America in April 1924. He completed High School at Woonsocket, R. I., in 1941 when the war drums were beating loudest. Godfrey tried to join the Air Corps but was turned down for lack of college training, so he turned to the RCAF and graduated with RCAF wings in October 1942, was assigned to an RAF Squadron and then in April 1943 was transferred to USAAF. Flying Gentile's wing, Godfrey shot down his first enemy plane in November 1943 and became an ace before his twenty-first birthday.

Over Berlin on 8 March 1944 Gentile and Godfrey attacked a formation of more than one hundred enemy aircraft preparing to engage a flight of Boeing Flying Fortresses. Together, they shot down six of the enemy planes and completely disrupted the attack on the B-17's allowing the bombers to succesfully complete their mission. Captain Hall further describes that action:

Gentile and Godfrey singled out two of the five 109's and made six or seven turns with them, sparring and feeling them out. Godfrey maneuvered onto the tail of one.

"Okay, I'll cover you," Gentile said.

Godfrey gave the 109 a few short bursts and got

179

strikes. The veteran Gentile pressed the transmitter button and said into his mask mike:

"Give 'im more . . . More!" The 109 rolled over and Godfrey clobbered him. He watched the German bail out. . . .

Gentile clobbered a 109 from 75 yards line astern.

"Gimme cover, Johnny, while I go after that 109 at 2 o'clock to us," Gentile said.

"I'm with you," Godfrey came back.

Using combat flaps for tighter turns, Gentile, with Godfrey guarding his tail . . . gave the 109 a squirt at 100 yards. The Hun's cockpit filled with smoke. He jumped from his plane.

By this time there were 50-plus Jerry fighters going up and down, in and out, in pairs. The bombers sprayed the sky with green flares to signal for help from the fighters. In these first Berlin shows, bomber pilots complained that the fighters, busy keeping their own heads above water, often ignored their distress signals. But they weren't talking about Gentile and Godfrey.

"All right, Johnny, there're two flying abreast at 1 o'clock. See 'em?"

"Yep."

"Okay," Gentile said, looking over at Godfrey, "you take the one on the right and I'll take the one on the left."

"Reet."

Gentile and Godfrey pushed the throttle to the firewall to overtake the two 109's. . . . The quarry were not the crafty, resolute killers like the 190 pilot who had stalked Gentile down by the railroad track a year before, or like they were to encounter later. The 109's took no evasive action, maintaining a duck-on-pond formation. It was possible the Jerries knew they were being followed and planned a violent Immelmann which would bring them down on the tails of their pursuers. If so, they waited too long to pull the stick. The wings of the two Mustangs flamed as two thumbs pressed down on the red firing tit —the same movement you use on a cigarette lighter.

Gentile's 109 rolled port and went down burning. Godfrey's rolled starboard and went down burning. Shooting them down was like pressing a dynamite detonator and seeing two bridges in the distance blow up.

Gentile and Godfrey had destroyed five Huns between them. They climbed back to 22,000 feet to get close to the bombers. Suddenly Godfrey looked over his right shoulder and saw it.

"Break! Break! One coming in at 4 o'clock to you!"

"Okay, break starboard," said Gentile.

They broke together and the 109 made a head-on pass.

"All right, Johnny," said Gentile, "when he comes back around on the next turn you break right and I'll break left."

They circled and the 109 came boring in for another head-on attack. He looked mean and vicious. He was bold enough to joust with two Mustangs. As the planes bored straight at each other's spinner, Gentile ordered the foxing maneuver:

"Now!"

Gentile broke sharply to the left; Godfrey to the right. They honked their sticks back, climbed and came barreling down on the 109's tail.

Thus trapped, the Jerry reacted fast. He pushed the stick forward and went into a steep dive for the clouds below. The Mustangs followed, firing and peppering the 109. Godfrey finally got in a solid burst as the 109 began pulling out of his dive at 500 feet, after a four-mile chase downward, and it gave off smoke.

"You take him, Don, I'm out of ammo," yelled Godfrey.

The German was weaving across the treetops. Gentile closed in and the next burst punctured the 109's belly tank. The German pulled up to 1,000 feet, jettisoned his canopy and crawled out the right side. He had the distinction of being No. 6 in the series.

The two aces were sent home together in June of 1944 to stress teamwork to the American people. After a series of war-bond tours they were separated: Gentile went to Wright-Patterson AFB as a test pilot and Godfrey returned to Europe.

In August 1944, back in combat, Godfrey, with only a wingman for support, destroyed eight locomotives, strafed a small enemy airbase destroying three and damaging three other aircraft. Returning to his base, with all but one gun knocked out, he spotted a ME-109 and shot it down in flames less than 200 feet over the streets of Hanover, Germany. For this action a grateful nation added a cluster to Major Godfrey's Silver Star.

On 24 August 1944, while strafing at Herzberg Air Base in Germany, he was downed by enemy flak. Going through pretty rough maltreatment at the hands of civilians he was finally rescued by the German *Luftwaffe*. (It was reliably reported after the war that Hitler wanted all U. S. flyer prisoners executed but that Hermann Goering, head of the *Luftwaffe*, talked him out of it.)

Godfrey escaped from prison and eventually reached American lines near Nuremberg on 17 April 1945. He went on inactive duty in January 1946. (Retired from the Air Force, Major Godfrey is now in the lace manufacturing business and is the youngest owner and operator of a lace mill.) In the same month, January 1946, Gentile received the honorary degree of Doctor of Aeronautics from Ohio Northern University at Ada, Ohio.

Official War Department combat intelligence reports show that Gentile and Godfrey were past masters of the "you-hold-him-and-I'll-hit-him" fighter system. In one report Gentile commented, "Without a good wingman, you are likely to be much more cautious and much less effective."

Gentile was attending the University of Maryland under an Air Force university program when he was killed in a T-33 (jet training plane) accident while flying between Andrews AFB, Maryland, and Wright-Patterson AFB, Ohio.

Major Robert S. Johnson, who made twenty-eight air-to-air kills, attributed his phenomenal success to athletic training before the war. The 24-year-old Oklahoman, who was a Golden Gloves boxer and a better-than-average football player at school, pointed out in an interview that the American sports scheme instills team spirit in a man. That spirit, he pointed out, is the difference between winning and losing in the sky battles with the Nazis.

"Fighting those Jerries is like playing football and who wants to be on a losing team?" Johnson said. "The way I figure it, when you compete in an athletic contest you realize that the other guy is no better than you. You go on trying because you can never tell when you'll get the break."

Major Johnson returned from one mission with a rudder control shot away which placed his ship in a position that it could only be flown straight ahead. He was headed back for England, starting to cross the Channel, when a Messerschmitt pilot spotted his P-47. The ME-109 made stern, side, bottom and top attacks, firing many rounds each pass. Bob crouched in his armor seat and could feel the slugs hit the plating but the P-47 kept tooling right on to England. Finally, the German, out of ammunition, drew alongside and waved a gesture of exasperation at Johnson, turned around and went home. Major Johnson got his Thunderbolt back to England without too much more trouble. Incidentally, Major Johnson after leaving the service went to work for Republic Aircraft as an executive—he liked the way Republic made its Thunderbolts.

George Preddy, high-ranking 8th Air Force ace and first ETO pilot to shoot down six German planes in one day, crashed to his death on 25 December 1944 during a spectacular dogfight over Belgium in which he downed two ME-109's. He was chasing an FW-109 when American antiaircraft gunners put up a stream of flak in an effort to trap the fleeing German pilot. It struck Major Preddy's P-51 and sent it spinning to the ground. The Focke-Wulf escaped both Major Preddy's guns and the fire thrown up by the doughboy ground gunners. Major Preddy officially had 25.8 kills in the air and five on the ground. Preddy was a veteran of combat in the Pacific and 13 months in Europe. He got six planes in a little over six minutes over Hamburg on 6 August 1944.

On 17 April 1945, Lieutenant Colonel Elwyn G. Reghetti was shot down over Germany as he hung up a new record becoming the second leading 8th Air Force ace and destroying nine planes on the ground during his last mission. As Commander of the 55th Fighter Group, he was leading his formation on a strafing mission in southern Germany when he sent his mate after a lone German plane while he buzzed an airfield to draw fire away from the other craft. This brought his total to twenty-seven on the ground. He had 7½ more bagged in the air.

Among the aces of the 8th Air Force was Lieutenant Clinton Burdick of Brooklyn, who was determined to break his father's World War I ace record of seven German planes. By April 1945, young Burdick had drawn near his father's record with three speared on the ground and 3½ in the air. Still only twenty years old, he had been overseas (8th AF) since October 1944. By the end of his tour he had topped his father's record with 5½ in the air and 3½ on the ground for a general total of nine. Dad never had a chance.

One of the most unusual incidents of the 8th Air Force's war was that of Lieutenant Vernon A. Boehle, an ex-Eagle Squadron pilot from Indianapolis, who actually lost the engine out of his P-47.

Lieutenant Boehle was jumped by four FW-190's while on an escort mission over France. He shook them pretty well, but one persistent one got in a few rounds. "I started back alone at 19,000 feet," he related. "I was about 30 miles from Dieppe and could see the French coast when I noticed a slight roughness in my ship. Then it began to vibrate and the whole plane shook like a toy. Then the engine dropped off the mounts and out of the plane. I saw her drop. My plane did a couple of tight loops, then started into a flat spin. I tried to transmit a distress signal, but the radio was dead. I got ready to bail out and climbed out of the cockpit, but I just flopped around on the wing. I thought I would bounce off, but the centrifugal force kept me glued to the wing and I believe I would have stayed there all the way down if I hadn't kicked myself off with my feet."

During the two days in his dinghy, Boehle kept warm sipping the whiskey in his emergency kit, but he couldn't smoke the cigarettes because they stayed too wet in the cold, choppy water. Rescue came two days later when a British motor torpedo boat pulled him out of the water.

The bombardment by the heavies; the air strikes by the mediums; the air sweeps by the fighters pressed on and German air power—in spite of the fact that they had perfected jet fighters to the operational stage—was on the verge of collapse. In a final effort they rose groggily from the canvas to throw one final, desperate blow. As General H. H. Arnold described this last effort:

During the Ruhr campaign, the Luftwaffe was heard from once more. Goering had begun plans for this last try in March. In a special order of the day Luftwaffe pilots were asked to volunteer for a secret, dangerous duty. Some 300 were selected and sent to Stendal for a 10-day course in ramming training, most of which consisted of getting them into the right frame of mind by lectures, films and Nazi indoctrination. They were taught ramming technique—the technique of flying out of the sun on a line astern of the bombers, opening fire at extreme range, and holding it until the final sharp ramming dive aimed just forward of the bomber's tail. Unlike the Japs, the pilots were allowed to bail out if possible. Eighty pilots were equipped with FW-190's and sent to Prague to operate against the Fifteenth Army Air Force heavies. The remainder were given ME-190's and organized into a unit of four groups known as Sonder-kommando Elbe and given such fancy names as Falken and Raubvogel, or birds of prey. On April 7, these groups were ready. At 9:30 A.M. they were alerted; our Eighth Air Force was forming. Thirteen hundred heavies and 850 fighters were in the air; at 11:16 A.M. Sonder-kommando Elbe rose to do and/or die. In their ears were dinned patriotic music and exhortations, and the pilots' radio transmitters had been removed from their planes so that they could not talk back.

When it was over, 65 German planes had gone down before our fighters; the bombers' guns brought the total to 104, and there is no estimate of how many enemy planes were destroyed by our 22 bombers and three fighters which were lost. The final "Big Blow" had failed. And we went on. In the two-week period of April 5-19, the Eighth and Ninth Air Forces almost annihilated the Luftwaffe, between them destroying 3,484 planes in the air and on the ground.

A month later the military might of Germany was in total ruin and the second great war on the Continent within the twentieth century was over. The final tabulations on V-E Day showed that in the European Theater the AAF had lost 11,687 airplanes while destroying 20,419 enemy aircraft—of which 9,275 were destroyed by the three fighter wings of the 8th Air Force. The U. S. Army Air Forces emerged from the slaughter as the "largest and most effective striking force the world has known" and the 8th Air Force had played a deadly, effective and vital role in bringing to pass the final Allied triumph.

CONFIRMED VICTORIES BY FIGHTER PILOTS OF THE EIGHTH AIR FORCE

This tabulation, prepared from reports of an officially constituted Fighter Victory Credits Board, covers the entire period of fighter operations from August 1942 to April 1945.

For reason of simplicity, partial victories are listed in decimals, i.e., 1½ is shown as 1.50; 2⅓ as 2.33, etc. In some cases a single victory has been credited to 2, 11 or as many as 23 individuals, thereby creating unusual percentages such as .83 or .59. In the Eighth Air Force air-to-ground kills as well as air-to-air-kills were credited.

NAME	RANK	HOME	AIRCRAFT DESTROYED IN THE AIR	ON THE GROUND	TOTAL
Meyer, John C.	Lt. Col.	Forest Hills, N. Y.	24	13	37
Godfrey, John T.	Captain	Woonsocket, R.I.	18	18	36
Righetti, Elwyn G.	Lt. Col.	San Antonio, Tex.	7.50	27	34.50
Gabreski, Francis S.	Lt. Col.	Oil City, Pa.	31	2.50	33.50
Schilling, David C.	Colonel	Traverse City, Mich.	22.50	10.50	33
Brown, Henry W.	Captain	Washington, D. C.	17.20	14.50	31.70
Preddy, George E.	Major	Greensboro, N. C.	25.83	5	30.83
Hofer, Ralph K.	1st Lt.	Salem, Mo.	16.50	14	30.50
Gentile, Don S.	Captain	Piqua, Ohio	23	7	30
Landers, John D.	Lt. Col.	Joshua, Tex.	8.50	20	28.50
Goodson, James A.	Major	Toronto, Canada	15	13	28
Johnson, Robert S.	Captain	Lawton, Okla.	28	..	28
Zemke, Hubert	Colonel	Missoula, Mont.	19.50	8.50	28
Cullerton, Wiliam J.	1st Lt.	Chicago, Ill.	6	21	27
Duncan, Glenn E.	Colonel	Houston, Tex.	19	7.80	26.80
Kinnard, Claiborne H.	Colonel	Franklin, Tenn.	8	17	25
Wetmore, Ray S.	Captain	Kerman, Calif.	22.59	2	24.59
Beeson, Duane W.	Major	Boise, Idaho	19.33	4.75	24.08
Litge, Raymond H.	Captain	Altenburg, Mo.	10.50	13	23.50
Olds, Robin	Major	Beverly Hills, Calif.	12	11	23

CONFIRMED VICTORIES BY FIGHTER PILOTS OF THE EIGHTH AIR FORCE (continued)

NAME	RANK	HOME	AIRCRAFT DESTROYED IN THE AIR	ON THE GROUND	TOTAL
Glover, Fred W.	Major	Asheville, N.C.	10.30	12.50	22.80
Carson, Leonard K.	Major	Ayreshire, Iowa	18.50	3.50	22
Heller, Edwin L.	Captain	Schneeksville, Pa.	5.50	16.50	22
McKennon, Pierce W.	Major.	Fort Smith, Ark.	12	9.68	21.68
Christensen, Fred J.	Captain	Watertown, Mass.	21.50	..	21.50
Compton, Gordon B.	Major	Dallas, Texas	6.50	15	21.50
Elder, John L.	Lt. Col.	Ebensburg, Pa.	8	13	21
Foy, Robert W.	Major	Oswego, N.Y.	17	3	20
Mahurin, Walker M.	Major	Fort Wayne, Ind.	19.75	..	19.75
Thornell, John F.	1st Lt.	East Walpole, Mass.	17.25	2	19.25
Peterson, Richard A.	Major	Alexandria, Minn.	15.50	3.50	19
England, John B.	Captain	Caruthersville, Mo.	17.50	1	18.50
Whisner, William T.	Captain	Shreveport, La.	15.50	3	18.50
Beckham, Walter C.	Major	DeFuniak Springs, Fla.	18	..	18
Johnson, Gerald W.	Lt. Col.	Owenton, Ky.	18	..	18
Welch, Robert E.	Captain	Brown City, Mich.	6	12	18
Bankey, Ernest E., Jr.	Captain	Toledo, Ohio	9.50	8	17.50
Carpenter, George	Major	Oil City, Pa.	13.33	4	17.33
Anderson, Clarence E.	Captain	New Castle, Calif.	16.25	1	17.25
Quirk, Michael J.	Major	Washington, D.C.	12	5	17
Graham, Gordon M.	Lt. Col.	Taft, Calif.	7	9.50	16.50
Lowell, John H.	Lt. Col.	Denver, Colo.	7.50	9	16.50
Norley, Louis H.	Major	Conrad, Mont.	11.33	5	16.33
Anderson, Charles F., Jr.	1st Lt.	Gary, Ind.	10.50	5.50	16
Clark, James A.	Colonel	Westbury, N.Y.	11.50	4.50	16
Juchheim, Aldwin M.	Captain	Grenada, Miss.	10	6	16

Name	Rank	Location	13	3	16
Moran, Glennon T.	1st Lt.	Granite City, Ill.	13	3	16
Megura, Nicholas	Captain	Ansonia, Conn.	11.84	3.75	15.59
Rinerman, Ben	Lt. Col.	Omaha, Nebr.	7	8.50	15.50
Luksic, Carl J.	1st Lt.	Joliet, Ill.	8.50	7	15.50
Haviland, Fred R., Jr.	Captain	Chicago, Ill.	9	6	15
Bostwick, George E.	Major	Wausau, Wis.	9	6	15
Millikan, Willard W.	Captain	Rock Port, Mo.	13	2	15
Schlegel, Albert L.	Captain	Cleveland, Ohio	10	5	15
Bochkay, Donald H.	Captain	N. Hollywood, Calif.	14.84		14.84
Andrew, Stephen W.	Major	Dallas, Texas	8	6.50	14.50
Gleason, George W.	Captain	Montrose, Colo.	12	2.50	14.50
Hively, Howard D.	Major	Athens, Ohio	12	2.50	14.50
Powers, Joe H., Jr.	Captain	Tulsa, Okla.	14.50		14.50
Brown, Quince L.	Major	Bristow, Okla.	12.34	2	14.34
Duffy, James E., Jr.	Captain	Montclair, N. J.	5.20	9	14.20
Ammon, Robert H.	Captain	Stinking Springs, Pa.	5	9	14
Jeffrey, Arthur F.	Lt. Col.	San Francisco, Calif.	14		14
Schreiber, LeRoy A.	Major	Plymouth, Mass.	12	2	14
Jackson, Michael J.	Major	Plainfield, N. J.	8	5.50	13.50
Stewart, James C.	Major	Corona, Calif.	12.50	1	13.50
Strait, Donald J.	Major	Verona, N. J.	13.50		13.50
Bryan, Donald S.	Captain	Paicines, Calif.	13.34		13.34
Blakeslee, Donald J. M.	Colonel	Fairport Harbor, Ohio	11.50	1.50	13
Miklajoyk, Henry J.	Captain	Syracuse, N. Y.	7.50	5.50	13
Williamson, Felix D.	Captain	Cordele, Ga.	13		13
Dregne, Irwin H.	Colonel	Viroquqa, Wisc.	7	5.50	12.50
Halton, William T.	Lt. Col.	Brooklyn, N. Y.	10.50	2	12.50
Hovde, William J.	Major	Crookston, Minn.	10.50	2	12.50
Waggoner, Horace Q.	Captain	Waggoner, Ill.	5	7.50	12.50
Starnes, James R.	Captain	Wilmington, N. C.	6	6.50	12.50
Dade, Lucian A., Jr.	Lt. Col.	Hopkinsville, Ky.	6	6	12

CONFIRMED VICTORIES BY FIGHTER PILOTS OF THE EIGHTH AIR FORCE (continued)

NAME	RANK	HOME	AIRCRAFT DESTROYED IN THE AIR	ON THE GROUND	TOTAL
Kirla, John A.	1st Lt.	Port Chester, N.Y.	11.50	.50	12
Storch, John A.	Lt. Col.	Long Beach, Calif.	10.50	1.50	12
Lang, Joseph L.	Captain	Hyde Park, Mass.	7.84	4	11.84
Conger, Paul A.	Major	Piedmont, Calif.	11.50		11.50
Cutler, Frank A.	Captain	Cleveland, Ohio	8.50	3	11.50
Karger, Dale E.	1st Lt.	McKees Rock, Pa.	7.50	4	11.50
Smith, Leslie C.	Lt. Col.	Caruthers, Calif.	7	4.50	11.50
Yeager, Charles E.	Captain	Hamlin, West Va.	11.50		11.50
Fortier, Norman J.	Major	Nashua, N. H.	5.83	5.50	11.33
Biel, Hipolitus T.	1st Lt.	St. Paul, Minn.	5.33	6	11.33
Doersch, George A.	Captain	Seymour, Wisc.	10.50	.50	11
Edens, Billy C.	1st Lt.	Tyronza, Ark.	8	3	11
Elder, Robert A.	Major	Memphis, Tenn.	9	2	11
Fiebelkorn, Ernest C.	Captain	Los Angeles, Calif.	9	2	11
Gallup, Kenneth W.	Lt. Col.	Clint, Texas	7	4	11
Jackson, Willie O., Jr.	Lt. Col.	Converse, La.	6	5	11
Jones, Cyril W., Jr.	1st Lt.	Athens, Tenn.	5	6	11
McElroy, James N.	Captain	Orlando, Fla.	5	6	11
Merritt, George L., Jr.	Major	Cumming, Ga.	7	4	11
Poindexter, James N.	Captain	Milville, N. J.	8	3	11
Weaver, Charles E.	Captain	Detroit, Mich.	8	3	11
Ceuleers, George F.	Lt. Col.	Los Angeles, Calif.	10.50		10.50
Jenkins, Otto D.	2nd Lt.	Kermit, Texas	8.50	2	10.50
Jones, Frank C.	Captain	Montclair, N. J.	5	5.50	10.50
Morris, James M.	Captain	Detroit, Mich.	7.33	2.83	10.16
Bille, Henry S.	Major	Paradise, Calif.	6	4	10

Name	Rank	Home			
Blickenstaff, Wayne K.	Captain	Chinco, Calif.	10		10
Broadhead, Joseph E.	Major	Rupert, Idaho	10		10
Carlson, Kendall E.	Captain	Red Bluff, Calif.	6	4	10
Crenshaw, Claude J.	1st Lt.	Monroe, La.	7	3	10
Hopkins, Wallace E.	Lt. Col.	Washington, Ga.	6	4	10
Keen, Robert J.	Captain	Jacksonville, Fla.	6	4	10
Lines, Ted E.	1st Lt.	Mesa, Ariz.	10		10
Meroney, Virgil K.	Captain	Pine Bluff, Ark.	8	2	10
Murphy, Alva C.	Captain	Knoxville, Tenn.	10		10
Rankin, Robert J.	1st Lt.	Washington, D. C.	9.50	.50	10
Spencer, Dale F.	1st Lt.	Corry, Pa.	9.50		9.50
Sykes, William J.	1st Lt.	Atlantic City, N. J.	5	5	9.50
Bryan, William E., Jr.	Major	Flint, Mich.	7.50	2	9.50
Cramer, Darrell S.	Major	Ogden, Utah	7.50	2	9.50
Riley, Paul S.	1st Lt.	York, Pa.	6.50	3	9.50
Adams, Fletcher E.	Captain	Ida, La.	9.50		9.50
Stewart, Everett W.	Colonel	Winfield, Kans.	7.83	1.50	9.33
Baccus, Donald A.	Lt. Col.	Los Angeles, Calif.	5	4	9
Beyer, William R.	Captain	Danville, Pa.	5		9
Burdick, Clinton D.	1st Lt.	Brooklyn, N. Y.	5.50	3.50	9
Chandler, Van E.	1st Lt.	Wachachie, Texas	5	4	9
Crombie, William F.	Major	El Paso, Texas	5	4	9
Davis, Clayton E.	Captain	Brookfield, Vt.	5	4	9
Larson, Donald A.	Major	Yakima, Wash.	6	3	9
Morrill, Stanley B.	1st Lt.	Willimantic, Conn.	9		9
Myers, Raymond B.	Lt. Col.	Dundee, Miss.	5	4	9
Roberts, Eugene P.	Lt. Col.	Spokane, Wash.	9		9
Scheible, Wilbur R.	Captain	Akron, Ohio	6	3	9
Sublett, John L.	Captain	Odessa, Texas	7	1	9
Wilkinson, James W.	Captain	Swarthmore, Pa.	8	2	9
Woods, Sidney S.	Lt. Col.	Somerton, Ariz.	8	1	9

CONFIRMED VICTORIES BY FIGHTER PILOTS OF THE EIGHTH AIR FORCE (continued)

NAME	RANK	HOME	AIRCRAFT DESTROYED IN THE AIR	ON THE GROUND	TOTAL
Woody, Robert E.	Captain	Roanoke, Va.	7	2	9
Cesky, Charles J.	Captain	Baltimore, Md.	8.50	. .	8.50
Hayes, Thomas L., Jr.	Lt. Col.	Brooks, Ore.	8.50	. .	8.50
Howe, David W.	1st Lt.	East Hickory, Pa.	6	2.50	8.50
McGrattan, Bernard L.	Captain	Chicago, Ill.	8.50	. .	8.50
Moats, Sanford K.	1st Lt.	Mission, Kans.	8.50	. .	8.50
Vanden Heuval, George R.	1st Lt.	Staten Island, N. Y.	5.50	3	8.50
Hockery, John J.	1st Lt.	Independence, Mo.	7	1.12	8.12
Booth, Robert J.	1st Lt.	Waukesha, Wisc.	8	. .	8
Collins, William F.	Captain	Janesville, Wisc.	5	3	8
Evans, Andrew J.	Lt. Col.	San Antonio, Texas	6	2	8
Fowle, James M.	Captain	San Francisco, Calif.	8	. .	8
Fryer, Earl R.	Captain	Boyertown, Pa.	7	1	8
Gerard, Francis R.	Captain	Lyndhurst, N. J.	8	. .	8
Howes, Bernard H.	Major	Staughton, Pa.	6	2	8
Julian, William H.	Captain	Dallas, Texas	5	3	8
Lewis, William H.	Captain	Pasadena, Calif.	8	. .	8
Maguire, William J.	Captain	Boston, Mass.	7	1	8
Olson, Norman E.	Captain	Fargo, N. Dak.	6	2	8
Pierce, Joseph F.	1st Lt.	Duncan, Okla.	7	1	8
Schlitz, Glenn D., Jr.	Captain	N. Canton, Ohio	8	. .	8
Schimanski, Robert G.	Captain	Spokane, Wash.	6	2	8
Shaw, Robert M.	1st Lt.	Pittsburgh, Pa.	8	. .	8
Trulock, John H.	Captain	Lynchburg, S. C.	7	1	8
Vogt, John W., Jr.	Major	Elizabeth, N. J.	8	. .	8
Whalen, William E.	1st Lt.	Hamilton, N. Y.	6	2	8

192

Amoss, Dudley M.	2nd Lt.	Greenwich, Conn.	5.50	1.50	7
Davis, Glendon V.	Captain	Parma, Idaho	7.50	.	7.50
Garrison, Vermont	1st Lt.	Mt. Victory, Kentucky	7.33	.25	7.58
Lenfest, Charles W.	Major	Boise, Idaho	5	2.50	7.50
Pompetti, Peter E.	1st Lt.	Philadelphia, Pa.	5.50	2	7.50
Smith, Donovan F.	Major	Niles, Mich.	5.50.	2	7.50
Becker, Robert H.	Captain	Hollywood, Calif.	7	.	7
Bonebreak, Robert R.	Captain	Taylor, Texas	5	2	7
Browning, James W.	Captain	Syracuse, Kans.	5	.	7
Comstock, Harold E.	Major	Fresno, Calif.	5	2	7
Carder, John B.	Captain	Red Oak, Iowa	7	.	7
Drew, Urban L.	1st Lt.	Detroit, Mich.	6	1	7
Gerick, Steven	Flt. Off.	Pittsburgh, Pa.	5	2	7
Hanseman, Chris J.	1st Lt.	Mondovi, Wisc.	5	2	7
Jamison, Gilbert L.	Captain	Olympia, Wash.	7	.	7
Klibbe, Frank W.	2nd Lt.	Anderson, Ind.	7	.	7
Lamb, Robert A.	Major	Ridgewood, N. J.	7	.	7
Marshall, Bert W.	Major	Greenville, Texas	5	2	7
McMinn, Evan D.	Flt. Off.	Pittsburgh, Pa.	5	.	7
O'Brien, Gilbert M.	Captain	Charleston, S. C.	7	.	7
Pissanos, Spiros N.	1st Lt.	New York, N. Y.	6	1	7
Roberson, Arval J.	1st Lt.	Los Angeles, Calif.	6	1	7
Thwaites, David F	Captain	Conshohocken, Pa.	5	2	7
Tordoff, Harrison B.	Captain	Mechanicsville, N. Y.	5	.	7
Tyler, Gerald E.	1st Lt.	Houston, Texas	7	.	7
Wicker, Samuel J.	Major	Muskogee, Okla.	7	.	7
Bennett, Joseph H.	Captain	Morton, Texas	6.50	.50	6.50
Care, Raymond C.	Captain	Angola, Ind.	6	.	6.50
Gailer, Frank L.	1st Lt.	Long Island, N. Y.	5.50	1	6.50
Horne, Francis H.	1st Lt.	Rucilla, Fla.	5.50	1	6.50
Malmstrom, Einar A.	Colonel	Spokane, Wash.	5	1.50	6.50

CONFIRMED VICTORIES BY FIGHTER PILOTS OF THE EIGHTH AIR FORCE (continued)

NAME	RANK	HOME	AIRCRAFT DESTROYED IN THE AIR	ON THE GROUND	TOTAL
Moseley, Mark L.	Captain	Atlanta, Ga.	6.50		6.50
Oberhansly, Jack J.	Lt. Col.	Spanish Fork, Utah	5	1.50	6.50
Stanley, Morris A.	1st Lt.	Alvin, Texas	5	1.50	6.50
Tanner, William F.	Captain	Canastota, N. Y.	5.50	1	6.50
Murphy, John B.	Lt. Col.	Darlington, S. C.	6.25		6.25
Bocquin, Victor E.	1st Lt.	Reading, Kans.	5	1	6
Brown, Harley L.	1st Lt.	Wichita, Kans.	6		6
Bryan, Gillespie	Major	Winona, Miss.	6		6
Candelaria, Richard G.	1st Lt.	Los Angeles, Calif.	6		6
Carter, James R.	Captain	Palouse, Wash.	6		6
Cook, Walter V.	Captain	Cincinnati, Ohio	6		6
Cooley, Warren C.	1st Lt.	Cashion, Okla.	6		6
Evans, Roy W.	Major	San Bernardino, Calif.	6		6
Hall, George F.	Captain	West Palm Beach, Fla.	6		6
Hart, Cameron M.	Captain	Westfield, N. J.	6		6
Kemp, William T.	2nd Lt.	East Peoria, Ill.	6		6
Mills, Henry L.	Major	Leonia, N. Y.	6		6
Minchew, Leslie D.	Captain	Miami, Fla.	5.50	.50	6
Pascoe, James J.	1st Lt.	Poughkeepsie, N. Y.	6		6
Pugh, John F.	Captain	Brogan, Ore.	6		6
Sears, Alexander F.	1st Lt.	Abilene, Texas	5	1	6
Starck, Walter E.	Captain	Milwaukee, Wisc.	6		6
Turley, Grant M.	2nd Lt.	Aripine, Ariz.	6		6
Wesson, Warren H.	1st Lt.	Brooklyn, N. Y.	6		6
Koraleski, Walter J., Jr.	Captain	Detroit, Mich.	5.54		5.54
Bennett, James H.	Captain	Morton, Texas	5.50		5.50

CONFIRMED VICTORIES BY FIGHTER PILOTS OF THE EIGHTH AIR FORCE (continued)

NAME	RANK	HOME	AIRCRAFT DESTROYED IN THE AIR	ON THE GROUND	TOTAL
Maloney, John T.	2nd Lt.	Washington, D. C.	5	..	5
Marsh, Lester C.	1st Lt.	Los Angeles, Calif.	5	..	5
Mason, Joe L.	Colonel	Columbus, Ohio	5	..	5
Maxwell, Chester K.	1st Lt.	Alva, Okla.	5	..	5
Price, Jack C.	Major	Grand Junction, Colo.	5	..	5
Priest, Royce W.	1st Lt.	San Antonio, Texas	5	..	5
Reese, William C.	1st Lt.	Bear River, Utah	5	..	5
Schank, Thomas D.	1st Lt.	Greely, Colo.	5	..	5
Schuh, Duerr H.	1st Lt.	Douglas, Wyo.	5	..	5
Stangel, William J.	Captain	Waubun, Minn.	5	..	5
Warren, Jack R.	Captain	San Jacinto, Calif.	5	..	5
Wilson, William F.	Captain	Strong City, Kans.	5	..	5
York, Robert M.	1st Lt.	Red Orchard, Me.	5	..	5

CONFIRMED VICTORIES BY FIGHTER PILOTS OF THE EIGHTH AIR FORCE

In the 8th Air Force air-to-ground kills as well as air-to-air kills were credited. The following is a list of those 8th Air Force flyers who received credit for five or more victories including ground kills.

This tabulation, prepared from reports of an officially constituted Fighter Victory Credits Board, covers the entire period of fighter operations from August 1942 to April 1945.

For reason of simplicity, partial victories are listed in decimals, i.e., 1½ is shown as 1.50; 2⅓ as 2.33, etc.

| | | | AIRCRAFT DESTROYED | | |
| | | | IN THE | ON THE | |
NAME	RANK	HOME	AIR	GROUND	TOTAL
Thury, Joseph L.	Lt. Col.	Clearwater, Fla.	2.50	25.50	28
Tower, Archie A.	Major	Winthrop, N. Y.	1.50	18	19.50
Everson, Kirke B., Jr.	Captain	Fort Wetherill, R. I.	1.50	16	17.50
Montgomery, Gerald E.	Major	Littlefield, Texas	3	14.50	17.50
Stewart, David	1st Lt.	Dallas, Texas		15	15
Boone, Walker L.	Major	Wyandotte, Okla.	2.67	12.13	14.80
Hightshow, Melville W.	1st Lt.	West Memphis, Ark.		14.50	14.50
Kolb, Herbert G.	Captain	Richmond, Va.		14.50	14.50
Anderson, Woodrow W.	Captain	Stockdale, Texas	4.50	9	13.50
Morris, Ray S.	1st Lt.	So. Birmingham, Ala.	3.50	10	13.50
Biggs, Oscar K.	1st Lt.	Wilmington, N. C.	.50	11.50	12
Corey, Harry R.	Captain	Niagara Falls, N. Y.	1	11	12
Harrington, Francis E.	1st Lt.	Randolph, Mass.	4	8	12
Lanoue, Ronald J.	1st Lt.	Lonsdale, R. I.	1	11	12
Murphy, Randel L.	2nd Lt.	Houston, Texas	2	10	12
Duffie, Claire A. P.	Major	York, Pa.	3	8.50	11.50
Gilbert, Olin E.	Lt. Col.	Collinsville, Ill.	2	9.50	11.50
Miller, Gerald J.	2nd Lt.	Lowville, N. Y.		11	11
Patillo, Charles G.	1st Lt.	Atlanta, Ga.	1	10	11

NAME	RANK	HOME	AIRCRAFT DESTROYED IN THE AIR	ON THE GROUND	TOTAL
Gustke, Richard N.	Flt. Off.	Battle Creek, Mich.		10.50	10.50
Jacobson, Gail E.	1st Lt.	Des Moines, Iowa	4.50	6	10.50
Malmsten, Donald M.	Captain	Burwell, Nebr.	3.50	7	10.50
Mansker, Joseph L.	1st Lt.	Long Beach, Calif.	3	7	10
Olson, Thomas C.	1st Lt.	Vancouver, Wash.	1	9.50	10.50
Burch, Harold W.	1st Lt.	Omaha, Nebr.		10	10
Duncan, John F.	Captain	Kokomo, Ind.	4	6	10
Johnson, Martin H., Jr.	1st Lt.	Ft. Worth, Texas	1	9	10
Kirk, John A.	1st Lt.	Baltimore, Md.	4	6	10
McCormick, Arthur B.	Captain	Fort Riley, Kan.	1	9	10
McMullen, Joseph D.	1st Lt.	Victoria, Texas		10	10
Mellen, Joseph E.	Captain	Booneville, Ind.	2	8	10
Peal, Charles M.	Captain	Nashville, Tenn.	2	8	10
Waldron, Karl J.	1st Lt.	Hopkins, Minn.	3	7	10
Clark, William C.	Lt. Col.	Richmond, Va.	1	8	9
Cole, Charles H.	Captain	St. Joseph, Mo.	3	6	9
Cunnick, John W., III	1st Lt.	Waco, Texas	2	7	9
Emory, Frank N.	Captain	Mt. Vernon, Wash.	2	7	9
Gevorkian, Sam D.	Captain	Pasadena, Calif.	2	7	9
Giller, Edward B.	Major	White Hall, Ill.	3	6	9
Greenwood, Ray P.	1st Lt.	Sandy, Utah		9	9
Hatter, Robert B.	1st Lt.	Ottawa, Ill.	3	6	9
Hunter, John C.	Captain	Ann Arbor, Mich.	3	6	9
Johnson, Clarence O.	Captain	Ada, Minn.	3	6	9
Kier, Edward L.	1st Lt.	Wyandot, Colo.	2	7	9
Kyler, Russell L.	1st Lt.	Huntingdon, Pa.	2	7	9
McDuffie, Duncan M.	1st Lt.	Aiken, S. C.	4	5	9

Name	Rank	Location			
Orcutt, Leon M., Jr.	1st Lt.	Huntington, Mass.	:	:	9	9
Taylor, Clyde E.	2nd Lt.	Jermyn, Pa.	:	:	9	9
Visconte, Romildo	Captain	Redwood City, Calif.	4	5	9
Webb, Roy A., Jr.	Lt. Col.	Pampa, Texas	4	5	9
Monroe, Shelton W.	1st Lt.	Waycross, Ga.	4.33	4.50	8.83
Happel, James R.	Captain	Paulsboro, N. J.	4.33	4.68	8.68
France, Victor J.	Captain	Oklahoma City, Okla.	4.33	4.33	8.66
Joiner, Joe H.	Captain	Corpus Christi, Tex.	4.50	4	8.50
Pierce, Donald J.	Captain	Alliance, Ohio		8.50	8.50
Slack, Henry R.	1st Lt.	Baltimore, Md.	1.50	7	8.50
Sowerby, Theodore J.	Captain	Murray, Utah	2	6.50	8.50
Hewitt, Richard A.	Captain	Lewiston, N. Y.	4	4.33	8.33
Alexander, Frederick H.	1st Lt.	Seattle, Wash.	2	6	8
Alfred, Carl R.	Captain	Atwater, Ohio	3	5	8
Ayers, James W.	1st Lt.	Tulsa, Okla.	1	7	8
Conner, Richard E.	Major	Vicksburg, Miss.	4.50	3.50	8
Flag, Walter L.	Captain	Connecticut, R. I.	2	6	8
Hermansen, Cephas	1st Lt.	Alden Station, Pa.		8	8
Jones, Reps. D.	1st Lt.	Miami Springs, Fla.	3	5	8
Josey, Danford E.	2nd Lt.	Scotland Neck, N. C.		8	8
Jurgens, Frederick H.	Flt. Off.	Long Island, N. Y.	:	8	8
MacClarence, Wm. R.	1st Lt.	Plainfield, N. J.		8	8
McGinnis, Keith R.	1st Lt.	Des Moines, Iowa	:2	6	8
Messinger, Richard A.	1st Lt.	Lynn, Mass.		8	8
Mudge, William P., Jr.	1st Lt.	Fall River, Mass.	:2	6	8
Orndorff, Roy W.	Captain	Casey, Ill.	4	4	8
Palson, Richard C. J.	2nd Lt.	Winchester, Mass		8	8
Pickering, Malcolm C.	1st Lt.	Detroit, Mich.	:4	4	8
Zetler, Vincent V.	1st Lt.	Canton, Ohio	1	7	8
Siems, Grover C., Jr.	1st Lt.	Woodside, N. Y.	4.33	3.50	7.83
Szaniawski, Edward W.	Major	Scarsdale, N. Y.	3	4.66	7.66

CONFIRMED VICTORIES BY FIGHTER PILOTS OF THE EIGHTH AIR FORCE (continued)

NAME	RANK	HOME	AIRCRAFT DESTROYED IN THE AIR	ON THE GROUND	TOTAL
Benjamin, Swift T.	1st Lt.	Philadelphia, Pa.	1	6.50	7.50
Falvey, Harold W.	Flt. Off.	Bridgeport, Conn.	1	6.50	7.50
Henley, Donald, Jr.	1st Lt.	Louisville, Ky.	3	4.50	7.50
Myers, Joseph	Major	Canton, Ohio	4.50	3	7.50
Wright, Robert C.	1st Lt.	Holdcroft, Va.	3.50	4	7.50
Smith, William B.	Captain	Bluefield, Va.	2.50	4.75	7.25
Antonides, William O.	2nd Lt.	Carbondale, Colo.		7	7
Boring, Lloyd D.	1st Lt.	Shelby, Ind.	.50	6.50	7
Caywood, Herbert L.	1st Lt.	Los Angeles, Calif.		7	7
Chetneky, Steve J.	1st Lt.	Trenton, N. J.	.1	6	7
Chinn, Claude A.	1st Lt.	Kansas City, Mo.		7	7
Diamond, Brack, Jr.	1st Lt.	Rices Landing, Pa.	.1	6	7
Eckfeldt, Robert T.	1st Lt.	Belmont, Mass.	3	4	7
Elmgren, Charles B.	1st Lt.	Sheridan, Wyo.		7	7
Emerson, Donald R.	Captain	Pembina, N. Dak.	.4	3	7
Farmer, Owen P.	Captain	Aberdeen, S. Dak.	2	5	7
Gresham, Walter V., Jr.	1st Lt.	Portsmouth, Va.	4	3	7
Hartley, Raymond E., Jr.	Captain	Kansas City, Mo.	3	4	7
Hepner, Neal	2nd Lt.	Detroit, Mich.	:	7	7
Hollingsworth, Jas. M.	Captain	Montesano, Wash.	:	7	7
Hopcroft, Ernest J.	1st Lt.	Bay City, Mich.	.4	3	7
Johnston, Ben D., Jr.	1st Lt.	Jacksonville, Fla.	2	5	7
Jones, William A.	1st Lt.	Phoenix, Ariz.	:	7	7
Kulik, Edward R.	Captain	Bessemer, Mich.	:	7	7
Mahany, Howard, Jr.	2nd Lt.	Jersey City, N. J.	.4	3	7
Martin, William D.	1st Lt.	Fort Smith, Ark.		7	7
Murphy, Jerome T.	1st Lt.	Brainerd, Minn.	:	7	7

Name	Rank	Location			
Price, William I.	Major	Pittsburgh, Pa.	3	4	7
Shupe, Joseph E.	1st Lt.	Bristol, Tenn.	2	5	7
Silva, Stanley H.	Captain	Pinole, Calif.	1	6	7
Smith, Robert E., Jr.	Captain	Seney, Mich.		6	7
Weber, Carl W.	1st Lt.	Mt. Airy, Pa.		7	7
Wilson, John H.	Major	New Rochelle, N. Y.	3.50	3.50	7
Witzell, George H.	1st Lt.	Rochester, N. Y.		7	7
Coleman, John B., Jr.	Captain	Milwaukee, Wisc.	4.34	2.50	6.84
Gilbertson, Merle J.	Major	Flora, N. Dak.	2.83	4	6.83
Cles, Leslie P.	Captain	Powell, Wyo.			6.50
Furr, William W.	1st Lt.	Raleigh, N.C.	3.50	3	6.50
Gansberg, Raymond H.	1st Lt.	Downers Grove, Ill.	2.50	4	6.50
Golden, John T.	1st Lt.	Nicalestes, Okla.	1	5.50	6.50
Goodman, Orville E.	1st Lt.	Alhambra, Calif.	4.50	2	6.50
Grasshoff, Hans J.	1st Lt.	Los Angeles, Calif.	2.50	4	6.50
Green, Robert T.	Captain	Long Beach, Calif.	4.50	2	6.50
Henry, Carroll D.	Captain	Taylorsville, Ky.	1.50	5	6.50
Jones, Thomas W.	1st Lt.	Meherrin, Va.	.50	6	6.50
Mayo, Ben I., Jr.	Major	Little Rock, Ark.	4	2.50	6.50
Moseley, Mark L.	Captain	Atlanta, Ga.	6.50		6.50
Olander, Richard B.	Captain	Racine, Wisc.	1.50	5	6.50
Rich, George T.	Captain	Wilmington, N. C.	1.50	5	6.50
Stepelton, Mark H.	Captain	Chicago, Ill.	4.50	2	6.50
Truett, Jesse L.	Colonel	Artesia, N. Mex.		6.50	6.50
Montgomery, Robert P.	2nd Lt.	Bethlehem, Pa.	3.34	3	6.34
Barger, Clarence R.	Major	Allendale, Mo.	.33	6	6.33
Gatterdam, Richard P.	1st Lt.	Columbus, Ohio	3.70	2.50	6.20
Adams, Louis W.	2nd Lt.	Kingsville, Texas	4	2	6
Apple, George A.	Lt. Col.	Waldron, Ind.		6	6
Bailey, William B.	1st Lt.	Rochester, N. Y.	3	3	6
Blizzard, Robert V. E.	1st Lt.	Detroit, Mich.		6	6

CONFIRMED VICTORIES BY FIGHTER PILOTS OF THE EIGHTH AIR FORCE (continued)

NAME	RANK	HOME	AIRCRAFT DESTROYED IN THE AIR	ON THE GROUND	TOTAL
Bosworth, Robert R.	1st Lt.	Oskaloosa, Iowa	1	5	6
Boulet, William P.	1st Lt.	New Orleans, La.	3	3	6
Bowers, Arthur R.	2nd Lt.	Tiskilwa, Ill.		6	6
Butler, George H.	1st Lt.	Los Angeles, Calif.	3	3	6
Chenez, Gordon H.	1st Lt.	Lakewood, Ohio		6	6
Clifton, Frank A.	1st Lt.	Boise City, Okla.		6	6
Colletti, Anthony T.	1st Lt.	Rego Park, N. Y.	1	5	6
DeAnda, Louis	2nd Lt.	Bakersfield, Calif.		6	6
DeVilliers, Donald J.	1st Lt.	Rochester, Minn.		6	6
Dissette, Lawrence J.	Captain	Buffalo, N. Y.	1	5	6
Einhaus, Lowell E.	Captain	Austin, Minn.		6	6
Frisch, Robert J.	1st Lt.	Cincinnati, Ohio		6	6
Frum, Rollin W.	Flt. Off.	Richwood, Ohio		6	6
Gordon, Ray C.	1st Lt.	Ligonier, Kans.	1	5	6
Gould, Clifford C.	1st Lt.	Pleasant Ridge, Mich.	2	4	6
Hansen, John W.	1st Lt.	Altadena, Calif.	4	2	6
Herren, James M., Jr.	Lt. Col.	Ashland, Ala.	2	4	6
Hooker, Verne E.	Captain	Great Falls, Mont.		6	6
Horner, Kenneth R.	1st Lt.	Laughlintown, Pa.	1	5	6
Irion, Robert E.	1st Lt.	Axtel, Kans.		6	6
Lennings, Loton G.	1st Lt.	Medford, Mass.		6	6
Jordan, William J.	1st Lt.	East Orange, N. J.	1.50	4.50	6
Kirby, Henry H., Jr.	Major	Little Rock, Ark.	1	5	6
Kucheman, Henry B., Jr.	Major	Richmond, Va.	4	2	6
Lee, Louis W.	1st Lt.	Houston, Texas	4	2	6
Long, Thurman C.	1st Lt.	Fort Wayne, Ind.	2	4	6
Mayden, James D.	Colonel	Junction City, Kans.	2	4	6

Name	Rank	Location			
McMahan, Bruce D.	2nd Lt.	Houston, Texas	.50	5.50	6
Miller, Edwin H.	2nd Lt.	Carson City, Nev.	4	2	6
Neely, Tom D.	1st Lt.	Edmonds, Wash.	2	4	6
Nelson, Robert F.	Flt. Off.	Long Beach, Calif.	1	5	6
Poage, Charles E., Jr.	1st Lt.	San Jose, Calif.		6	6
Pederson, Douglas P.	1st Lt.	Long Beach, Calif.		6	6
Pogue, Edward F.	1st Lt.	Chattanooga, Tenn.	2.50	3.50	6
Powell, Lawrence J., Jr.	1st Lt.	Southgate, Calif	2	4	6
Prescott, Walter A. S.	1st Lt.	Brooklyn, N. Y.		3	6
Paul, Robert H.	1st Lt.	Baltimore, Md.	3	3	6
Rafferty, Vernon G.	1st Lt.	Menomonie, Wisc.	2	2	6
Reynolds, Garth L.	1st Lt.	Omaha, Neb.	4	4	6
Shafer, Dale E., Jr.	Lt. Col.	Waynesville, Ohio		2	6
Shope, Herbert K.	1st Lt.	Coachella, Calif.	1	6	6
Speer, Frank E.	2nd Lt.	Alburtis, Pa.		5	6
Tracy, Richard M.	Captain	Washington, D. C.	3	6	6
Uttenweiler, Fred. L.	Captain	Bridgeport, Conn.	3	6	6
Wallace, Alton J.	Captain	Southington, Conn.	1	3	6
Whinnem, Donald W.	1st Lt.	Hartford, Conn.	4.50	5	6
Wiggins, Howard E.	1st Lt.	Tunkhammock, Pa.		1.50	6
Williams, Gene L.	2nd Lt.	Indianapolis, Ind.		6	6
Woolery, James C.	1st Lt.	Bloomington, Ind.		6	6
Yannell, Michael P.	Major	Summit, N. J.	2	4	6
Abbott, Earl L.	Captain	Erie, Pa.	4.75	1	5.75
Williamson, Brady C.	Captain	Parkersburg, W. Va.	1.70	4	5.70
Adams, Thomas H.	1st Lt.	Eldorado, Ark.	4.50	1	5.50
Armsby, Sherman	1st Lt.	Baltimore, Md.	4.50	1	5.50
Ashby, Clifford T.	1st Lt.	Nyssa, Ore.	3.50	2	5.50
Bell, Thomas R.	Captain	Shawboro, N. C.		5.50	5.50
Bennette, Charles H.	1st Lt.	Oldtown, Me.	2	3.50	5.50
Berkshire, Robert H.	1st Lt.	Tarzana, Calif.	4.50	1	5.50

NAME	RANK	HOME	AIRCRAFT DESTROYED IN THE AIR	ON THE GROUND	TOTAL
Bledsoe, Marvin	Captain	Los Angeles, Calif.	..	5.50	5.50
Capp, Merle R.	1st Lt.	Arlington, Va.	2	3.50	5.50
Carter, Joseph D.	1st Lt.	Sherman, Texas	.50	5	5.50
Chatterley, Archie W.	Captain	San Diego, Calif.	4.50	1	5.50
Clark, Jack W.	1st Lt.	Jacksonville, Fla.	2.50	3	5.50
Cooper, Randolph W.	2nd Lt.	Jacksonville, Fla.	..	5.50	5.50
Dix, Gerald J.	Colonel	Sullivan, Ind.	4	1.50	5.50
Izor, Edward F.	Captain	Farmersville, Ohio	4.50	1	5.50
Jabara, James	1st Lt.	Wichita, Kan.	..	5.50	5.50
Kurtz, Robert G.	Captain	Denver, Colo.	..	5	5.50
Lamb, Huie H.	1st Lt.	Abilene, Texas	2.50	3	5.50
Loveless, Philip M., Jr.	Captain	Warren, Ohio	.50	5	5.50
McMahan, Darrel E.	1st Lt.	Paso Robles, Calif.	1.50	4	5.50
Miller, Harold O.	1st Lt.	Santa Rosa, Calif.	2	3.50	5.50
Morgan, Frank A.	Captain	Portland, Ore.	.50	5	5.50
Peel, Eugene L.	1st Lt.	Fort Wayne, Ind.	.50	5	5.50
Ramm, Albert J.	Captain	Jamaica, N.Y.	.50	5	5.50
Richards, Vernon R.	1st Lt.	Felts Mills, N.Y.	2	3.50	5.50
Smith, Robert C.	1st Lt.	Davison, Mich.	2.50	3	5.50
Fiedler, Clemens A.	1st Lt.	Fredericksburg, Tex.	4.33	1	5.33
Johnson, Wilton W.	Major	Dassel, Minn.	3.33	2	5.33
Brookins, Richard C.	1st Lt.	Los Angeles, Calif.	4.25	1	5.25
Zellner, Edmond	1st Lt.	Hazelton, Pa.	3.25	2	5.25
Armstrong, Clifford F.	1st Lt.	New Baltimore, N.Y.	3	2	5
Baker, George F.	Captain	Fulton, N.Y.	4.50	.50	5
Ball, Sanborn N., Jr.	1st Lt.	Salem, Mo.	1.50	3.50	5
Barnaby, Harold T.	Captain	Waco, Texas	4	1	5

Name	Rank	Location			
Baugh, Donald P.	Flt. Off.	Blanca, Colo.			5
Baughn, Richard M.	1st Lt.	Omaha, Nebr.	1	4	5
Beason, Eugene M.	1st Lt.	Granite City, Ill.	1	4	5
Becraft, Myron A.	1st Lt.	Horseheads, N.Y.	1	4	5
Birtcel, Frank E.	Captain	Sylvia, Kan.		4	5
Bline, Brooks J.	Captain	Annapolis, Ill.	1	4	5
Blodgett, Burton O.	1st Lt.	Detroit, Mich.		5	5
Bodiford, Hugh	1st Lt.	Montgomery, Ala.	2	3	5
Braley, Byron K.	1st Lt.	Chicago, Ill.	3	2	5
Byers, John R.	1st Lt.	University City, Mo.		5	5
Caldwell, Merle F.	1st Lt.	Greenville, Pa.	2	3	5
Ceglarski, George W.	1st Lt.	Library, Pa.	1	4	5
Chase, Harold W.	Captain	Bradford, Vt.	1	4	5
Denson, Gordon A.	2nd Lt.	Rockville, Conn.		5	5
Dickey, Melvin N.	1st Lt.	Tampa, Fla.		5	5
Doss, Gene C.	1st Lt.	McAlester, Okla.	1	4	5
DuFree, Charles W.	1st Lt.	Stillwater, Okla.		5	5
Fletcher, Jack M.	1st Lt.	Moultrie, Ga.		5	5
Fulton, Joseph O., Jr.	1st Lt.	Paoli, Pa.	1	4	5
Gibbs, Richard G.	1st Lt.	Nantucket, Mass.	4	1	5
Gilbert, William T., Jr.	1st Lt.	Woodbridge, Conn.	4.50	.50	5
Grove, Lindsay W.	1st Lt.	New Hartford, N.Y.	1	4	5
Guyton, William R.	1st Lt.	Pittsburgh, Pa.		5	5
Hagan, Harry N.	Captain	Yorkville, Ohio	2	3	5
Hahn, Robert F.	2nd Lt.	Weissport, Pa.	1	4	5
Hall, Thomas H., Jr.	1st Lt.	Miami, Fla.	3	2	5
Hamilton, Ralph W.	Captain	Des Moines, Iowa	4	1	5
Hansen, Kenneth J.	1st Lt.	Arapahoe, Wyo.		5	5
Helfrecht, Kenneth G.	1st Lt.	Madison, Wisc.		5	5
Hewitt, Sidney H.	Captain	Absecon, N.J.	2.50	2.50	5
Higgins, Donald H.	Major	New Orleans, La.	1.50	3.50	5

CONFIRMED VICTORIES BY FIGHTER PILOTS OF THE EIGHTH AIR FORCE (continued)

NAME	RANK	HOME	AIRCRAFT DESTROYED IN THE AIR	ON THE GROUND	TOTAL
Hobart, Robert D.	Captain	Woodland, Wash.	2	3	5
Hunt, Harlan F.	1st Lt.	Meriden, Conn.	..	5	5
Jackson, Boyd O.	1st Lt.	Harlem, Mont.	..	5	5
John, Leedom K.	1st Lt.	Coatesville, Pa.	..	5	5
Jure, James M.	2nd Lt.	Dallas, Texas	3.50	1.50	5
Kesler, Gilbert L.	1st Lt.	Washington, D. C.	..	5	5
Kissell, William F.	1st Lt.	San Mateo, Calif.	..	5	5
Krauss, William H.	1st Lt.	Lynchburg, Va.	.50	4.50	5
Kuhn, Philip G.	2nd Lt.	Dearborn, Mich.	1	4	5
Ledington, Dorian	Captain	Wichita, Kan.	2	3	5
Lynch, William J.	2nd Lt.	Kennedy, Texas	..	5	5
MacKean, Robert C.	Captain	Yonkers, N. Y.	..	5	5
Marsh, Halbert G.	2nd Lt.	Birmingham, Ala.	..	5	5
Marts, Jay F	1st Lt.	Salem, N. J.	2	3	5
McCasland, Darwin D.	2nd Lt.	Morton, Texas	2	3	5
McClure, James H.	1st Lt.	Springfield, Ky.	..	5	5
McCollom, Francis N.	1st Lt.	Los Angeles, Calif.	..	5	5
McCubbin, James L.	1st Lt.	Kansas City, Mo.	4	1	5
McFadden, Jack D.	1st Lt.	Brookville, Pa.	..	5	5
McGraw, Charles L.	Captain	Warrensburg, Mo.	3	2	5
McHugh, Philip M. N.	1st Lt.	Trenton, N. J.	..	5	5
McKee, Daniel D.	Lt. Col.	Greenville, Miss.	2	3	5
Moroney, Edward J.	1st Lt.	Highland Park, Ill.	3	2	5
Murr, John N.	1st Lt.	Oxnard, Calif.	2	3	5
Nagel, Jerome K.	1st Lt.	Denver, Colo.	1	4	5
Neal, Thomas F., Jr.	Captain	Chatham, Va.	4.50	.50	5
North, Albert B.	2nd Lt.	Massillon, Ohio	3	2	5

Name	Rank	Location			
O'Donnell, William J.	Captain	Philadelphia, Pa.	2	3	5
Parmelee, Charles E.	1st Lt.	Lakewood, Ohio	3	2	5
Patterson, Roy L.	1st Lt.	Roanoke, Va.	1	4	5
Perry, Emil F.	1st Lt.	Lebanon, N. H.	2	3	5
Peterburs, Joseph A.	1st Lt.	West Allis, Wisc.	:	5	5
Peters, Robert O.	1st Lt.	Bexley, Ohio	3	2	5
Phaneuf, Richard E.	1st Lt.	Flint, Mich.	:	5	5
Phillips, Raymond G.	1st Lt.	Newton, Iowa	2	3	5
Pierini, Donald J.	1st Lt.	Trenton, N. J.	1	4	5
Pryer, Thomas P., Jr.	1st Lt.	Joliet, Ill.	:	5	5
Queen, Thomas W.	Lt. Col.	San Diego, Calif.	:	5	5
Randolph, John P.	Lt. Col.	Schertz, Texas	1	4	5
Rau, Harold J.	1st Lt.	Hempstead, N. Y.	1	4	5
Reinhardt, Edwin D.	Flt. Off.	Brocksville, Ohio	:	5	5
Rice, John J.	1st Lt.	Hartford, Conn.	:	5	5
Rigsby, Alden P.	1st Lt.	Logan, Utah	4	1	5
Shane, Presson S.	Captain	Junction City, Kan.	:	5	5
Sharbo, Walter J.	2nd Lt.	Williston, N. Dak.	3	2	5
Smith, Kenneth B.	Captain	Watsontown, Pa.	3	2	5
Smeltz, Kenneth C.	1st Lt.	Lancaster, Pa.	1	4	5
Smigel, Alfred J.	1st Lt.	Garwood, N. J.	:	5	5
Smith, Vernon A.	2nd Lt.	Phillipsburg, N. J.	:	5	5
Stewart, Henry M.	Captain	So. Braintree, Mass.	4	1	5
Sweat, Dale S.	1st Lt.	Lafayette, Ill.	:	5	5
Sykes, Henry S.	1st Lt.	Burlington, Iowa	:	5	5
Taylor, Willis B.	Captain	Sarasota, Fla.	3	2	5
Timony, Eugene J.	1st Lt.	Lakewood, Ohio	1	4	5
Wilkerson, William F.	Captain	Cincinnati, Ohio	1	4	5
Wolski, Victor	1st Lt.	Glendale, Calif.	3	2	5

12

KOREAN CONFLICT

DURING THE FIVE short years following the last fading echoes of the atomic blasts that had jarred the world to peace new and sinister forces were taking shape. While jubilant America welcomed home her weary warriors and dismantled her war machines a new form of tyranny was building new armies and new weapons for yet another cycle of blood and turmoil in the bellicose twentieth century.

During these short peaceful years the leaders of the military air arm, while de-activating war units, releasing men and dismantling planes with their right hands, were with their left hands building, experimenting and developing new vehicles in preparation for a novel air war yet to come —the jet war. Under the skillful guidance of General Hoyt S. Vandenberg the Air Force was forming a strong nucleus of modern air machines while at the same time slashing its size and relaxing its pace in the languid atmosphere of the newly found peace.

Then on a Sunday, 25 June 1950, armed aggression reared its ugly head and the Communist troops of North Korea poured over the 38th Parallel to once again herald America to arms.

The next afternoon the airmen of the 5th Air Force, headquartered in Japan, were over Seoul in every available aircraft evacuating Americans from Korea via Kimpo Airfield and carrying dependents and other noncombatants out of the beleaguered Korean capital. The enemy pressed hard and fast. American flyers who only that morning had been combat ready in nothing more perilous than swivel chairs were winging over the wrinkled blue-green mountains of Korea.

Above the droning transports—C-54's, C-47's, C-46's—

prop-driven F-51 Mustangs and F-82 Twin Mustang night fighters formed a protective fighter cover. Lieutenant Colonel James W. Little and First Lieutenant William G. Hudson were on such a cover mission on 27 June 1950 when two North Korean YAK fighters slipped out of a cloud and made a long, sweeping fighter pass. The Americans replied with blazing guns, flaming the YAKs and scoring America's first aircraft kills of the Korean conflict. After careful study, the Air Force has given Lieutenant Hudson the nod for the first official kill at 1150 hours that day.

On the same day, under orders from Washington, the 5th Air Force went into the war business in earnest and in the subsequent three years flew over three-fourths of the combat missions flown during the Korean conflict. They were aided in their air missions by shore-based Marines attached to the 5th Air Force; carrier-based Marine and Navy aircraft; attached Royal Australian Meteorjets; Republic of Korea and South African fighter bombers, plus Greek and Thailand transport units.

While the savage ground war raged up and down the ill-fated peninsula the aircraft of the Far East Air Forces waged an almost ceaseless air war against the enemy, destroying his aircraft, attacking his supply and troop centers, shattering his critical transportation facilities and routes, burning his vehicles, locomotives and rail cars, destroying his other modes of supply movement and relentlessly pounding his front-line dug-in positions.

Into this fresh violence went America's flyers bolstered greatly by an abundance of battle-tested World War II aviators. With the veteran group went veteran aircraft: the time-proven F-51 Mustang which had become a most formidable fighter-bomber; the B-26 light bomber and the grand old lady, the B-29 Superfortress. Added to these effective propeller-driven warships was the new jet F-80 Shooting Star, which was later supplanted in Korea by the F-84 Thunderjet, a speedy fighter-bomber, and the "Mig Killer," F-86 Sabrejet, plus the many Navy, Marine and Royal Australian jets and prop-driven machines.

In the air-to-air war, with which this book is primarily concerned, it was, at the final bell, the Sabrejet that had made the biggest noise in the contrail skies. Early in the war it was the North Korean YAKs that tangled with the

American Mustangs and Shooting Stars, but as the Chinese Communists moved into the battle during that historic winter along the Yalu, the swept-wing MIG entered the air picture, as did the American equal weapon, the F-86. Although a few of the speedy MIGs were shot from the sky by the slower American F-80s, it was in the ensuing encounters with the F-86 that the MIGs met their nemesis.

Of the 839 MIG-15s shot down in air-to-air combat during the Korean conflict eight hundred of them were brought down by American Sabrejets while the Communists shot down only fifty-eight F-86s. (Sixteen of the remaining thirty-nine kills were credited to B-29 gunners of the FEAF Bomber Command, while the remaining twenty-three went to the other fighters and fighter-bombers of the Far East Air Forces.) And of this impressvie tally of aircraft destroyed the forty aces of the Korean Conflict accounted for over 41 per cent of the MIGs destroyed.

As a rule the jet aces were not the youthful, stripling pilots, but the old-timers, the retreads of World War II. The vaunted 21-year-old colonels were no longer the vogue and the now ancient concepts of young, reckless aviators had to be revised. The new machines—machines of precision and complication—were no longer a fighter weapon for the novice. Consequently it was the experienced hands who were able to put the sleek, swept-wing warrior through the tricky paces to give America air superiority and a better than 14 to 1 average against the equally speedy and well-built Communist MIG. (There were, of course, exceptions to the rule, such as Second Lieutenant James F. Low, who downed nine MIGs for acedom.)

The unique problems of the new jet war are best described by the classic description of a routine fighter mission over Korea by J. H. Kindelberger, chairman of North American Aviation (the manufacturers of the Sabrejet):

At an altitude of about eight miles above the earth, the pilot and his airplane are in a very thin and very cold atmosphere. The temperature is about sixty below zero and the pressure is about two pounds per square inch, as compared with almost fifteen pounds per square inch at sea level. . . . Breathing free in this atmosphere, the pilot could not remain conscious more than about thirty seconds and could not survive more than a few minutes.

He must be enclosed in a heated and pressurized compartment, and he must have pure oxygen pushed into his lungs under pressure. The thin air also handicaps the engine, to the extent that its effective thrust is barely enough to win the fight against the weight and drag of the airplane. Therefore the pilot must make every maneuver with delicate precision.

Now let's take a look at the pilot. He finds himself packed into the sleek fuselage of a jet fighter with about 100 controls to operate and twenty-four instruments to observe plus a dozen indicators of warning lights to keep an eye on. In the fuselage with him is electrical and electronic gear equal in complexity to the combined circuits of a city power system, a radio broadcasting station, a television broadcasting station, and the fire control system of a battleship. Under him and behind him run hydraulic lines, fuel lines, cooling and heating ducts, and oxygen lines. A few feet away is a giant blowtorch delivering as much effective power as three large Diesel locomotives. And there he sits, loaded down with protective clothing, parachute, G-suit, crash helmet, oxygen mask, and an acute bellyache caused by the expansion of his body gas at high altitude.

Now the reason he is eight miles above the Korean landscape is to find another airplane and if possible shoot it down. Here his senses prove pretty inadequate, for the reasons that both his airplane and the enemy airplane are moving fast, and that his spatial perception is impaired by such things as lack of reference points, most of the clouds being below and even the horizon being just an indistinct haze far in the distance. Also, the sky above is very dark blue in which it is almost impossible to see anything unless he catches a glint of sun on metal. Not only are his senses inadequate to see the other airplane and judge its relative position and speed, but his reaction time is often too slow for proper control of his airplane and his guns.

In all this there is a pretty strong psychological factor, also. Remember that the pilot is in a very intricate machine moving fast through an environment in which he cannot exist without the aid of his equipment. In the back of his mind is the emergency in which he may have to leave the aircraft by actuating the controls which blow off the canopy and fire his ejection seat away from the airplane, after which comes the prospect of a perilous and very cold descent to enemy territory....

Thus, with the added complexities of high-speed and high-altitude flying great new problems had been added to the already arduous art of aerial combat. But if the air war was strange in the matter of aircraft, it was even stranger in the unique set of unwritten rules by which the American jet pilots fought. The location of the big air battles was "MIG Alley," a small section in Northwestern Korea near the Yalu River (which divides North Korea from Chinese Manchuria). To this battlefield the American airmen had to fly over 250 miles while the Chinese were conveniently located nearby. The Americans had to return the same 250 miles and thus had limited fuel for patrolling, seeking the enemy and dogfighting. At the same time the battlefield was over North Korean territory bordered on one side by a one-way boundary and a sanctuary from which the enemy could dart at will and with extreme freedom of action. Nevertheless, in spite of these one-sided rules the American aviators took an enormous toll of Communist aircraft and chased the MIGs from the sky.

A clearer picture of this singularly unique air war can be seen through the personal account of a typical engagement as related by an experienced jet ace, Colonel Harrison R. Thyng. Colonel Thyng, a 34-year-old World War II ace, with eight German planes and one Jap to his credit, served as a combat commander of the 4th Fighter-Interceptor Wing in Korea and flamed five MIGs in the process. Wrote Colonel Thyng:

Like olden knights the F-86 pilots ride up over North Korea to the Yalu River, the sun glinting off silver aircraft, contrails streaming behind, as they challenge the numerically superior enemy to come on up and fight. With eyes scanning the horizon to prevent any surprise, they watch avidly while MIG pilots leisurely mount into their cockpits, taxi out onto their runways for a formation take-off.

"Thirty-six lining up at Antung," Black Leader calls.

"Hell, only twenty-four taking off over here at Tatungkou," complains Blue Leader.

212

"Well, it will be at least three for everybody. I count fifty at Takushan," calls White Leader.

"I see dust at Fen Cheng, so they are gathering up there," yells Yellow Leader.

Once again the Commie leaders have taken up our challenge, and now we may expect the usual numerical odds as the MIGs gain altitude and form up preparatory to crossing the Yalu.

Breaking up into small flights, we stagger our altitude. We have checked our guns and sights by firing a few warm-up rounds as we crossed the bomb line. Oxygen masks are checked and pulled as tight as possible over our faces. We know we may exceed eight "G's" in the coming fight, and that is painful with a loose mask. We are cruising at a very high Mach. Every eye is strained to catch the first movement of an enemy attempt to cross the Yalu from their Manchurian sanctuary into that graveyard of several hundred MIGs known as "MIG Alley." Several minutes pass. We know the MIG pilots will become bolder as our fuel time limit over the Alley grows shorter.

Now we see flashes in the distance as the sun reflects off the beautiful MIG aircraft. The radio crackles, "Many, many coming across at Suiho above forty-five thousand feet." Our flights starts converging toward that area, low flights climbing, yet keeping a very high Mach. Contrails are now showing over the Antung area, so another enemy section is preparing to cross at Sinuiju, a favorite spot.

We know the enemy sections are now being vectored by GCI, and the advantage is theirs. Traveling at terrifically high speed and altitude, attackers can readily achieve surprise. The area bound by the horizon at this altitude is so vast that it is practically impossible to keep it fully covered with the human eye.

Our flights are well spread out, ships line abreast, and each pilot keeps his head swiveling 360 degrees. Suddenly MIGs appear directly in front of us at our level. At rates of closure of possibly 1200 miles an hour we pass through each other's formations.

Accurate radar range firing is difficult under these conditions, but you fire a burst at the nearest enemy anyway. Immediately the MIGs zoom for altitude, and you break at maximum "G" around toward them. Unless the MIG wants to fight and also turned as he climbed, he will be lost from sight in the distance before the turn is completed. But if he shows an inclination to scrap, you immediately trade head-on passes again. You "sucker" the MIG into a position where the outstanding advantage of your aircraft will give you the chance to outmaneuver him.

For you combat has become an individual dogfight. Flight integrity has been lost, but your wingman is still with you, widely separated but close enough for you to know that you are covered. Suddenly you go into a steep turn. Your Mach drops off. The MIG turns with you, and you let him gradually creep up and outturn you. At the critical moment you reverse your turn. The hydraulic controls work beautifully. The MIG cannot turn as readily as you and is slung out to the side. When you pop your speed brakes, the MIG flashes by you. Quickly closing the brakes, you slide onto his tail and hammer him with your "50's." Pieces fly off the MIG, but he won't burn or explode at that high altitude. He twists and attempts to dive away, but you will not be denied. Your 50's have hit him in the engine and slowed him up enough so that he cannot get away from you. His canopy suddenly blows and the pilot catapults out, barely missing your airplane. Now your wingman is whooping it up over the radio, and you flash for home very low on fuel. At this point your engine is running very rough. Parts of the ripped MIG have been sucked into your engine scoop, and the possibility of its flaming out is very likely. Desperately climbing for altitude you finally reach forty thousand feet. With home base now but eighty miles away, you can lean back and sigh with relief for you know you can glide your ship back and land, gear down, even if your engine quits right now. You hear over the radio, "Flights re-forming and returning—the last MIGs chased back across the Yalu." Everyone is checking in, and a few scores are being discussed. The good news of no losses, the tension which gripped you before the battle, the wild fight, and the "G" forces are now being felt. A tired yet elated feeling is overcoming you, although the day's work is not finished. Your engine finally flames out, but you have maintained forty thousand feet and are now but twenty miles from home. The usual radio calls are given, and the pattern set up for a dead-stick landing. The tower calmly tells you that you are number three deadstick over the field, but everything is ready for your entry. Planes in front of you continue to land in routine and uninterrupted precision, as everyone is low on fuel. Fortunately this time there are no battle damages to be crash landed. Your altitude is decreasing, and gear is lowered. Hydraulic controls are still working beautifully on the pressure maintained by your windmilling engine. You pick your place in the pattern, land, coast to a stop, and within seconds are tugged up the taxi strip to your revetment for a quick engine change.

This mission is the type most enjoyed by the fighter pilot. It is a regular fighter sweep, with no worries about escort or providing cover for fighter-bombers. The mission had been well planned and well executed. Best of all, the MIGs had come forth for battle. Our separate flights had probably again confused the enemy radarscope readers, and, to an extent, nullified that tremendous initial advantage which radar plotting and vectoring gives a fighter on first sighting the enemy. We had put the maximum number of aircraft into the target area at the most opportune time, and we had sufficient fuel to fool the enemy. Our patrolling flights at strategic locations had intercepted split-off MIGs returning toward their sanctuary in at least two instances. One downed MIG had crashed in the middle of Sinuiju, and another, after being shot up, had outrun our boys to the Yalu, where they had to break off pursuit. But they had the satisfaction of seeing the smoking MIG blow up in his own traffic pattern. Both instances undoubtedly did not aid the morale of the Reds.

America's first jet ace, and by the end of the war the second highest scoring fighter pilot in Korea with fifteen air-to-air kills, Captain James Jabara, stepped over the threshold of jet acedom with his fifth victory on 20 May 1951. Captain Jabara tells of that mission in the June 1951 issue of *Air Force:*

About five o'clock in the afternoon of May 20, fourteen of our F-86 Sabres from the 4th Fighter Interceptor Group were jumped by fifty Commie jets over Sinuiju, near the Yalu River.

I was in the second wave of the fourteen. I tacked on to three MIGs at 35,000 feet, picked out the last one and bored straight in. My first two bursts ripped up his fuselage and left wing. At about 10,000 feet the pilot bailed out. It was a good thing he did because the MIG disintegrated.

Then I climbed back to 20,000 feet to get back into the battle. I bounced six more MIGs. I closed in and got off two bursts into one of them, scoring heavily both times. He began to smoke.

Then when my second burst caught him square in the middle he burst into flames and fell into an uncontrolled spin. All I could see was a whirl of fire. I had to break off then because there was another MIG on my tail.

That was my bag for the day and it made me feel pretty good to know that I was the first jet ace in the history of aerial warfare.

On 30 November 1951 F-86s of the 4th Fighter Interceptor Wing caught thirty Russian-built bombers and forty-six other Communist aircraft, destroying eleven and damaging four. Major Winton W. "Bones" Marshall, a jet ace and one of the squadron commanders involved in the battle, described the action:

We entered the area right on schedule and sighted two large formations of MIG-15 jets coming across the Yalu River high above us. They were apparently out on their own fighter sweep, but they didn't come down on us. We held formation and turned south in hopes of cutting into them.

Just then Colonel Thyng called out bogies coming across the river dead ahead of us and about 10,000 feet below. He said he was going down to look and instructed me to cover them as the air above was filled with MIGs and there were more coming every minute.

The bogies turned out to be a large formation of TU-2 bombers and their fighter escort. There were several "boxes" of bombers in groups of three. They were surrounded by an escort of LA-9 propeller-driven fighters. Another formation of MIGs was flying top cover. The colonel called for a head-on pass by two squadrons of the Sabres.

I came over the bombers just as the Sabres struck. It was better than a seat on the 50-yard line at a football game. As our fighters poured it on, the whole sky became alive with smoke and flame. It was really a sight —our boys scoring hits all over the bombers, and their fighters could do nothing because of the Sabres' superior speed.

Right after the Sabres made their first pass on the bombers Colonel Preston called me and said, "Bones, come on down and get 'em." We were in a perfect spot for an overhead pass. The entire squadron went over on its back and came in on the bombers from six o'clock high, right on the Mach.

As we dove, the remaining bombers turned their guns on us and their fighters nosed toward us in an attempt to turn us from the battle. The whole area was alive with bullets. The bombers that hadn't been hit still held a tight formation and straight course. They were like sitting ducks.

I lined up the bomber on the right side of the last "box." My first burst set him afire.

As I continued to fire, he fell out of formation and the crew began bailing out. Then two LA-9s came into my sights and I gave the leader a short burst from my .50-calibers. He seemed to come apart at the seams and dropped like a stone to the ocean.

Our first pass on the TU-2s was over in a matter of seconds. I glanced to see if my squadron was still with me and then turned into them again for another pass. It gave me a thrill, for this was the first bomber formation I've ever tangled with.

By this time the area was so crowded with fighters I had to weave in and out between them to get in position for another pass. Finally, I squared away on the lead "box" of bombers, and fired my remaining ammunition into one of them. He started smoking as my bursts cut into his wings and fuselage . . . I pulled away.

While these air battles were raging over the little peninsula a thirty-year-old jet pilot was on the North American continent fighting a personal battle to get to Korea and into the shooting war. He was Captain Joseph McConnell Jr., who seemed to have been directing his entire life toward this one place for his big chance. A veteran of World War II, McConnell had served in the European theater as a navigator (after having been turned down for pilot training) on a B-24, and had returned with a very satisfactory war record. After the war, when the opportunity presented itself, he reapplied for pilot training, was accepted and finally won his pilot's wings in February 1948 as part of the first group of specially trained F-80 jet pilots.

When the war broke out in Korea McConnell was in Alaska and he immediately began applying for a transfer into combat. The Air Force deemed his assignment in Alaska to be equally as important as one in Korea and he remained in the cold north country. At the end of his Alaskan tour he was transferred to George, AFB, California, where he continued his efforts to get into battle. He was finally rewarded in the fall of 1952 when he was assigned to the 51st Fighter Interceptor Wing in Korea.

Once in combat Captain McConnell began to build up his experience and skill until his efforts paid off on 14 January 1953 when he flamed his first Red MIG. From then on he laced enemy planes with hot lead in his meteoric rise to the top of the jet ace list. Slightly over a month after his first kill he shot down his 5th MIG for acedom.

After bagging his eighth kill, his Sabrejet was struck by anti-aircraft fire and McConnell bailed out over enemy waters. The close teamwork of his fellow pilots and the brave men of air-sea rescue had him safely aboard the helicopter and headed home only two minutes after McConnell had touched down in the freezing sea.

The following day McConnell was back in the battle, popping his ninth Red jet from the sky. By the end of April McConnell had become a double jet ace and was getting better and better at his deadly profession.

On the morning of 18 May 1953 in a furious battle in MIG Alley Joe McConnell brought down two of the swept-wing MIGs, to set a new Air Force record and to win triple jet acedom. That afternoon he was again in the warring skies and another MIG-15—McConnell's sixteenth kill—was knocked down. *Newsweek* Magazine recorded the incident: "The short, slim, 31-year-old Captain seemed 'a little wild' to fellow Sabre pilots in Korea until he was forced to bail out last month over the Yellow Sea. But if the dunking 'settled' him, it didn't cool off his blazing record: On May 18 Joe McConnell of Apple Valley, Calif., shot down three Red MIG's to stretch his string to sixteen and become the first 'triple jet ace' in history."

McConnell himself said of his acedom: "It's the team-work out here that counts, the lone wolf stuff is out. Your life always depends on your wingman and his life on you. I may get credit for a MIG. But it's the team that does it . . . not myself alone."

Then on 25 August 1954, back in the United States, Joe McConnell was applying his exceptional flying ability to the development and improvement of a newly modified F-86 in a test flight over the Mojave Desert. The plane failed, Joe McConnell tried to save the ship and perished in the hot, dusty desert.

Although the speedy jet air war was being fought and won at fantastic speeds high above the Communist terrain, another, smaller air war was taking place over the United Nations' territory in South Korea. Routinely the Reds would send out slow, bi-winged, single-engined planes to drop small bombs on American installations in nightly nuisance raids. These attacks were not for strategical or tactical purposes, but rather to keep the troops awake at night running to shelters and in general lower the efficiency and morale of the American and other United Nations forces.

Nicknamed "Bed Check Charlies," these planes were too slow for the jets to shoot down—they being able to turn inside of and away from any jet. Lieutenant Guy Pierre Bordelon went to war with these Bed Check Charlies and in his radar-equipped, propeller-driven Corsair (F4U-5N) he polished off two YAK-18s on 29 June 1953 near Seoul. On 1 July he bagged two more YAKs south of Suwon. On 16 July he blasted one more Bed Check Charlie to become the first and only Navy ace in Korea and to finally dampen the spirits of all but the most reckless of the Bed Check Charlies.

On 22 July 1953 Second Lieutenant Sam P. Young was

returning from a patrol along the south bank of the Yalu River with two other Sabrejets. As they swept through MIG Alley they had encountered heavy ground fire but no MIGs —MIGs having become scarce in the closing days of the war, remaining safely behind the protective barrier of the Yalu. Pushing their patrol to the last possible minute the three American fighters were low on fuel when they turned southward for their base. This was Lieutenant Young's 34th combat mission with the 51st Fighter Interceptor Wing, but the young officer had not engaged a single enemy aircraft. Then it happened:

"Coming out of the turn I spotted a bunch of four MIGs cutting along below us. Three veered off, but I lined up behind one and poured in about 1600 rounds. Finally he flopped over, began smoking and went down."

It was over that quickly and Lieutenant Young had made his first kill and had shot down the last MIG destroyed in the Korean conflict.

Four days later the truce was signed and the peace, though uneasy, hushed the booming cannons and silenced the chattering guns of the war birds.

ACES OF THE KOREAN CONFLICT

25 June 1950—27 July 1953

NAME	DATE OF BIRTH	HOMETOWN	WW II AIR TO AIR	KOREA AIR TO AIR
Capt. Joseph McConnell, Jr., USAF[1]	30 Jan. 22	Dover, New Hampshire		16
Lt. Col. James Jabara, USAF	10 Oct. 23	Wichita, Kansas	3.5 Ger.	15
Capt. Manuel J. Fernandez, USAF	19 Apr. 25	Miami, Florida		14.5
Lt. Col. George A. Davis, Jr., USAF[2]	1 Dec. 20	Lubbock, Texas	7 Jap.	14
Col. Royal N. Baker, USAF	27 Nov. 18	McKinney, Texas	3.5 Ger.	13
Maj. Frederick C. Blesse, USAF	22 Aug. 21	Phoenix, Arizona		10
Capt. Harold E. Fischer, USAF	8 May 25	Swea City, Iowa		10
Col. James K. Johnson, USAF	30 May 16	Phoenix, Arizona	1 Ger.	10
Lt. Col. Vermont Garrison, USAF	20 Oct. 15	Mt. Victory, Kentucky	11 Ger.	10
Maj. Lonnie R. Moore, USAF[3]	13 July 20	Ft. Walton, Florida		10
Capt. Ralph S. Parr, Jr., USAF	1 July 24	Washington, D. C.		10
1st Lt. James F. Low, USAF	10 Sept. 25	Sausalito, California		9
1st Lt. Cecil G. Foster, USAF	30 Aug. 25	San Antonio, Texas		9
Lt. Col. James P. Hagerstrom, USAF	14 Jan. 21	Waterloo, Iowa	6 Jap.	8.5
Maj. Robinson Risner, USAF	16 Jan. 25	Oklahoma City, Oklahoma		8
Col. George I. Ruddell, USAF	21 Jan. 19	Riverside, California		8
Capt. Clifford D. Jolley, USAF	4 May 21	Salt Lake City, Utah		7
Capt. Leonard W. Lilley, USAF	24 Oct. 23	Manchester, New Hampshire		7
1st Lt. Henry Buttelmann, USAF	26 June 29	Bayside, Long Island, N. Y.		7
Lt. Col. Winton W. Marshall, USAF	6 July 19	Beverly Hills, California		6.5
Col. Francis S. Gabreski, USAF	28 Jan. 19	Oil City, Pennsylvania	31 Ger.	6.5
Maj. Donald E. Adams, USAF[4]	23 Feb. 21	Mount Clemens, Michigan	4 Ger.	6.5
Col. George L. Jones, USAF	12 May 18	Vero Beach, Florida		6.5
Capt. Robert J. Love, USAF	28 Dec. 17	San Bernardino, California		6
Lt. Col. John F. Bolt, USMC	19 May 21	Sanford, Florida	6 Jap.	6
1st Lt. James H. Kasler, USAF	2 May 26	Indianapolis, Indiana		6

ACES OF THE KOREAN CONFLICT (continued)

NAME	DATE OF BIRTH	HOMETOWN	WW II AIR TO AIR	KOREA AIR TO AIR
Maj. William T. Whisner, USAF	17 Oct. 23	Shreveport, Louisiana	15.5 Ger.	5.5
Capt. Richard S. Becker, USAF	4 Dec. 26	Fleetwood, Pennsylvania	..	5
Capt. Ralph D. Gibson, USAF	7 Nov. 24	Mount Carmel, Illinois	..	5
Lt. Col. Richard D. Creighton, USAF	25 Jan. 24	Baton Rouge, Louisiana	2 Ger.	5
Capt. Robert H. Moore, USAF	13 May 24	Houston, Texas	..	5
Capt. Iven C. Kincheloe, Jr., USAF[5]	2 July 28	Cassapolis, Michigan	..	5
Maj. William H. Wescott, USAF	1 Sept. 22	New Lisbon, Wisconsin	..	5
Capt. Robert T. Latshaw, Jr., USAF[6]	20 Aug. 25	Amarillo, Texas	8 Ger.	5
Col. Harrison R. Thyng, USAF	12 Apr. 18	Barnstead, New Hampshire	1 Jap.	5
Capt. Dolphin D. Overton, III, USAF	8 Apr. 26	Andrews, South Carolina	..	5
Col. Robert P. Baldwin, USAF	19 Oct. 17	Los Angeles, California	..	5
Capt. Clyde A. Curtin, USAF	25 Oct. 20	Portland, Oregon	1 Ger.	5
Maj. Stephen L. Bettinger, USAF	28 Apr. 24	West Caldwell, New Jersey	..	5
Lt. Guy P. Bordelon, Jr., USN[7]	....	Ruston, Louisiana	..	5

1 McConnell was killed in an F-86 test flight at Edwards AFB, Calif. in 1954.

2 KIA, Davis was awarded the Congressional Medal of Honor posthumously.

3 Killed in F-101 accident at Eglin AFB, Fla., January 10, 1956.

4 Adams was killed in an Air Show at Detroit in 1952.

5 Kincheloe flew Bell X-2 rocket research plane to new world record of 126,000 ft. (unconfirmed) and exceeded 1500 mph on 7 September 1956 flight for which he was awarded the 1956 Mackay Trophy.

6 Killed in F-86 accident at Boca Del Rio Air Base, Venezuela, 20 April 1956.

7 Lt. Bordelon flew a propeller driven aircraft.

A list of the more notable military pilots, who, although not aces in the Korean conflict, served the United Nations forces by shooting down Russian-built MIGs.

NAME	GRADE	SSN	E/A DEST
Emmert, Benjamin J.	Lt. Col.	9578A	1
Best, Jack R.	Lt. Col.	7631A	1
Bertram, William E.	Lt. Col.	4310A	1
Gibson, Harold	Lt. Col.	4814A	1
Arnell, Zane S.	Major	22706A	3
Dickinson, R. T. F.	Flt. Off. (RAF)	58764	1
Eagleston, Glenn T.	Lt. Col.	9438A	2
Glover, Earnest A.	Flt. Off. (RCAF)	17484	3
Gogerly, Bruce	Flt. Off. (RAAF)	0–11402	1
Granville-White, John H.	Flt. Lt. (RAF)	3039274	1
Harvey, Julian A.	Lt. Col.	8470A	½
Heller, Edwin L.	Major	9900A	3½
Hulse, Graham S.	Flt. Lt. (RAF)	52935	2
Kelly, Albert S.	Lt. Col.	5082A	2½
Keyes, Ralph E.	Lt. Col.	AO–388609	1
La France, Claude A.	1st Lt. (RCAF)	30003	1
Levesque, J. A. O.	Flt. Lt. (RCAF)	19794	1
Lindsay, James D.	Sq. Ldr. (RCAF)	20361	1
Lovell, John H. J.	Flt. Lt. (RAF)	607020	1
Mahurin, Walker M.	Col.	8658A	3½
Markham, Theon E.	Lt. Col.	9180A	1½
Martin, Maurice L.	Col.	1015A	1
Meyer, John C.	Col.	4496A	2
McElroy, Carrol B.	Lt. Col.	10517A	2
McHale, Robert V.	Lt. Col.	7259A	1
McKay, John	Sq. Ldr. (RCAF)	19727	1
Mitchell, John W.	Col.	3741A	4
Ola, George J.	Lt. Col.	3630A	1
Payne, J. S.	Lt. Col. (Marine)	0–11234	1
Preston, B. S., Jr.	Col.	4283A	4
Price, Harold L.	Lt. Col.	AO–437222	4
Pugh, Paul E.	Lt. Comdr. (USN)	106211	1
Raebel, James B.	Lt. Col.	9017A	3
Samways, William T.	Lt. Col.	AO–397432	4
Schinz, Albert W.	Col.	4646A	½
Van Etten, Chester L.	Lt. Col.	AO–663442	1
Vetort, Francis J.	Lt. Col.	4195A	1

13

IN CONCLUSION

IF A SINGLE word had to be selected as the one word most closely allied with the *ace,* that word would be *attack.* For in every war, in every theater, and in every service the one common denominator among all aces has been their attitude of relentless attack. As a rule the defensive fighter pilot won few victories, while the aviator who pressed the battle, who grabbed the offensive regardless of odds, was the man who scored the aerial triumphs. It was the difference between the hunter and the hunted; and in the wars in the sky the advantage has been with the hunter.

The Air Force itself has already recognized the importance of the development of this attitude of attack through their "tiger" programs in the aviation cadet and pilot training schools. Through careful indoctrination—in the classroom as on the flight line—the embryo aviators are being taught the importance of the "every-man-a-tiger" approach to flying a fighter aircraft and the difference in the margin of victory between the tiger and the lamb.

It was at one time thought that the secret of the ace was his eyes. It was even figured that perhaps it was the distance the eyes were set apart that gave the ace special perception for seeing the enemy aircraft. This study was moving in the right direction; for indeed, the ability to see the enemy has played a large and important role in the ace's accomplishments in battle. However, it has not been so much the acuteness of the aviator's vision, as his "experienced" vision. On great fighter sweeps across the Korean mountains, over the German-occupied countryside, and above the hostile Japanese islands of the Pacific, the new and inexperienced fighter pilots have seen no enemy planes, while in the same flights the old hands observed them in all directions.

Captain Joseph McConnell, top Korean ace, once commented: "You have to go looking for them. Sometimes even this doesn't help. I know of pilots who have flown 100 missions and haven't brushed with the MIGs once." And yet while others saw no enemy aircraft Captain McConnell, with his experienced vision, had no difficulty spotting and destroying the enemy in the fuzzy light of the upper air.

A third important aspect in the creation of the ace has been teamwork and tactics. Occasionally in the statistics on aces, an unusually high percentage of aces appears in one particular organization. For example, over 50% of the pilots who flew for the Flying Tigers became aces. Why? Because of exceptional leadership and the development of new tactics. In every instance where the leaders of fighter units showed unusual genius and fresh vision in the field of aerial tactics the percentage of aces in that outfit has shown a marked increase. There was Lufbery with his Escadrille, Rickenbacker with his Hat-in-the-Ring Squadron, Chennault with his Flying Tigers, Zemke with his 56th Fighter Group, Cochran with his Red Scarf Guerrillas, Foss with his Flying Circus, Valencia with his close-knit Division, Johnny Meyer with his 4th Fighter Interceptor Wing, the MIG killers in Korea, and on and on. In each case the leaders have employed clever, unique and advanced fighter tactics with a unit that they have drawn together into a closely co-ordinated team.

Thus we have the creature, the ace. He was neither always young nor always old: age was no criterion. Nor did size, nor height, nor physical build matter. He was not necessarily an extrovert nor an introvert; a braggart nor a shy recluse. But though there were many things the ace was not, there were several things he seemed always to be.

The ace flew aggressively and always pressed his attack. He was not necessarily reckless nor foolhardy, but he was daring and a fighter. He loved to fly and knew his business when he had the flying machine strapped on by the safety belt. He was constantly on the alert for the enemy and his experienced eyes were able to catch that flicker of motion, that flashing speck on the horizon, that almost unseen movement that was sometimes the only indication that an enemy was sharing the same sky. In some cases aces have been able to run up an impressive number of victories because of their exceptional shooting abilities, but while this ability often made a difference in final totals, it seldom, alone, made a flyer an ace. The ace understood his business, learned from his own experience and from that of others, carefully employing those tactics which put to greatest advantage his fighting vehicle. With this combination of fighting attributes the ace seized the advantage to sweep the enemy before him.

The aces, as a group, did not merely represent one of the more colorful aspects of military aviation, but rather formed the all-important keystone to America's air supremacy. Generally speaking less than 1 per cent of the military pilots have become aces, yet they accounted for roughly between thirty per cent to forty per cent of the enemy aircraft shot down!

America's Armed Forces cannot operate in war unless the troops, the supplies, the vehicles, the airplanes, the railroads and the sea vessels can move without interference from the foe. This demands American control of the sky. And control of the sky is the job of the fighter pilot whose mission is to seek the enemy and destroy him. Thus in the sky, it is the ace who is the margin of victory. He is a member of that elite group of men who proudly hold the key to American air supremacy. The age of the aerial warrior is now; and the ace is the twentieth-century knight.

STATISTICS OF ACES AND ENEMY AIRCRAFT
DESTROYED—BY THEATER

THEATER	EAD* IN THE AIR	EAD ON THE GROUND	NUMBER OF ACES	AIR TO AIR EAD BY ACES	% OF TOTAL EAD BY ACES
1. Lafayette Escadrille	199	d	12	106	53%
2. World War I	854	d	80	578	55%
3. Flying Tigers	299	d	37	279	93%
4. Eagle Squadron	74	d	d	d	d
5. Navy	9282	6221	331	2388	37%
6. Marines	a	a	122	990	a
7. Far East AF	2709	299	154	1239	39%
8. Pacific Ocean Areas	370	131	c	c	c
9. Alaskan	34	13	c	c	c
10. 20th Air Force	80	17	c	c	c
11. China-Burma-India	847	620	51	372	44%
12. Mediterranean	3569	1364	178	1294	26%
13. European	7422	6796	259	1584	b
14. Korea	800(e)	d	42(f)	328	41%

(a) Marine statistics are included in Navy totals.
(b) E.T.O. statistics are included in Mediterranean totals.
(c) Included in Far East Air Force totals.
(d) Data not available.
(e) MIG-15s only.
(f) Jet aces only.
   * Enemy aircraft destroyed.

APPENDICES

CONGRESSIONAL MEDAL
OF HONOR ACES

A HISTORY OF military aces is necessarily a chronicle of brave men; a record of flyers to whom daring and extraordinary skill are routine; a registry of aviators to whom courage and heroism are commonplace. However, occasionally from these select lists came those rare men who exceed even the high bounds of gallantry and self-sacrifice ordinarily practiced by the military aces. These men are the aces who, for their conspicuous heroism, have been decorated with the highest military award for bravery the United States can bestow upon a fighting man: The Congressional Medal of Honor. There are only a few American military aces who have been so honored and it is for these outstanding aces that this section has been designed.

The Congressional Medal of Honor can be won in only one way: by a deed of personal bravery or self-sacrifice above and beyond the call of duty. The accomplishment must be proved by incontestable evidence of at least two eyewitnesses; it must be so outstanding that it clearly distinguishes the gallantry beyond-the-call-of-duty from lesser forms of bravery; it must involve the personal risk of life; and it must be the type of deed which, if it had not been performed, would not have subjected the recipient to any justified criticism.

(Apart from the great honor which it conveys, there are certain small privileges which accompany the Medal of Honor. Its winners are entitled to free available military air transportation whether or not they are on active duty. Enlisted personnel winners are given $2 additional pay each month, and upon reaching the age of sixty-five each holder of the Medal of Honor receives a special pension of $120 a year. It has become an honored and traditional custom for all American Armed Forces personnel to salute any service person, regardless of his rank, who wears the light blue silken ribbon with five white stars representing the Medal of Honor.)

The military aces who have received this highest military honor are listed here along with a description of the exploits that won for them the Congressional Medal of Honor.

BAUER, HAROLD WILLIAM, Lieutenant Colonel, USMC. Born 20 November 1908, Woodruff, Kans. Appointed from Nebraska.

For extraordinary heroism and conspicuous courage as Squadron Commander of Marine Fighting Squadron TWO HUNDRED TWELVE in the South Pacific Area during the period 10 May to 14 November 1942. Volunteering to pilot a fighter plane in defense of our positions on Guadalcanal, Colonel Bauer participated in two air battles against enemy bombers and fighters outnumbering our force more than two-to-one, boldly engaged the enemy and destroyed one Japanese bomber in the engagement of 28 September and shot down four enemy fighter planes in flames on 3 October, leaving a fifth smoking badly. After successfully leading 26 planes on an over-water ferry flight of more than 600 miles on 16 October, Colonel Bauer, while circling to land, sighted a squadron of enemy planes attacking the *U. S. S. McFarland*. Undaunted by the formidable opposition and with valor above and beyond the call of duty, he engaged the entire squadron and, although alone and his fuel supply nearly exhausted, fought his plane so brilliantly that four of the Japanese planes were destroyed before he was forced down by lack of fuel. His intrepid fighting spirit and distinctive ability as a leader and an airman, exemplified in his splendid record of combat achievement, were vital factors in the successful operations in the South Pacific Area.

BONG, RICHARD I. (Air Mission), Major, Air Corps. Over Borneo and Leyte, 10 October to 15 November 1944. Entered Service at: Poplar, Wisconsin. Birth: Poplar, Wisconsin. G. O. No. 90, 8 December 1944.

For conspicuous gallantry and intrepidity in action above and beyond the call of duty in the Southwest Pacific Area from 10 October to 15 November 1944. Though assigned to duty as gunnery instructor and neither required nor expected to perform combat duty, Major Bong voluntarily and at his own urgent request engaged in repeated combat missions, including unusually hazardous sorties over Balikpapan, Borneo, and in the Leyte area of the Philippines. His aggressiveness and daring resulted in his shooting down eight enemy airplanes during this period.

BOYINGTON, GREGORY, Major, USMCR. Born 4 December 1912, Coeur D'Alene, Idaho. Accredited to Washington. Other Navy awards: Navy Cross.

For extraordinary heroism and valiant devotion to duty as Commanding Officer of Marine Fighting Squadron TWO HUNDRED FOURTEEN in action against enemy Japanese forces in the Central Solomons Area from 12 September 1943, to 3 January 1944. Consistently outnumbered throughout successive hazardous flights over heavily defended hostile territory, Major Boyington struck at the enemy with daring and courageous persistence, leading his squadron into combat with devastating results to Japanese shipping, shore installations and aerial forces. Resolute in his efforts to inflict crippling damage on the enemy, Major Boyington led a formation of 26 fighters over Kahili on 17 October and, persistently circling the airdrome where 60 hostile aircraft were grounded, boldly challenged the Japanese to send up planes. Under his brilliant command, our fighters shot down 20 enemy craft in the ensuing action without the loss of a single ship. A superb airman and determined fighter against overwhelming odds, Major Boyington personally destroyed 26 of the many Japanese planes shot down by his squadron and, by his forceful leadership, developed the combat readiness in his command which was a distinctive factor in the Allied aerial achievements in this vitally strategic area.

DAVIS, GEORGE A., JR., Lieutenant Colonel, USAF. Born 1 December 1920 at Hale Center, Texas.

Col. Davis, of Lubbock, Tex., was shot down February 10, 1952, while flying his 60th Korean combat mission. On this date, Col. Davis and his wingman unhesitatingly attacked a formation of 12 MIG-15's in order to protect friendly fighter-bombers who were conducting low-level operations against enemy lines. After destroying two of the MIGs, Col. Davis deliberately sacrificed the superior speed which would have permitted him to evade the concentrated fire of the enemy formation and, slowing his plane by use of dive brakes, pressed the attack against a third MIG. During this attack, his F-86 was hit and crashed out of control into a mountain.

DeBLANC, JEFFERSON JOSEPH, Captain, USMCR. Born 15 February 1921, Lockport, La. Appointed from

Louisiana. Other Navy awards: Distinguished Flying Cross, Air Medal with four Gold Stars.

For conspicuous gallantry and intrepidity at the risk of his life above and beyond the call of duty as Leader of a Section of Six Fighter Planes in Marine Squadron ONE HUNDRED TWELVE, during aerial operations against enemy Japanese forces off Kolombangara Island in the Solomons Group, 31 January 1943. Taking off with his section as escort for a strike force of dive bombers and torpedo planes ordered to attack Japanese surface vessels, First Lieutenant DeBlanc led his flight directly to the target area where, at 14,000 feet, our strike force encountered a large number of Japanese Zeros protecting the enemy's surface craft. In company with other fighters, First Lieutenant DeBlanc instantly engaged the hostile planes and aggressively countered their repeated attempts to drive off our bombers, persevering in his efforts to protect the diving planes and waging fierce combat until, picking up a call for assistance from the dive bombers under attack by enemy float planes at 1,000 feet, he broke off his engagement with Zeros, plunged into the formation of float planes and disrupted the savage attack, enabling our dive bombers and torpedo planes to complete their runs on the Japanese surface disposition and withdraw without further incident. Although his escort mission was fulfilled upon the safe retirement of the bombers, First Lieutenant DeBlanc courageously remained on the scene despite a rapidly diminishing fuel supply and, boldly challenging the enemy's superior number of float planes, fought a valiant battle against terrific odds, seizing the tactical advantage and striking repeatedly to destroy three of the hostile aircraft and to disperse the remainder. Prepared to maneuver his damaged plane back to base, he had climbed aloft and set his course when he discovered two Zeros closing in behind. Undaunted, he opened fire and blasted both Zeros from the sky in a short, bitterly fought action which resulted in such hopeless damage to his own plane that he was forced to bail out at a perilously low altitude atop the trees on enemy-held Kolombangara. A gallant officer, a superb airman and an indomitable fighter, First Lieutenant DeBlanc had rendered decisive assistance during a critical stage of operations, and his unwavering fortitude in the face of overwhelming opposition reflects the highest credit upon himself and adds new luster to the traditions of the United States Naval Service.

FOSS, JOSEPH JACOB, Captain, USMCR. Born 17 April 1915, Sioux Falls, S. D. Appointed from South Dakota. Other Navy awards: Distinguished Flying Cross.

For outstanding heroism and courage, above and beyond the call of duty as Executive Officer of Marine Fighting Squadron ONE TWENTY ONE, First Marine Aircraft Wing, at Guadalcanal. Engaging in almost daily combat with the enemy from 9 October to 19 November 1942, Captain Foss personally shot down 23 Japanese planes and damaged others so severely that their destruction was extremely probable. In addition, during this period, he successfully led a large number of escort missions, skillfully covering reconnaissance, bombing and photographic planes as well as surface craft. On 15 January 1943, he added three more enemy planes to his already brilliant successes for a record of aerial combat achievement unsurpassed in this war. Boldly searching out an approaching enemy force on 25 January, Captain Foss led his eight F4F Marine planes and four Army P-38's into action and, undaunted by tremendously superior numbers, intercepted and struck with such force that four Japanese fighters were shot down and the bombers were turned back without releasing a single bomb. His remarkable flying skill, inspiring leadership and indomitable fighting spirit were distinctive factors in the defense of strategic American positions on Guadalcanal.

GALER, ROBERT EDWARD, Major, USMC. Born 23 October 1913, Seattle, Wash. Accredited to Washington. Other Navy awards: Distinguished Flying Cross, Air Medal with four Gold Stars.

For conspicuous heroism and courage above and beyond the call of duty as Leader of a Marine Fighter Squadron in aerial combat with enemy Japanese forces in the Solomon Islands Area. Leading his squadron repeatedly in daring and aggressive raids against Japanese aerial forces, vastly superior in numbers, Major Galer availed himself of every favorable attack opportunity, individually shooting down 11 enemy bomber and fighter aircraft over a period of 29 days. Though suffering the extreme physical strain attendant upon protracted fighter operations at an altitude above 25,000 feet, the squadron under his zealous and inspiring leadership, shot down a total of 27 Japanese planes. His superb airmanship, his outstanding skill and personal valor reflect great credit upon Major Galer's gallant fighting spirit and upon the United States Naval Service.

HANSON, ROBERT MURRAY, First Lieutenant, USMCR. Born 4 February 1920, Lucknow, India. Accredited to Massachusetts. Other Navy awards: Navy Cross, Air Medal.

For conspicuous gallantry and intrepidity at the risk of his life and above and beyond the call of duty as Fighter Pilot attached to Marine Fighting Squadron TWO HUNDRED FIFTEEN in action against enemy Japanese forces at Bougainville Island, 1 November 1943; and New Britain Island, 24 January 1944. Undeterred by fierce opposition, and fearless in the face of overwhelming odds, First Lieutenant Hanson fought the Japanese boldly and with daring aggressiveness. On 1 November, while flying cover for our landing operations at Empress Augusta Bay, he dauntlessly attacked six enemy torpedo bombers, forcing them to jettison their bombs and destroying one Japanese plane during the action. Cut off from his division while deep in enemy territory during a high cover flight over Simpson Harbor on 24 January, First Lieutenant Hanson waged a lone and gallant battle against hostile interceptors as they were orbiting to attack our bombers and, striking with devastating fury, brought down four Zeroes and probably a fifth. Handling his plane superbly in both pursuit and attack measures, he was a master of individual air combat, accounting for a total of 25 Japanese aircraft in this theater of war. His great personal valor and invincible fighting spirit were in keeping with the highest traditions of the United States Naval Service.

HOWARD, JAMES H. Rank and Organization: Lieutenant Colonel, Air Corps. Place and Date: Over Oschersleben, Germany, 11 Jan. 1944. Entered Service at: St. Louis, Mo. Birth: Canton, China. G. O. No. 45, 5 June 1944.

For conspicuous gallantry and intrepidity above and beyond the call of duty in action with the enemy near Oschersleben, Germany, on 11 Jan. 1944. On that day Colonel Howard was the leader of a group of P-51 aircraft providing support for a heavy bomber formation on a long-range mission deep in enemy territory. As Colonel Howard's group met the bombers in the target area the bomber force was attacked by numerous enemy fighters. Colonel Howard, with his group, at once engaged the enemy and himself destroyed a German ME 110. As a result of this attack Colonel Howard lost contact with his group and at once returned to the level of the bomber formation. He then saw that the bombers were being heavily attacked by enemy airplanes and that no other friendly fighters were at hand. While Colonel Howard could have waited to attempt to assemble his group before engaging the enemy, he chose instead to attack single-handed a formation of more than 30 German airplanes. With utter disregard for his own safety he immediately pressed home determined attacks for some 30 minutes, during which time he destroyed three enemy airplanes and probably destroyed and damaged others. Toward the end of this engagement three of his guns went out of action and his fuel supply was becoming dangerously low. Despite these handicaps and the almost insuperable odds against him, Colonel Howard continued his aggressive action in an attempt to protect the bombers from the numerous fighters. His skill, courage, intrepidity on this occasion set an example of heroism which will be an inspiration to the armed forces of the United States.

KEARBY, NEEL E. (Air Mission). Rank and Organization: Colonel, Air Corps. Place and Date: Near Wewak, New Guinea, 11 Oct. 1943. Entered Service at: Dallas, Tex. Birth: Wichita Falls, Tex. G. O. No. 3, 6 Jan. 1944.

For conspicuous gallantry and intrepidity above and beyond the call of duty in action with the enemy. Colonel Kearby volunteered to lead a flight of four fighters to reconnoiter the strongly defended enemy base at Wewak. Having observed enemy installations and reinforcements at four airfields, and secured important tactical information, he saw an enemy fighter below him, made a diving attack and shot it down in flames. The small formation then sighted approximately 12 enemy bombers accompanied by 36 fighters. Although his mission had been completed, his fuel was running low, and the numerical odds were 12 to 1, he gave the signal to attack. Diving into the midst of the enemy airplanes he shot down three in quick succession. Observing one of his comrades with two enemy fighters in pursuit, he destroyed both enemy aircraft. The enemy broke off in large numbers to make a multiple attack on his airplane but despite his peril he made one more pass before seeking cloud protection. Coming into the clear, he called his flight together and led them to a friendly base. Colonel Kearby brought down six enemy aircraft in this action, undertaken with superb daring after his mission was completed.

KNIGHT, RAYMOND L. (Air Mission), First Lieutenant, Air Corps. In Northern Po Valley, Italy, 24-25 April 1945. Entered Service at: Houston, Texas, G. O. No. 81, 24 September 1945.

He piloted a fighter-bomber aircraft in a series of low-level strafing missions, destroying 14 grounded enemy aircraft and leading attacks which wrecked ten others during a critical period of the Allied drive in northern Italy. On the morning of 24 April, he volunteered to lead two other aircraft against the strongly defended enemy airdrome at Ghedi. Ordering his fellow-pilots to remain aloft, he skimmed the ground through a deadly curtain of antiaircraft fire to reconnoiter the field, locating eight German aircraft hidden beneath heavy camouflage. He rejoined his flight, briefed them by radio, and then led them with consummate skill through the hail of enemy fire in a low-level attack, destroying five aircraft, while his flight accounted for two others. Returning to his base, he volunteered to lead three other aircraft in reconnaissance of Bergamo airfield, an enemy base near Ghedi and one known to be equally well defended. Again ordering his flight to remain out of range of antiaircraft fire, Lieutenant Knight flew through an exceptionally intense barrage, which heavily damaged his Thunderbolt, to observe the field at minimum altitude. He discovered a squadron of enemy aircraft under heavy camouflage and led his flight to the assault. Returning alone after this strafing, he made ten deliberate passes against the field despite being hit by antiaircraft fire twice more, destroying six fully loaded enemy twin-engine aircraft and two fighters. His skillfully led attack enabled his flight to destroy four other twin-engine aircraft and a fighter plane. He then returned to his base in his seriously damaged plane. Early the next morning, when he again attacked Bergamo, he sighted an enemy plane on the runway. Again he led three other American pilots in a blistering low-level sweep through vicious antiaircraft fire that damaged his plane so severely that it was virtually nonflyable. Three of the few remaining enemy twin-engine aircraft at that base were destroyed. Realizing the critical need for aircraft in his unit, he declined to parachute to safety over friendly territory and unhesitatingly attempted to return his shattered plane to his home field. With great skill and strength, he flew homeward until caught by treacherous air conditions in the Apennines Mountains, where he crashed and was killed. The gallant action of Lieutenant Knight eliminated the German aircraft which were poised to wreak havoc on Allied forces pressing to establish the first firm bridgehead across the Po River; his fearless daring and voluntary self-sacrifice averted possible heavy casualties among ground forces and the resultant slowing of the German drive culminated in the collapse of enemy resistance in Italy.

LUKE, FRANK, JR. Rank and Organization: Second Lieutenant, 27th Aero Squadron, First Pursuit Group, Air Service. Place and Date: Near Murvaux, France, 29 Sept. 1918. Entered Service at: Phoenix, Ariz. Birth: Phoenix, Ariz. G. O. No. 59, W. D. 1919.

After having previously destroyed a number of enemy aircraft within 17 days, he voluntarily started on a patrol after German obervation balloons. Though pursued by eight German planes which were protecting the enemy balloon line, he unhesitatingly attacked and shot down in flames three German balloons, being himself under heavy fire from ground batteries and the hostile planes. Severely wounded, he descended to within 50 meters of the ground, and flying at this low altitude near the town of Murvaux opened fire upon enemy troops, killing six and wounding as many more. Forced to make a landing and surrounded on all sides by the enemy, who called upon him to surrender, he drew his automatic pistol and defended himself gallantly until he fell dead from a wound in the chest.

McCAMPBELL, DAVID, Commander, USN. Born 16 January 1910, Bessemer, Alabama. Appointed from Florida. Other Navy awards: Navy Cross, Silver Star Medal, Legion of Merit, Distinguished Flying Cross with two Gold Stars, Air Medal.

For conspicuous gallantry and intrepidity at the risk of his life above and beyond the call of duty as Commander, Air Group FIFTEEN, during combat against enemy Japanese aerial forces in the First and Second Battles of the Philippine Sea. An inspiring leader, fighting boldly in the face of terrific odds, Commander McCampbell led his fighter planes against a force of 80 Japanese carrier-based aircraft bearing down on our fleet on 19 June 1944. Striking fiercely in valiant defense of our surface force, he personally destroyed seven hostile planes during this single engagement in which the outnumbering attack force was utterly routed and virtually annihilated. During a major fleet engagement with the enemy on 24 October, Commander McCampbell assisted by but one plane, intercepted and daringly attacked a formation of 60 hostile land-based craft approaching our forces. Fighting desperately but with superb skill against such overwhelming air power, he shot down nine Japanese planes and, completely disorganizing the enemy group, forced the remainder to abandon the attack before a single aircraft could reach the fleet. His great personal valor and indomitable spirit of aggression under extremely perilous combat conditions reflect the highest credit upon Commander McCampbell and the United States Naval Service.

McGUIRE, THOMAS B., JR. (Air Mission), Major, 13th Air Force. Over Luzon, Philippine Islands, 25-26 December 1944. Entered Service at: Sebring, Florida. Birth: Ridgewood, New Jersey. G. O. No. 24, 7 March 1946.

He fought with conspicuous gallantry and intrepidity over Luzon, Philippine Islands. Voluntarily, he led a squadron of 15 P-38's as top cover for heavy bombers striking Mabalacat Airdrome, where his formation was attacked by 20 aggressive Japanese fighters. In the ensuing action he repeatedly flew to the aid of embattled comrades, driving off enemy assaults while himself under attack and at times outnumbered three to one, and even after his guns jammed, continuing the fight by forcing a hostile plane into his wingman's line of fire. Before he started back to his base he had shot down three Zeros. The next day he again volunteered to lead escort fighters on a mission to strongly defended Clark Field. During the resultant engagement he again exposed himself to attacks so that he might rescue a crippled bomber. In rapid succession he shot down one aircraft, parried the attack of four enemy fighters, one of which he shot down, single-handedly engaged three more Japanese, destroying one, and then shot down still another, his thirty-eighth victory in aerial combat. On 7 January 1945, while leading a voluntary fighter sweep over Los Negros Island, he risked an extremely hazardous maneuver at low altitude in an attempt to save a fellow flyer from attack, crashed, and was reported missing in action. With gallant initiative, deep and unselfish concern for the safety of others, and heroic determination to destroy the enemy at all costs, Major McGuire set an inspiring example in keeping with the highest traditions of the military service.

O'HARE, EDWARD HENRY, Lieutenant, USN. Born 13 March 1914, St. Louis, Missouri. Appointed from Missouri. Other Navy awards: Navy Cross, Distinguished Flying Cross with one Gold Star.

For conspicuous gallantry and intrepidity in aerial combat, at grave risk of his life above and beyond the call of duty, as Section Leader and Pilot of Fighting Squadron THREE, on 20 February 1942. Having lost the assistance of his teammates, Lieutenant O'Hare interposed his plane between his ship and an advancing enemy formation of nine attacking twin-engined heavy bombers. Without hesitation, alone and unaided, he repeatedly attacked this enemy formation, at close range in the face of intense combined machine-gun and cannon fire. Despite this concentrated opposition, Lieutenant O'Hare, by his gallant and courageous action, his extremely skillful marksmanship in making the most of every shot of his limited amount of ammunition, shot down five enemy bombers and severely damaged a sixth before they reached the bomb release point. As a result of his gallant action—one of the most daring, if not the most daring, single action in the history of combat aviation—he undoubtedly saved his carrier from serious damage.

RICKENBACKER, EDWARD V. Rank and Organization: First Lieutenant, 94th Aero Squadron, Air Service. Place and Date: Near Billy, France, 25 Sept. 1918. Entered Service at: Columbus, Ohio. Birth: Columbus, Ohio. G. O. No. 2, W. D., 1931.

For conspicuous gallantry and intrepidity above and beyond the call of duty in action against the enemy near Billy, France, 25 September 1918. While on a voluntary patrol over the lines, Lieutenant Rickenbacker attacked seven enemy planes (five type Fokker, protecting two type Halberstadt). Disregarding the odds against him, he dived on them and shot down one of the Fokkers out of control. He then attacked one of the Halberstadts and sent it down also.

SHOMO, WILLIAM A. (Air Mission). Rank and Organization: Major, 82d Tactical Reconnaissance Squadron. Place and Date: Over Luzon, Philippine Islands, 11 Jan. 1945. Entered Service at: Westmoreland County, Pa. Birth: Jeannette, Pa. G. O. No. 25, 7 Apr. 1945.

For conspicuous gallantry and intrepidity at the risk of his life above and beyond the call of duty. Major Shomo was lead pilot of a flight of two fighter planes charged with an armed photographic and strafing mission against the Aparri and Laoag airdromes. While en route to the objective, he observed an enemy twin-engine bomber, protected by 12 fighters, flying about 2,500 feet above him and in the opposite direction. Although the odds were 13 to 2, Major Shomo immediately ordered an attack. Accompanied by his wingman he closed on the enemy formation in a climbing turn and scored hits on the leading plane of the third element, which exploded in midair. Major Shomo then attacked the second element from the left side of the formation and shot another fighter down in flames. When the enemy formed for counterattack, Major Shomo moved to the other side of the formation and hit a third fighter which exploded and fell. Diving below the bomber, he put a burst into its under side and it crashed and burned. Pulling up from this pass he encountered a fifth plane firing head on and destroyed it. He next dived upon the first element and shot down the lead plane; then diving to 300 feet in pursuit of an-

241

other fighter he caught it with his initial burst and it crashed in flames. During this action his wingman had shot down three planes, while the three remaining enemy fighters had fled into a cloudbank and escaped. Major Shomo's extraordinary gallantry and intrepidity in attacking such a far superior force and destroying seven enemy aircraft in one action is unparalleled in the Southwest Pacific Area.

SMITH, JOHN LUCIAN, Major, USMC. Born 26 December 1914, Lexington, Okla. Accredited to Oklahoma. Other Navy awards: Legion of Merit, Air Medal with four Gold Stars.

For conspicuous gallantry and heroic achievement in aerial combat above and beyond the call of duty as Commanding Officer of Marine Fighting Squadron TWO HUNDRED TWENTY THREE during operations against enemy Japanese forces in the Solomon Islands Area, August-September 1942. Repeatedly risking his life in aggressive and daring attacks, Major Smith led his squadron against a determined force, greatly superior in numbers, personally shooting down 16 Japanese planes between 21 August and 15 September 1942. In spite of the limited combat experience of many of the pilots of this squadron, they achieved the notable record of a total of 83 enemy aircraft destroyed in this period, mainly attributable to the thorough training under Major Smith and to his intrepid and inspiring leadership. His bold tactics and indomitable fighting spirit, and the valiant and zealous fortitude of the men of his command not only rendered the enemy's attacks ineffective and costly to Japan, but contributed to the security of our advance base. His loyal and courageous devotion to duty sustains and enhances the finest traditions of the United States Naval Service.

SWETT, JAMES ELMS, First Lieutenant, USMC. Born 15 June 1920, Seattle, Wash. Accredited to California. Other Navy awards: Distinguished Flying Cross with Gold Star, Air Medal with three Gold Stars.

For extraordinary heroism and personal valor above and beyond the call of duty, as Division Leader of Marine Fighting Squadron TWO HUNDRED TWENTY ONE with Marine Aircraft Group TWELVE, First Marine Aircraft Wing, in action against enemy Japanese aerial forces in the Solomon Islands Area, 7 April, 1943. In a daring flight to intercept a wave of 150 Japanese planes, First Lieutenant Swett unhesitatingly hurled his four-plane division into action against a formation of 15 enemy bombers and personally exploded 3 hostile planes in midair with accurate and deadly fire during his dive. Although separated from his division while clearing the heavy concentration of antiaircraft fire, he boldly attacked six enemy bombers, engaged the first four in turn and, unaided, shot down all in flames. Exhausting his ammunition as he closed the fifth Japanese bomber, he relentlessly drove his attack against terrific opposition which partially disabled his engine, shattered the windscreen and slashed his face. In spite of this, he brought his battered plane down with skillful precision in the water off Tulagi without further injury. The superb airmanship and tenacious fighting spirit which enabled First Lieutenant Swett to destroy seven enemy bombers in a single flight were in keeping with the highest traditions of the United States Naval Service.

WALSH, KENNETH AMBROSE, First Lieutenant, USMC. Born 24 November 1916, Brooklyn, N. Y. Accredited to New York. Other Navy awards: Distinguished Flying Cross with five Gold Stars, Air Medal with 13 Gold Stars.

For extraordinary heroism and intrepidity above and beyond the call of duty as a Pilot in Marine Fighting Squadron ONE HUNDRED TWENTY FOUR in aerial combat against enemy Japanese forces in the Solomon Islands Area. Determined to thwart the enemy's attempt to bomb Allied ground forces and shipping at Vella Lavella on 15 August 1943, First Lieutenant Walsh repeatedly dived his plane into an enemy formation outnumbering his own division 6 to 1 and, although his plane was hit numerous times, shot down two Japanese dive bombers and one fighter. After developing engine trouble on 30 August during a vital escort mission, First Lieutenant Walsh landed his mechanically disabled plane at Munda, quickly replaced it with another, and proceeded to rejoin his flight over Kahili. Separated from his escort group when he encountered approximately 50 Japanese Zeros, he unhesitatingly attacked, striking with relentless fury in his lone battle against a powerful force. He destroyed four hostile fighters before cannon shellfire forced him to make a dead-stick landing off Vella Lavella where he was later picked up. His valiant leadership and his daring skill as a flier served as a source of confidence and inspiration to his fellow pilots and reflect the highest credit upon the United States Naval Service.

POST-WORLD WAR I ACES

World War I was over and the fury in the European skies had produced nearly eighty American aces, eleven of whom had been killed in combat. The remaining men, having reached the pinnacle of acedom, did not choose to fall back into the complacent role of yesterday's heroes basking in the ebb tide of their past glories. Rather, they turned to the future and faced the challenges of the robust nation that had come of age. For the most part these aces were men of aviation, and in aviation they became the leaders in the growth of this expanding industry in both military and civilian fields. Others climbed to success as captains in different spheres of activity, such as Elliott White Springs in the cotton textile industry and Sumner Sewall, who became Governor of Maine.

Because of the outstanding contributions these men have made to this country, above and beyond their war achievements, the following brief summaries have been designed to include biographical sketches of some of the more prominent. These sketches of World War I aces in their postwar careers are of even further interest when it is considered that the accomplishments of these men may well be indicative of the future promise of the aces of World War II and the Korean Conflict.

These sketches have been prepared from information contained in *Blue Book of American Aviation, Who's Who in the Industry*, Aviation Statistics Institute of America, Asheville, North Carolina, 1942; Lester D. Gardner's *Who's Who in American Aeronautics, the Blue Book of American Airmen*, Gardner, New York, 1922-1928, three editions; *Blue Book of Aviation, a Biographical History of American Aviation*, Hoagland, Los Angeles, California, 1932, edited by Roland W. Hoagland; *Writers' Program—Who's Who in Aviation,* Ziff Davis, Chicago, Illinois, 1942; and *U.S. Air Services,* Air Services Publishing Co., Inc., Washington, D.C.

Rickenbacker, Edward Vernon—President, General Manager and Director Eastern Air Lines Incorporated, New York City. Born in Columbus, Ohio, on 8 October 1890. Parents are William and Elizabeth (Barcler) Rickenbacker. Education: Hon. Dr. Ae. Sc. Pa. Military College 1938, Brown University 1940, University of Miami 1941. Married Adelaide Frost Durant, 16 September 1922. Pilot Record: Learned to fly, France, 1917. Aviat. Bus. rec: Vice-President and Director of Sales, General Aviation Manufacturing Company; Vice-President, American Airways 1932, North-American Aviation Incorporated 1933; General Manager 1935, President-General Manager since 1938, Eastern Air Lines Incorporated; President and Director of Indianapolis Motor Speedway Corporation; Director Air Transport Association of America; member, Advisory Committee for Aeronautics, National Safety Council, New York City. Military Record: Sgt. U.S. Army 1917; Staff Driver for General Pershing, later transferred to Air Corps; Chief Engin. Off. Issoudon Aviation School with rank of Lieutenant; Commissioned officer with rank of Captain, Ninety-fourth Aero Squadron 1918; won distinction as America's "Ace of Aces" officially credited with twenty-six enemy planes; honorably discharged with rank of Major. Awards: Croix de Guerre with four palms, Legion of Honor Medal, Distinguished Service Cross with nine Oak Leaves, Congressional Medal of Honor. Author: *Fighting the Flying Circus,* 1919, and other publications.

Vaughn, George Augustus, Jr.—Aviation Executive, Newark, New Jersey. Residence—Helena Road, Dongan Hills, S. I., New York. Born in Brooklyn, New York, on May 20, 1897. Parents are George Augustus and Grace (Sours) Vaughn. Education: Adelphi Academy, Brooklyn, New York, 1915; B. S. Princeton University 1920. Married Marion Perkins of East Orange, New Jersey, on October 9, 1925. Pilot record: Learned to fly Princeton, New Jersey 1917; Pvt. pilot Certificate No. 5027. Aviation Bus. rec: Aviation Salesman, Westinghouse Elec. & Manufacturing Company 1923-1938; President Eastern Aero. Corporation 1928-1940; New York State Aviation Commissioner 1931-1934; Vice-President and Director of Casey Jones School of Aero., Secretary-Treasurer, Director J. V. W. Corps of Canada Ltd. and J. V. W. Corps Ltd. of Great Britain since 1932; Secretary-Treasurer, Director Acad. of Aero. Incorporated since 1940. Military Record: Flight Commander, 17th Aero Squadron, A.E.F., 1917-1919;

Second ranking U. S. War ace; Major, New York National Guard Air Service, 1921-1930; Lt. Colonel, New York National Guard Air Corps 1930-1940. Awards: Distinguished Service Cross, U. S.; Distinguished Flying Cross, England. Memberships, Princeton Engin. Association, Quiet Birdmen, Veteran Air Pilots Association. Clubs: Princeton Club of N. Y., Richmond County, Dongan Hills, New York City.

Springs, Elliott White—Owner and Director of the Spring Cotton Mills, Lancaster, South Carolina; Colonel, USAAF. Residence at Fort Mill, South Carolina. Born in Lancaster, South Carolina, on July 31, 1896. Parents are Leroy and Grace (White) Springs. Education: Graduate Calves Military Academy 1913, A. B. Princeton, 1917; studied Military Aviation, Oxford University, 1917. Married Frances Hubbard Ley on 4 October 1922. Pilot record: Test Pilot, 1919, participated in first cross country airplane race 1919. Military record: Private Aviation section, Sign. Offrs. Res. Corps, 1917; Executive officer of Charlotte Air Base: World War II. Awards: Distinguished Flying Cross, Distinguished Service Cross. Memberships: National Aeronautics Association, Reserve Officers Association, American Legion. Author: Nocturne Militaire 1927; Leave Me with a Smile 1928; Contact 1930; In the Cool of the Evening 1930; Rise and Fall of Carol Burke 1931; Pent up on a Penthouse 1931; Warbirds and Ladybirds 1931 and numerous current publications. Commander, South Carolina Wing of Civil Air Patrol.

Landis, Reed Gresham—Colonel, U. S. Army, Office of Chief of Air Forces, Washington, D.C. (retired). Residence—Harvard Hall, 1630 Harvard Avenue, Washington, D.C. Born in Ottawa, Illinois, on July 17, 1896. Parents are Kenesaw Mountain and Winifred (Reed) Landis. Married Marion Keehn of Kenilworth, Illinois, on September 20, 1919. Pilot record: Learned to fly in England, 1917. Aviation Rec: Regional Vice-President of American Airlines Incorporated 1940-1941; Aviation consultant to Director, Office of Civil Defense, Washington, D.C., 1941-1942. Military record: Pvt. First Illinois Cav., Mexican Border 1916; advanced through grades to Major U. S. Army Air Services 1917-1918; attached to RAF 1917-1918; Commander Twenty-fifth Aero Squadron, A. E. F. 1918; Major, U. S. Army, Office of Chief of Air Forces since March 1942. Awards: American Distinguished Service Cross, British Flying Cross, Commander Italian Order of the Royal Crown. Memberships: Institute of the Aero Services, American Legion, Beta Theta Pi. Clubs: Chicago Athletic Association; Skokie Country Club (Glencoe, Illinois).

Hunter, Frank O'D.—Maj. General (retired). Born Savannah, Ga., 8 December 1894. Enlisted as flying cadet, and commissioned 1st Lt. Aviation Section, Signal Corps Reserve, 12 September 1917. Reg. Army commission as 1st Lt. Air Service, 1 July 1920. Shot down 9 planes in World War I. Military Observer in London 1940. In May 1942 became Commanding General of the 8th Air Force Fighter Command. Returned to U. S. in September 1943 and designated Commanding General 1st Air Force. Ratings: Command Pilot, Aircraft Observer, Technical Observer. Decorations: DSC with 4 Oak Leaf Clusters, Silver Star, Legion of Merit, Purple Heart, French Croix de Guerre with Palm. Hunter Air Force Base, Savannah, Ga., named in his honor.

Larner, G. de Freest—Secretary and General Manager National Aeronautics Association, Washington, D. C. Residence: Army and Navy Club, Washington, D. C. Born in Washington, D. C., on 5 July 1897. Parents are Robert Martin and Adelaide (de Freest) Larner. Education: A. B. Columbia University 1921. Pilot record: Learned to fly in France 1917; Military Pilot, instrument rating. Aviation Business record: Secretary and General Manager—National Aeronautical Association since 1940. Military record: Pilot Lafayette Escadrille, 103rd Pursuit Squadron, U. S. and French Army Air Service, 1917-1918; member of Peace Comm., France, 1918; Chief of Pursuit Training Division U. S. Army Air Corps 1919; Colonel U. S. Army Air Corps Reserve; active duty U. S. Army Air Corps in London—World War II. Awards: Distinguished Service Cross with Bronze Oak Leaf; Croix de Guerre with two Palms, France; three Silver Star Citations. Memberships: Delta Kappa Epsilon. Clubs: Chevy Chase, Army and Navy (Washington, D. C.)

Chambers, Reed McKinley—Vice-President and Treasurer, U. S. Aviation Underwriters Incorporated, New York City. Residence: Bay Avenue, Huntington, New York. Born in Onaga, Kansas, in August 1894. Parents are Jeremiah Sherman and Winifred (Saunders) Chambers. Married Myrtle Blonnquist of Joliet, Illinois, on October 1, 1919. Pilot Record: Learned to fly at Ashburn and Rantoul Fields, Illinois; Military aviator —logged 2000 hours in 1920-1925; Aviation business record: Commercial paid pilot 1920-1925. Founder of Florida Airways 1925; co-founder U. S. Aircraft Insurance Group 1928; President Canadian Aviation Insurance Managers Ltd.; Vice-President and Treasurer U. S. Aviation Underwriters Incorporated. Military Record: 1st Lt. U. S. Army Signal Reserve Corps 1917; instructor at Rantoul Field, Illinois, 1917; Training School Issoudun and Cazaux, France; Commander 94th U. S. Army Aero Squadron 1918-1919; Major U. S. Army Air Corps. Awards: Distinguished Service Cross with three Oak Leaves; Legion of Honor, Croix de Guerre with Palm and two Stars, France. Memberships—Institute of the

Aero Sciences, Aero. Chamber of Commerce, Quiet Birdmen, Insurance Soc. of New York, A. F. A. M. Clubs: Downtown Athletic, Bankers of America (New York City); Crescent (Huntington, New York)—(Hartford, Connecticut).

Campbell, Douglas—Vice-President Pan American—Grace Airways Incorporated, New York City. Residence: 52 Gramercy Park North, New York City. Born in San Francisco, California on June 7, 1896. Parents are William Wallace and Elizabeth Ballard (Thompson) Campbell. Education: A. B. Harvard University 1917. Pilot Record: Learned to fly Issoudun, France, 1917; Military aviator. Aviation Business Record: Assistant Treasurer 1935-1939, Vice-President in charge of Peru and New York Divisions since 1939, Pan American-Grace Airways Incorporated. Military Record: 1st Lt. 1917-1918, Captain 1918-1919 U. S. Army Air Service, A. E. F., France. Awards: Distinguished Flying Cross, Legion of Honor, Croix de Guerre, France. Memberships: Institute of Aero Sciences. Clubs: Club Nacional (Lima, Peru); Harvard (New York City).

Stenseth, Martinus—Colonel, United States Army Air Forces (retired). Born in Minnesota on 11 June 1890. Pilot Record: Learned to fly United States Army Air Service, 1917-1918; Command Pilot and combat observer. Military Record: Advanced through grades of 1st Lt. to Colonel, United States Army Air Forces since 1920; graduated Air Corps Tactical School, 1927; Cavalry School, 1928. Awards: Distinguished Service Cross: Silver Star.

Stovall, William Howard—Brig. Gen.—USAFR. Plantation owner, Stovall, Mississippi.

Robertson, Wendel A.—Colonel, United States Army Air Force (retired).

Curtis, E. P.—Colonel, United States Army Air Force (retired).

Sewall, Sumner—Governor of Maine, 1942; Residence: 1132 Washington Street, Bath, Maine. Born in Bath, Maine, on 17 June 1897. Parents: William Dunning and Mary Lock (Sumner) Sewall. Education: Howard—1916 to 1917; Yale —1919 to 1920. Married Helen Ellena Evans on 16 March 1929. Pilot Record: Learned to fly Tours, France, 1917; Military Aviator. Aviation Business Record: General Traffic Manager, Colonial Air Transport Company, 1926-1929; Passenger Traffic Manager, Aviation Corporation, New York City, 1930; Director, United Air Lines Transport Corporation, Chicago since 1934. President of Maine State Senate, 1939. Military Record: 95th Aero Squadron, AEF, France, 1917-1918; seven victories. Awards: Distinguished Service Cross with Oak Leaf, Legion of Honor Medal, Croix de Guerre, French-Order of the Crown, Belgium. Memberships:

BPOE, Delta Kappa Epsilon. Clubs: Tennis and Racquet, New York City. Assistant Director, Bath National Bank, Maine.

Vasconsells, Jerry C.—Investment Banker. Residence: 425 Humboldt, Denver, Colorado. Born in Lyons, Kansas, on 3 December 1892. Parents are Frank Quintal and Anna (Dun Brac) Vasconsells. Education: B. S. & LLB, University of Denver. Married Marietta C. Cassell of Denver, Colorado, on 18 October 1922. President, Vasconsells, Hicks & Company. Flying Record: Learned to fly RFC, Toronto, Canada, and Hicks Field, Texas, 1917 and Issoudun, France, 1918; Military Aviator. Military Record: First Officer, Training Camp, Fort Logan, 1916-1917; Flying Cadet, Toronto, Canada, 1917; with 1st Pursuit Group, Toul, France, 1918; Commander, B Flight, 27th Division Squadron; Commander 185th Aero Squadron; Commander 2nd Pursuit Group; Brought down six (6) gunner planes and 1 balloon in combat, 1918; Commander 120th Aero Squadron, Colorado. National Guard. Memberships: Sigma Chi; Chmn., State Aero Association of Colorado; Sec., Traders Association; Chmn., National Association of Security Dealers. Clubs: Denver Club. Awards: Croix de Guerre, Nieuport Medal, General Pershing Citation for "Hero of the Day," NAA Medal, only Colorado man credited as ace (WW I).

Knotts, Howard Clayton—Attorney, Residence: 1303 South Sixth Street, Springfield, Illinois. Born in Girard, Illinois, on August 25, 1895. Parents are Edward Clay and Elizabeth (Routzahn) Knotts. Education: Blackburn College, Illinois, 1912-1915; A. B. Knox College, 1916; LLB Harvard Law School 1921. Married Charlotte Ann Sterling of Bloomington, Illinois, on 25 June 1921. Pilot Record: Learned to fly at Toronto, Canada, 1917; Military Aviator. Aviat. Bus. Record: Secretary, Illinois Aerial Navigation Comm., 1929-1931; Aviat. Supervisor, Illinois Commerce Comm. since 1930; Member of editorial staff 1931-1937, editor-in-chief since 1937, Journal of Air Law and Commerce, Chicago; consulting expert to Bureau of Air Commerce and C. A. A., 1937-1939; secretary, National Association of State Aviation Officials, 1937-1939; member of Advisory Comm., Amer. Sect. of Comité International Teqnique d'Experts Juridiques Aeriens since 1937; general counsel NAA, 1939-1940; lecturer on Economics of Air Transportation, 1938-1940, lecturer on Illinois Public Utility Law. Managing Director, Air Law Institute, Northwestern University; counsel Presidents' Interdepartmental Committee on Civil Aviation; counsel American Association of Airport Executives since 1940. Military Record: 2nd Lt., 182nd Aero. Squadron, Aviation Section, U. S.

Army Signal Corps, Fort Wood, New York, and Fort Worth, Texas, 1917-1918; pilot RFC, Toronto, Canada, and 17th Pursuit Squadron, 13th Wing, RAF, Flanders, Cambrai and Somme, France, 1918-1919. Awards: U. S. Distinguished Service Cross, Silver Star Medal and 2 Oak Leaf clusters, Purple Heart, British Distinguished Flying Cross. Memberships: National Association of State Aviation Officials; American Association of State Aviation Officials; American Association of Airport Executives; Quiet Birdmen; Private Flyers Association; Disabled American War Vets; VFW Sangamon County; Illinois State and American Bar Associations; Beta Theta Pi, AFAM Club, Sangamo Illinois Country Club (Springfield, Illinois). Author: Civil Air Regulations (co-authors Fred D. Fagg, Jr. and John H. Wigmore) 1937; revised 1938.

Healy, James A.—Colonel, USAAF (retired). Born in Kansas, on March 26, 1895. Education: A. B., St. Peters College, New Jersey, 1914. Pilot Record: Learned to fly, U. S. Army Air Service, 1917-1918. Military Record: Advanced through grades 2nd Lt. to Lt. Colonel, U. S. Army Corps, since 1918; graduated from Army Balloon School, 1921; Air Service Balloon and Airship School, 1924. Awards: Distinguished Service Cross.

Strahm, Victor H.—Brigadier General, USAAF (retired). Born in Tennessee, on 26 October 1895. Pilot Record: Learned to fly, U. S. Army Air Service, 1917; Command Pilot and Combat Observer. Military Record: Advanced through grades 1st Lt. to Colonel, USAAF since 1920. Graduated from Air Service Engineers School, 1923; Air Corps Tactical School, 1932; Command and General Staff School, 1936; Army War College, 1939. Retired 31 July 1953, permanent Colonel, Base Commander at various bases including Barksdale Air Force Base. Chief of Staff, 9th Air Force, 1943, under M/Gen. Brereton, and on 7 September 1943 succeeded him as Commanding General.

Lindsay, Robert Opie—Colonel, U. S. Army Air Forces (retired).

Ingalls, David S.—Vice-President Pan American Air Ferries Incorporated. Born 28 January 1899, Cleveland, Ohio. Education: Yale (1920) B. A.; Harvard Law School 1923 LL. B. ATT: Ohio House of Representatives 1926-1929; Assistant Secretary of Navy for Aeronautics 1929-1932; Director, Division of Public Health & Welfare of Cleveland, Ohio 1934-1935. Member: University Club, New York; Union Club, Cleveland, Ohio; Chagrin Valley Hunt Club, Gate Mills, Ohio; American Legion; Masonic Order. Add. Bus., Chrysler Building, New York, New York. Residence, Storybrook Farm, Chagrin Falls, Ohio.

250

Brooks, Arthur Raymond—Research Engineer, Bell Telephone Laboratories Incorporated, New York City. Residence: Wayside, Short Hills, New Jersey. Born in Framingham, Massachusetts, on 1 November 1895. Parents are Frank Emelsin and Josephine (LeVasseur) Brooks. Education: B. S., MIT, 1917. Married Ruth M. Connery of Nashua, New Hampshire, on 25 September 1920. Pilot Record: Learned to fly, United States Army Air Service, 1917-1918. Transport pilot #1738. Avia. Bus. Record: Assistant to the President, Florida Airways Corporation, 1925-1926; associate airways engineer, North East Section, United States Department of Commerce, 1926-1928. Organizer-Supervisor of Air Operation Group, 1928-1938, research engineer and member of tech. staff since 1928, Bell Telephone Laboratories Incorporated. Military Record: Advanced through grades 2nd Lt., to Captain, U. S. Army, 1918-1919; Pilot and Flight Commander, 139th & 22nd Pursuit Squadrons and Second Pursuit Group; AEF, France, 1918; Commanding Officer, 95th Pursuit Squadron and 1st Pursuit Group, 1919-1921; Air Corps Tac. School, 1921-1922. Awards: Distinguished Service Cross, Aero Club of America Medal of Merit.

George, Harold H.—Major General. Born in Lockport, New York, in 1892. Commissioned 1st Lt., Air Service in 1920; Commanding Officer of 31st Pursuit Group, 1940; Chief of Staff, Far Eastern Air Force, 1941; Commanding Officer, 5th Interceptor Command, 1941. Commanded all Air Corps troops in Philippine Islands, December, 1941-March, 1942. Killed in airplane crash, Darwin, Australia, April, 1942. Awards and decorations include DSC and DSM. George Air Force Base, Victorville, California named in his honor.

Bissell, Clayton Lawrence—Major General (retired). Born in Kane, Pennsylvania, 1896. Graduated from Valparaiso University. Enlisted as Flying Cadet, 1917. Commissioned 1st Lt., Air Service, 1920. Served overseas during World War I with 148th and 42nd Aerial Squadrons and credited with destruction of 5 enemy aircraft. Graduated from Army War College, 1934. Duty with War Plans Division, Washington 1939. Commanding General, 10th Air Force, CBI, 1942-1943. Duty with WDGS G2, 1943, 1946. Military attaché to Great Britain, 1946. Awards and decorations include DSC, DSM with 2 clusters, Silver Star DFC, and British DFC.

Donaldson, John O.—Born at Fort Yates, N. D., on May 14, 1897; primary and high school education, Greenville, S. C.; Furman University, Greenville; ground training school, Cornell University. Awarded: Distinguished Service Cross, Distinguished Flying Cross (British) and World War I Victory Medal with the Aisne-Marne-Somme Offensive, Ypres-Lys and Defensive Sector Battle Clasps. Lt. Belvin W. Maynard and Captain Donaldson were selected as co-winners of the Mackay Trophy for 1919, for making the fastest round-trip flights from New York to San Francisco and return, in a race in which 64 airplanes of all types competed. Lt. Maynard made the roundtrip in 9 days, 4 hours, 26 min., and Captain Donaldson came in second by finishing it in 9 days, 21 hours, 5 min. In the November, 1919 issue of *U. S. Air Services* appeared two interesting articles by these famous flyers, "Twice Across the Continent in a Single-Seater," by Capt. J. O. Donaldson and "Most Dramatic Incident in My Flight," by Lt. B. W. Maynard. Following his discharge in 1920, Capt. Donaldson spent the next ten years in commercial aviation. On September 7, 1930 he was killed while stunt flying at an air show held near Philadelphia.

Easterbrook, Arthur E.—Born, Amsterdam, N. Y.; son of Chaplain and Mrs. Edmund Easterbrook; father served as Chief of Army Chaplains from 1928 to 1929. Only observer to have been rated as an ace during World War I; died on July 24, 1954 in Long Beach Veterans Administration Hospital, Long Beach, Calif.; brother of Mrs. J. Lawton Collins, wife of the Army Chief of Staff. Twice decorated with the Distinguished Service Cross and recommended for the Congressional Medal of Honor for heroism in aerial combat in World War I; Distinguished Service Cross and an Oak Leaf cluster were awarded for his work as an observer and for successfully completing a mission despite five encounters with enemy planes; recommended for the Medal of Honor for attacking enemy planes from an observation aircraft; Gen. Billy Mitchell, in 1919, said of General Easterbrook, "This officer's record is second to none in this war." Active pilot between World Wars; he served as Executive Officer of the Army Air Corps Training Center at Randolph Field, Texas, and on the staff of the late General of the Army, H. H. Arnold, as Chief of Training and Operations. Retired in 1939 but was recalled to active service early in 1940; was Chief of Staff of the West Coast Air Corps Training Center in California until 1944; served as Commanding General of the Amarillo Army Air Field, Texas, and later as Chief of Staff of the Western Technical Training Command at Denver, until 1945; commanded the Santa Ana (Calif.) Air Base until he retired again in 1946. Besides Mrs. Collins, his sister, he is survived by his wife, Mrs. Gertrude Louise Augustine; a son, Lieut. Arthur E. Easterbrook, Jr., both of Santa Ana; three brothers, Wilfred G. and William E., both of Seattle, and Col. Ernest F. Easterbrook, of the Joint Chiefs of Staff in Washington.

Haight, Edward M.—Colonel, USAF (retired). Last surviving WW I ace on active duty with the Air Force to retire; won his wings at an Allied flying school in France in 1917; spent some time in the Regular Army Air Service as a pursuit pilot; resigned his commission in 1923; president of the South Florida Realty Co.; chief pilot and manager, Central American Airlines; consultant to an airport engineering service; licensed as both a pilot and a mechanic. Recalled to duty in 1940 as a major and spent 17 months at Randolph Air Force Base, Texas, sometimes acting as base commander; Air Attaché, Central America. Last year of WW II, commander of the 30th Air Service Gp., England; only son, Lt. Edward L. Haight, a photo reconnaissance pilot, failed to return from a mission over Europe; military government officer, Bavaria; chief of the War Plans Division in the Directorate of Installations, Pentagon.

Kindley, Field E.—Kindley Air Force Base, Bermuda, was named in honor of Capt. Field E. Kindley who was killed in an air crash at Kelly Field, San Antonio, Texas, in 1920.

WORLD WAR I OFFICIAL SUMMARY OF AIR OPERATIONS

When hostilities ceased on November 11, 1918 there were actually assigned to the Army 45 American squadrons and 767 pilots, 481 observers, 23 aerial gunners, and the complement of soldiers. These squadrons were equipped with 740 airplanes, with armament of the latest type, and the flying personnel, trained in Air Service schools, was second to none in the world for aggressiveness and skill. Twelve of these squadrons were equipped with American built airplanes and Liberty engines. . . .

On the Marne, at St. Mihiel, and in the Argonne our air forces were pitted against the best which Germany could produce, and the results show that the enemy more than met his match. Our pilots shot down 781 enemy airplanes which were officially confirmed, and many others, too far behind the lines to be confirmed by our own witnesses, but which were nevertheless undoubtedly destroyed. They also destroyed 73 (confirmed) enemy balloons. Our total losses in air battles were 289 airplanes and 49 balloons brought down by the enemy.

Our squadrons, in round numbers took part in 150 bombing raids, during which they dropped over 275,000 pounds of explosives on the enemy. They flew 35,000 hours over the lines and took 18,000 photographs of enemy positions, from which 585,000 prints were made by the photographic sections attached to observation groups. On innumerable occasions they regulated the fire of our artillery, flew in contact with infantry during attacks, and from a height of only a few yards from the ground they machine-gunned and bombed enemy batteries, convoys and troops on the march.

Of the 35 balloon companies then in France, with 466 officers and 6365 men, there were 23 companies serving with the armies at the front. Our balloons at the front made 1642 ascensions, and were in the air a total of 3111 hours. They made 316 artillery adjustments, each comprising all the shots fired at one target; they reported 12,018 shell blasts, sighted 11,856 enemy airplanes, reported enemy balloon ascensions 2649 times, enemy batteries 400 times, enemy traffic and roads and railroads (movements) 1113 times, explosions and destructions 587 times.

Our balloons were attacked by enemy planes on 89 occasions: 35 of them were burned during such attacks, 12 others were destroyed by shell fire, and one blown over enemy lines. Our observers jumped from the baskets 116 times; in no case did the parachute fail to open properly. One observer lost his life because pieces of the burning balloon fell on his descending parachute.

TOP USAF ACES—AIR-TO-AIR VICTORIES WORLD WAR I, WORLD WAR II, AND KOREAN CONFLICT

NAME	RANK	AIR TO AIR VICTORIES	THEATER	BIOGRAPHY
1. Bong, Richard I.	Major	40	FEAF	Congressional Medal of Honor; Killed in an F-80 accident, 6 Aug. 1945 at Los Angeles, Calif; Bong A.F.B., Wis. named in his honor.
2. McGuire, Thomas B., Jr.	Major	38	FEAF	Congressional Medal of Honor; Killed over Leyte, Philippine Islands in 1945; McGuire A.F.B., N.J. named in his honor.
3. Gabreski, Francis S.	Colonel	37½	8th AF and Korea	Top Ace 8th AF, World War II; Winner of record 12 Distinguished Flying Crosses; Active duty—USAF.
4. Johnson, Robert S.	Captain	28	8th AF	Not on active duty; executive with Republic Aviation Co.; Past president and one of the founders of the Air Force Association.
5. MacDonald, Charles H.	Colonel	27	FEAF	Active Duty—USAF.
6. Rickenbacker, Edward V.	Captain	26	WW I	Congressional Medal of Honor; Biography would require volumes. Presently Chairman of the Board, Eastern Air Lines.
7. Meyer, John C.	Colonel	26	8th AF and Korea	Active Duty—USAF.
8. Preddy, George E.	Major	25.83	8th AF	Killed in action over Brussels, Belgium 25 Dec. 1944.
9. Mahurin, Walker M.	Colonel	25½	ETO, FEAF and Korea	Not on active duty—executive with Northrop Aviation Co.
10. Gentile, Don S.	Captain	23	8th AF	Killed in a T-33 Jet accident near Andrews AFB, in 1950. AF installation at Dayton, Ohio, named in his honor.

#	Name	Rank	Score	AF	Notes
11.	Wetmore, Ray S.	Captain	22.59	8th AF	Killed in an aircraft accident near Otis A.F.B. Mass., on 14 Feb. 1951.
12.	Schilling, David C.	Colonel	22½	8th AF	Won Harmon Trophy in 1951. Member of 40th Air Div.; Recipient of Mackay Trophy, 1953. Killed in auto accident at Mildenhall, England on 14 August 1956. Schilling A.F.B., Kansas named in his honor.
13.	Johnson, Gerald R.	Lt. Col.	22	FEAF	Killed in accident shortly after WW II. Johnson A.F.B., Japan named in his honor.
14.	Kearby, Neel E.	Colonel	22	FEAF	Killed in Action 5 March 1944. Congressional Medal of Honor.
15.	Robbins, Jay T.	Colonel	22	FEAF	Active Duty—USAF.
16.	Christensen, Fred J.	Lt. Col.	21½	8th AF	Not on active duty. Assigned to Mass. Air National Guard.
17.	Davis, George A., Jr.	Lt. Col.	21	FEAF and Korea	Congressional Medal of Honor; Killed in Action in Korea in 1952.
18.	Garrison, Vermont	Lt. Col.	21	8th AF and Korea	Active duty—USAF.
19.	Herbst, John C.	Colonel	21	CBI	Top Ace CBI Theater WW II. Killed in air crash (F-80) 4 July 1946.
20.	Voll, John J.	Major	21	15th AF	Active duty—USAF; Top Ace—15th AF WW II.
21.	Whisner, William T., Jr.	Major	21	8th AF and Korea	Won Bendix Trophy in 1953. Active duty—USAF.
22.	Eagleston, Glenn T.	Colonel	20½	9th AF and Korea	Active duty—USAF; Top Ace 9th Air Force, WW II.
23.	Lynch, Thomas J.	Lt. Col.	20	FEAF	Killed in Action 9 March 1944.
24.	Westbrook, Robert B.	Lt. Col.	20	13th AF	Top Ace 13th AF-WW II. Killed in Action in Philippine Islands 22 Nov. 1944.
25.	Zemke, Hubert	Colonel	19½	8th AF	Active duty—USAF.
26.	Beeson, Duane W.	Major	19⅓	8th AF	Deceased, 1949, Wright-Patterson A.F.B., Ohio.
27.	Duncan, Glenn E.	Colonel	19	8th AF	Active duty—USAF.
28.	Fleming, Patrick	Colonel	19	Navy	Killed in B-52 accident, 16 February 1956.

TOP USAF ACES—AIR-TO-AIR VICTORIES
WORLD WAR I, WORLD WAR II, AND
KOREAN CONFLICT (continued)

NAME	RANK	AIR TO AIR VICTORIES	THEATER	BIOGRAPHY
29. Carson, Leonard K.	Major	18½	8th AF	Active duty—USAF.
30. Jabara, James	Lt. Col.	18½	9th AF and Korea	Active duty—USAF.
31. Hill, David L.	Colonel	18¼	CBI and Flying Tigers	Not on active duty; Commander 8707th Reserve Pilot Training Wg., Brooks AFB, Texas (1956).
32. Beckham, Walter C.	Colonel	18	8th AF	Active duty—USAF.
33. Godfrey, John T.	Captain	18	8th AF	Retired (Physical Ret.) from USAF; executive and owner of silk mills in New England.
34. Johnson, Gerald W.	Colonel	18	8th AF	Active duty—USAF. Member of 40th Air Div.; Recipient of Mackay Trophy—1953.
35. Luke, Frank, Jr.	2nd Lt.	18	WW I	Congressional Medal of Honor; Killed in Action 1918; Luke A.F.B., Ariz. named in his honor.
36. England, John B.	Lt. Col.	17½	8th AF	Kiled in an F-86 accident on 20 Nov. 1954 at Toul-Rosiere Air Base, France. England AFB, Alexandria, La. named in his honor.
37. Thornell, John F.	Major	17¼	8th AF	Active duty—USAF.
38. Brown, Henry W.	Lt. Col.	17.20	8th AF	Active duty—USAF.
39. Foy, Robert W.	Lt. Col.	17	8th AF	Active duty—USAF.
40. Hampshire, John F.	Captain	17	CBI	Killed in Action on 2 May 1943 in China.
41. Lufbery, Gervais Raoul	Major	17	WW I	Killed in Action—1918.
42. Baker, Royal N.	Colonel	16½	ETO and Korea	Active duty—USAF.
43. Hofer, Ralph K.	1st Lt.	16½	8th AF	Killed in Action during WW II.
44. Reed, William N.	Lt. Col.	16½	CBI and Flying Tigers	Killed in Action on 19 Dec. 1943 in China.

No. & Name	Rank	Score	Air Force	Notes
45. Anderson, Clarence E.	Lt. Col.	16¼	8th AF	Active duty—USAF.
46. Harris, Bill	Colonel	16	13th AF	Active duty—USAF.
47. McConnell, Joseph M.	Captain	16	Korea	Killed in F-86 test flight accident at Edwards AFB, Calif., in 1954. No USAF Record.
48. Neale, Robert H.	Captain	16	CBI and Flying Tigers	Killed while testing an F-100 for North American Aviation Co. on 11 Oct. 1954 at Edwards AFB, Calif.
49. Welch, George S.	Major	16	FEAF	Killed in Action—1944.
50. Beerbower, Don M.	Captain	15½	9th AF	Not on active duty.
51. Peterson, Richard A.	Major	15½	8th AF	Flew more combat missions than any other officer in USAF; Member 27 Fi. Escort Wg.; Recipient of Mackay Trophy—1950. Active duty—USAF.
52. Blakeslee, Donald J. M.	Colonel	15	8th AF and Eagle Sq.	Active duty—USAF.
53. Bochkay, Donald H.	Lt. Col.	15	8th AF	Active duty—USAF.
54. Bradley, Jack T.	Colonel	15	9th AF	Active duty—USAF.
55. Brown, Samuel J.	Captain	15	15th AF	Not on active duty.
56. Cragg, Edward	Major	15	FEAF	Killed in Action, 23 Dec. 1943.
57. Dunham, William D.	Colonel	15	FEAF	Active duty—USAF.
58. Goodson, James A.	Major	15	8th AF	Active duty—USAF.
59. Homer, Cyril F.	Major	15	FEAF	Not on active duty.
60. Fernandez, Manuel I., Jr.	Captain	14½	Korea	Active duty—USAF. Set new world record Bendix Trophy Race, Sept. 1956, flying F-100C Super Sabre at average speed of 666.661 mph.
61. Hagerstrom, James P.	Lt. Col.	14½	FEAF and Korea	Active duty—USAF. Placed, Thompson Trophy Race—1949.
62. Powers, Joe H., Jr.	Captain	14½	8th AF	Killed in Action in Korea 1951.
63. Carr, Bruce W.	Major	14	9th AF	Active duty—USAF.
64. Dahlberg, Kenneth H.	1st Lt.	14	9th AF	Not on active duty.
65. DeHaven, Robert M.	Major	14	FEAF	Not on active duty.—USAF. Position with Hughes Aircraft Corp. (unofficial) Winner of Bendix Jet Trophy Race—National Air Races 1948.

TOP USAF ACES—AIR-TO-AIR VICTORIES
WORLD WAR I, WORLD WAR II, AND
KOREAN CONFLICT (continued)

NAME	RANK	AIR TO AIR VICTORIES	THEATER	BIOGRAPHY
66. Emmer, Wallace N.	Captain	14	9th AF	Killed in Action—1944.
67. Head, Coatsworth B., Jr.	Captain	14	13th AF	MIA—18 Jan. 1944.
68. Jeffrey, Arthur F.	Colonel	14	8th AF	Active duty—USAF.
69. McComas, Edward O.	Colonel	14	CBI	Deceased, Washington, D. C., 1954.
70. Roberts, Daniel T., Jr.	Major	14	FEAF	Killed in Action 9 Nov. 1943.
71. Schreiber, Leroy A.	Major	14	8th AF	Killed in Action over Germany—1944.
72. Thyng, Harrison R.	Colonel	14	12th AF, FEAF and Korea	Active duty—USAF.
73. Bryan, Donald S.	Lt. Col.	13½	8th AF	Active duty—USAF.
74. Carpenter, George	Major	13½	8th AF	Active duty—USAF.
75. Strait, Donald J.	Colonel	13½	8th AF	Not on active duty—Deputy Assistant AF Secretary for Reserve Affairs (1957).
76. Brooks, James L.	2nd Lt.	13	15th AF	Not on active duty. Test pilot with North American Aviation Co.
77. East, Clyde B.	Major	13	9th AF	Active duty—USAF; Winner of record 43 Air Medals.
78. Hoefker, John H.	Major	13	9th AF	Not on active duty.
79. Holloway, Bruce K.	Maj. Gen.	13	CBI	Deputy Commander, 9th AF, Shaw AFB, S.C. (1957).
80. Millikan, Willard W.	Colonel	13	8th AF	Commander, 113th Ftr. Bomber Wg., District of Columbia Air National Guard. Set transcontinental air speed record in F-86 on 2 Jan. 1954. Air Force Association Regional Vice President.
81. Moran, Glennon T.	Lt. Col.	13	8th AF	Active duty—USAF.
82. Parker, Harry A.	Captain	13	15th AF	No USAF record.

260

		Rank	Score	Theater	Remarks
83.	Scott, Robert L.	Brig. Gen.	13	CBI	Chief, Office of Information Services, Hq., USAF (1956). Author of many aviation books and articles including best seller "God is my Co-Pilot."
84.	Stephens, Robert W.	Colonel	13	9th AF	Active duty—USAF.
85.	Vaughn, George A.	1st Lt.	13	WW I	Not on active duty—Associated with various aeronautical concerns.
86.	Williamson, Felix D.	Captain	13	8th AF	No USAF record.
87.	Brueland, Lowell K.	Lt. Col.	12½	9th AF	Active duty—USAF.
88.	Stewart, James C.	Colonel	12½	8th AF	Active duty—USAF.
89.	Brown, Quince L.	Major	12⅓	8th AF	No USAF record.
90.	Brezas, Michael	Major	12	15th AF	Killed in F-86 accident in Korea on 6 Feb. 1952.
91.	Chase, Levi R.	Colonel	12	NW African AF	Active duty—USAF. Top Ace North West African Air Force—WW II.
92.	Dalglish, James B.	Captain	12	9th AF	Not on active duty.
93.	Eastham, David B.	Captain	12	FEAF	No USAF record.
94.	Gleason, George W.	Major	12	8th AF	Active duty—USAF.
95.	Hively, Howard D.	Lt. Col.	12	8th AF	Active duty—USAF.
96.	Kindley, Field E.	Captain	12	WW I	Killed in air crash at Kelly Field, San Antonio, Texas in 1920. Kindley AFB, Bermuda named in his honor.
97.	Ladd, Kenneth G.	Captain	12	FEAF	No USAF record.
98.	McKennon, Pierce W.	Major	12	8th AF	Killed in aircraft accident—1946.
99.	Olds, Robin	Colonel	12	8th AF	Active duty—USAF. Placed 2nd in Thompson Jet Trophy Race—National Air Races 1946.
100.	Putnam, David E.	1st Lt.	12	WW I	Killed in action—World War I.
101.	Quirk, Michael J.	Lt. Col.	12	8th AF	Active duty—USAF.
102.	Rector, Edward F.	Colonel	12	Flying Tigers	Active duty—USAF.
103.	Shubin, Murray	Lt. Col.	12	13th AF	Deceased—1956.
104.	Skogstad, Norman C.	1st Lt.	12	15th AF	Not on active duty.
105.	Sloan, William J.	Major	12	12th AF	Active duty—USAF. Top Ace 12th Air Force, WW II.

TOP USAF ACES—AIR-TO-AIR VICTORIES WORLD WAR I, WORLD WAR II, AND KOREAN CONFLICT (continued)

NAME	RANK	AIR TO AIR VICTORIES	THEATER	BIOGRAPHY
106. Springs, Elliot W.	Captain	12	WW I	Not on active duty; Commander South Carolina Wing of Civil Air Patrol; Successful Author; Owner and Director of Spring Cotton Mills, South Carolina.
107. Turner, Richard E.	Lt. Col.	12	9th AF	Not on active duty.
108. Watkins, James A.	Colonel	12	FEAF	Active duty—USAF.
109. West, Richard L.	Captain	12	FEAF	Not on active duty.
110. Megura, Nicholas	Captain	11.84	8th AF	Not on active duty.
111. Clark, James A.	Colonel	11½	8th AF	Not on active duty.
112. Conger, Paul A.	Major	11½	8th AF	Not on active duty.
113. Kirla, John A.	Major	11½	8th AF	Not on active duty.
114. Yeager, Charles E.	Major	11½	8th AF	Winner Mackay Trophy 1947. Winner Collier Trophy 1948. Winner Harmon Trophy 1954. 1st man to fly faster than the speed of sound, 17 Oct. 1947 in XS-1, at Mach 1.86. On 17 Dec. 1953 flew Bell X1A at 1650 mph.
115. Norley, Louis H.	Lt. Col.	11⅓	8th AF	Active duty—USAF.
116. Frantz, Carl M.	1st Lt.	11	9th AF	Not on active duty.
117. Goebel, Robert J.	Major	11	15th AF	Active duty—USAF.
118. Green, Herschel H.	Colonel	11	15th AF	Active duty—USAF.
119. Johnson, James K.	Colonel	11	Korea and ETO	Active duty—USAF.
120. Lent, Francis J.	1st Lt.	11	FEAF	No USAF record.
121. Leverette, William L.	Colonel	11	15th AF	Active duty—USAF.
122. Loisel, John S.	Colonel	11	FEAF	Active duty—USAF.

No.	Name	Rank	Score	Unit	Notes
123.	McCorkle, Charles M.	Brig. Gen.	11	15th AF	Active duty—USAF. Dept. Asst. c/s for Guided Missiles, Hq. USAF (1956).
124.	Riddle, Robert H.	2nd Lt.	11	15th AF	No USAF record.
125.	Smith, Cornelius M., Jr.	Lt. Col.	11	FEAF	Active duty—USAF.
126.	Sparks, Kenneth C.	1st Lt.	11	FEAF	Killed in a P-38 flight at Ontario, Calif. 1944.
127.	Burgard, George T.	(Civ.)	10¾	Flying Tigers	Not on active duty in USAF.
128.	Adams, Donald E.	Major	10½	8th AF and Korea	Killed in Air Show, Detroit, 1952.
129.	Anderson, Charles F., Jr.	1st Lt.	10½	8th AF	USAF unable to identify.
130.	Cewleers, George F.	Colonel	10½	8th AF	Active duty—USAF.
131.	Doersch, George A.	Lt. Col.	10½	8th AF	Active duty—USAF.
132.	Halton, William T.	Colonel	10½	8th AF	Killed in Korea—1952.
133.	Hovde, William J.	Colonel	10½	8th AF	Active duty—USAF.
134.	Jernstedt, Kenneth A.	(Civ.)	10½	Flying Tigers	Not on active duty in USAF.
135.	Littge, Raymond H.	Captain	10½	8th AF	Killed in F-84 flight from Bangor, Maine, to Selfridge AFB, Mich.—1948.
136.	Little, Robert L.	(Civ.)	10½	Flying Tigers	Killed in accident in China on 22 June 1942.
137.	McGarry, William D.	(Civ.)	10½	Flying Tigers	Not on active duty in USAF.
138.	Newkirk, John V. K.	(Civ.)	10½	Flying Tigers	Killed in accident on 24 March 1942 in China.
139.	O'Connor, Frank Q.	Colonel	10½	9th AF	Active duty—USAF.
140.	Storch, John A.	Lt. Col.	10½	8th AF	Not on active duty.
141.	Glover, Fred W.	Major	10.30	8th AF	Killed in civilian aircraft accident at Hazlehurst, Ga.—7 July 1956.
142.	Older, Charles H.	(Civ.)	10¼	Flying Tigers	Not on active duty in USAF.

TOP USAF ACES—AIR-TO-AIR VICTORIES
WORLD WAR I, WORLD WAR II, AND
KOREAN CONFLICT (continued)

NAME	RANK	AIR TO AIR VICTORIES	THEATER	BIOGRAPHY
143. Alison, John R.	Colonel	10	CBI	USAF Reserves Brig. General; vice-president of Northrop Aircraft Co.; past vice-president—Air Force Association; former Assistant Secretary of Commerce for Air.
144. Aschenbrener, Robert W.	Major	10	FEAF	No USAF record.
145. Bleese, Frederick C.	Major	10	Korea	Captain of Training Command Team winning 1955 USAF Gunnery Meet. Author of book "No Guts—No Glory"; Won General Electric Trophy in 21 minute Chicago to Detroit race with 670.2 mph, the fastest speed of 1951 National Air Races.
146. Blickenstaff, Wayne K.	Captain	10	8th AF	No USAF record.
147. Broadhead, Joseph E.	Lt. Col.	10	8th AF	Not on active duty.
148. Coffey, Robert L.	Colonel	10	9th AF	Killed in P-80 accident at Kirtland AFB, Ariz. on 20 Apr. 1949, undergoing AF reserve activities; Was member of U. S. House of Representatives from Penna. at the time.
149. England, James J.	Lt. Col.	10	CBI	Active duty—USAF.
150. Fischer, Harold E.	Captain	10	Korea	Active duty—USAF.
151. Giroux, William K.	Captain	10	FEAF	Not on active duty.
152. Goehausen, Walter J., Jr.	2nd Lt.	10	15th AF	No USAF record.
153. Grosvenor, William, Jr.	Captain	10	CBI	Retired from USAF.
154. Harris, Ernest A.	Major	10	FEAF	Killed in Germany—1949.
155. Juchheim, Aldwin M.	Captain	10	8th AF	Not on active duty.
156. Landis, Reed G.	Captain	10	WWI	Col.—USAAF retired.
157. Lines, Ted E.	1st Lt.	10	8th AF	Not on active duty.

158. Lowry, Wayne L.	Major	10	15th AF	Not on active duty.
159. Meroney, Virgil K.	Lt. Col.	10	8th AF	Member of 4800 mile nonstop F-84F record flight from Tokyo to Australia, 18 May 1955.
160. Molland, Leland P.	Lt. Col.	10	15th AF	Killed in Korea—1951.
161. Moore, Lonnie R.	Major	10	Korea	Killed in F-101 flight at Eglin AFB, Fla., on 10 Jan. 1956.
162. Parr, Ralph S.	Captain	10	Korea	Active duty—USAF.
163. Rankin, Robert J.	Lt. Col.	10	8th AF	Active duty—USAF.
164. Reynolds, Andrew J.	Colonel	10	FEAF	Active duty—USAF.
165. Shlegel, Albert L.	Captain	10	8th AF	Killed in Action WW II.
166. Stanch, Paul M.	Major	10	FEAF	Active duty—USAF.
167. Summer, Elliot	Lt. Col.	10	FEAF	Not on active duty.
168. Swaab, Jacques M.	Captain	10	WW I	Not on active duty.

TOP NAVY ACES—AIR-TO-AIR VICTORIES
WORLD WAR II

NAME	SERIAL NO.	SERVICE/RANK	VICTORIES	BIOGRAPHY
1. McCampbell, David S.	072487	USN—Capt.	34	Winner of the Congressional Medal of Honor—Active duty.
2. Harris, Cecil E.	114286	USN—Lt. Cmdr.	24	Active duty.
3. Valencia, Eugene A.	113030	USN—Cmdr.	23	Active duty.
4. Vraciu, Alexander	124731	USN—Lt. Cmdr.	19	Active duty.
5. Kepford, Ira C.	145749	USNR—Lt.	17	Not on active duty.
6. Stimpson, Charles R.	121639	USNR—Lt.	17	Not on active duty.
7. Baker, Douglas			16	Missing in action.
8. Nooy, Cornelius N.	177027	USNR	15	Not on active duty.
9. Hawkins, Arthur R.	240489	USN—Lt. Cmdr.	14	Active duty.
10. McCuskey, Elbert S.	081585	USN—Cmdr.	14	Active duty.
11. Wirth, John L.	146937	USN	14	Not on active duty.
12. Duncan, George C.	082484	USN—Cmdr.	13½	Active duty
13. Mehle, Roger W.	078670	USN—Capt.	13 1/6	Active duty.
14. Carmichael, Daniel A., Jr.	250521	USNR	13	Not on active duty.
15. Rushing, Roy W.	263563	USNR	13	Not on active duty.
16. Strane, John R.	106001	USN—Cmdr.	13	Active duty.
17. Twelves, Wendell V.	283102	USN—Lt.	13	Active duty.
18. Craig, Clement M.	086053	USN—Cmdr.	12	Active duty.
19. Hedrick, Roger R.	077688	USN—Cmdr.	12	Active duty.
20. Henry, William E.	084181	USN—Cmdr.	12	Active duty.
21. Masoner, William J., Jr.	082264	USNR	12	Not on active duty.
22. O'Hare, Edward H.	078672	USN—Lt. Cmdr.	12	Killed in Action—1943; O'Hare International Airport, Ill. named in his honor; winner of Congressional Medal of Honor.
23. Shirley, James. A	112972	USNR	12	
24. Carr, George R.	243216	USNR	11½	
25. Bakutis, Fred E.	075028	USN	11	

266

26.	Blackburn, John T.	072292	USN—Lt. Cmdr.	11	
27.	Dean, William A., Jr.	073624	USN—Cmdr.	11	Active duty.
28.	French, James B.	305948	USNR	11	
29.	Mallory, Charles M.	251056	USNR	11	
30.	McWhorter, Hamilton, III	112968	USNR	11	
31.	Reber, James V., Jr.	354792	USNR	11	
32.	Rigg, James F.	079142	USN—Cmdr.	11	Active duty.
33.	Runyon, Donald E.	146644	USN—Lt. Cmdr.	11	Active duty.
34.	Stanbook, Richard E.	112421	USNR	11	
35.	Vejtasa, Stanley W.	081514	USN	11	
36.	Beebe, Marshall U.	077807	USN	11	
37.	Reiserer, Russell L.	112294	USNR	10½	
38.	Murray, Robert E.	315070	USNR	10½	
39.	Elliott, Ralph E.	104741	USNR	10⅓	
40.	Brown, Carl A., Jr.	114255	USNR	10¼	
41.	Coleman, Thaddeus T.	130401	USN	10	
42.	Mitchell, Harris E.	300998	USNR	10	
43.	Singer, Arthur, Jr.	263939	USNR	10	
44.	Swope, James S.	117177	USNR	10	

TOP MARINE ACES—AIR-TO-AIR VICTORIES
WORLD WAR II

NAME	RANK	E/A DEST.	BIOGRAPHY
1. Boyington, Gregory	Colonel	28	Flying Tigers—Congressional Medal of Honor—Retired, Military—Brewery Executive, San Diego, California.
2. Foss, Joseph J.	Brig. Gen	26	Congressional Medal of Honor—Air National Guard, Brig. Gen.—Governor of South Dakota.
3. Hanson, Robert M.	1st Lt.	25	Congressional Medal of Honor—Deceased (KIA).
4. Walsh, Kenneth A.	Major	21	Active duty—Congressional Medal of Honor.
5. Aldrich, Donald N.	Captain	20	Killed in aircraft accident in USA—1947.
6. Smith, John L.	Colonel	19	Congressional Medal of Honor—Active duty.
7. Carl, Marion E.	Lt. Col.	18½	Military Test Pilot—Flew Douglas "Skymaster" to record 83,235 feet in August 1953—Also set Jet speed record of 650.6 mph in August 1947 with Douglas "Sky Streak." Flew Douglas "Sky Rocket" to record 1143 mph on 2 September 1953.
8. Thomas, Wilbur J.	Captain	18½	Not on active duty.
9. Swett, James E.	Major	16½	Not on active duty—Congressional Medal of Honor.
10. Spears, Harold L.	Captain	15	Killed in aircraft accident in USA—1944.
11. Donahue, Archie G.	Major	14	Not on active duty.
12. Cupp, James N.	Lt. Col.	13	Active duty.
13. Galer, Robert E.	Colonel	13	Congressional Medal of Honor—Active duty.
14. Marontate, William P.	1st Lt.	13	Deceased (KIA).
15. Shaw, Edward O.	Captain	13	Deceased (KIA).
16. Frazier, Kenneth D.	Lt. Col.	12½	Active duty.
17. Bolt, John F., Jr.	Lt. Col.	12	Korea, 6 MIGs—Active duty.
18. Everton, Loren D.	Lt. Col.	12	Active duty.
19. Segal, Harold E.	Captain	12	Not on active duty.
20. Trowbridge, Eugene A.	Major	12	Not on active duty.
21. Snider, William N.	Captain	11½	Not on active duty.

22. Delong, Philip C.	Major	11 1/6	Active duty.
23. Bauer, Harold W.	Lt. Col.	11	Congressional Medal of Honor. Deceased (KIA).
24. Sapp, Donald H.	Lt. Col.	11	Active duty.
25. Conger, Jack E.	Lt. Col.	10½	Active duty.
26. Baldwin, Frank B.	Captain	10	Not on active duty.
27. Long, Herbert H.	Major	10	Not on active duty.
28. Mann, Thomas H., Jr.	Major	10	Active duty.

SELECTED ARMY AIR FORCE STATISTICS— WORLD WAR II

	1941	1942	1943	1944	1945	TOTAL
Combat Sorties	212	26,688	365,940	1,284,195	685,765	2,362,800
Against Germany		9,749	233,523	1,012,101	438,192	1,693,565
Against Japan	212	16,939	132,417	272,094	247,573	669,235
Tons Bombs Dropped	36	10,203	198,800	1,085,978	762,227	2,057,244
Enemy Aircraft Destroyed		935	10,837	19,442	8,477	39,691
In aerial combat		809	9,462	14,281	3,160	27,712
On the ground		126	1,375	5,161	5,317	11,979
Airplanes lost on combat missions[1]		482	3,847	13,289	5,330	22,948
Aircraft on Hand[2]	12,297	33,304	64,232	72,726	63,175	
Very Heavy Bombers		3	91	977	2,865	
Heavy Bombers	288	2,076	8,027	12,813	11,065	
Medium and Light Bombers	1,544	3,757	6,741	9,169	8,463	
Fighters	2,170	5,303	11,875	17,198	16,799	
Reconnaissance	475	468	714	1,804	1,971	
Transports	254	1,857	6,466	10,456	9,561	
Trainers	7,340	17,044	26,051	17,060	9,558	
Communications	226	2,796	4,267	3,249	3,433	
Total Personnel[3]	194,626	1,597,049	2,373,882	2,359,456	2,253,182	

1 Includes losses due to enemy aircraft, enemy anti-aircraft fire, and operational losses.
2 As of December 31, 1941 through 1944, as of August 30, 1945.
3 As of July 1941, as of December 1942 through 1944; as of August 1945.

Source: Aircraft Yearbook 1946, United States Air Force.

SELECTED NAVAL AVIATION STATISTICS—
WORLD WAR II

	1941	1942	1943	1944	1945	TOTAL
Combat Sorties[1]	⋮	5,277	21,274	135,722	121,482	283,755
Carrier Based Fighters	⋮	938	2,345	37,805	44,774	85,862
Carrier Based Bombers	⋮	1,735	2,784	31,002	25,392	60,913
Land Based Fighters	⋮	1,089	4,295	34,048	21,171	60,603
Land Based Dive and Torpedo	⋮	1,405	10,971	25,782	21,431	59,589
Patrol Bombers	⋮	110	879	7,085	8,714	16,788
Enemy Aircraft Destroyed[1]	⋮	1,156	1,458	6,891	5,998	15,503
In Aerial Combat	⋮	858	1,239	4,024	3,161	9,282
On Surface	⋮	298	219	2,867	2,837	6,221
Losses to Enemy Action[1]	⋮	332	363	1,165	1,016	2,886
To Enemy Aircraft	⋮	266	233	261	146	906
To Enemy Anti-Aircraft	⋮	76	130	904	870	1,980
Aircraft on Hand[2]	5,233	11,772	26,172	36,788	32,410	⋮
Fighters	514	1,253	5,516	12,034	10,320	⋮
Scout and Torpedo Bombers	809	1,565	6,185	9,338	7,761	⋮
Patrol Bombers	466	1,019	2,421	3,962	3,180	⋮
Scout Observation	682	1,594	1,512	1,104	819	⋮
Transports	303	624	1,397	2,445	2,942	⋮
Trainers	2,459	5,714	9,141	7,905	7,388	⋮

SELECTED NAVAL AVIATION STATISTICS—WORLD WAR II (continued)

	1941	1942	1943	1944	1945	TOTAL
Carrier Strength[1]	8	16	57	93	104	..
Battle Carriers	0	0		0	1	..
Carriers	7	4[3]	13	20	23	..
Light Carriers	0	0	9	8[5]	8	..
Escort Carriers	1	12	35[4]	65[5]	72[6]	..
Total Aviation Personnel[7]	29,402	122,172	284,452	400,147	437,524	..
Pilots Trained	N.A.	6,610[8]	20,842	21,067	7,149[9]	35,666

[1] Includes U. S. Marine Corps.
[2] Aircraft on hand as of December 31, 1941 through 1944, as of November 30, 1945; including U. S. Marine Corps.
[3] Carriers Hornet, Lexington, Yorktown, and Wasp sunk during 1942.
[4] Escort Carrier Liscome Bay sunk during 1943.
[5] Light Carrier Princeton and Escort Carriers Block Island, Gambier Bay, and St. Lo sunk during 1944.
[6] Escort Carriers Ommaney Bay and Bismarck Sea sunk during 1945.
[7] As of December 31, 1941 through 1944, as of August 31, 1945; includes Navy, Marine, and Coast Guard Aviation Personnel.
[8] July 1 to December 31 only.
[9] Through August.
Source: Aircraft Yearbook, 1946; Navy Department.

KOREAN CONFLICT STATISTICS

ENEMY AIRCRAFT LOSSES:

MIG-15:   839 destroyed; 154 prob. destroyed; 919 damaged
All Types: 1,020 destroyed; 182 prob. destroyed; 1,010 damaged
  (Incl. MIGs)

USAF AIRCRAFT LOSSES:

	AIR-TO-AIR	GROUNDFIRE	OTHER	TOTAL
Jet........	83	259	93	435
Prop.......	21	285	60	366
Total......	104	544	153	801

FRIENDLY FOREIGN

A/C..........	6	54	22	82

SHOREBASED MARINE

A/C..........	0	79	38	117
GRAND TOTAL.	110	677	213	1,000

Following are observed reported figures for USAF and attached units from beginning of Korean war to and including 10 P.M. July 27, 1953, the hour of cease-fire:

ITEMS	USAF	ATTACHED UNITS	TOTALS
Sorties Flown...................	716,979	119,898	836,877
Vehicles Destroyed............	74,589	8,331	82,920
Railcars Destroyed............	9,417	1,072	10,489
Bridges Destroyed.............	869	341	1,210
Tanks Destroyed..............	1,160	171	1,331
Troop Casualties..............	145,416	39,392	184,808
Locomotives Destroyed.........	869	94	963
Buildings Destroyed...........	89,639	29,690	119,329
Gun Positions Destroyed (not broken down)..........			18,324
Barges and Boats Destroyed (not broken down).......			592

Delivered as of June 30, 1953: (USAF and attached total).

Tons of bombs................................ 448,366
Rounds of ammunition.......................... 182,829,400
Number of rockets............................. 511,329
Gallons of napalm............................. 9,596,798
Tons of personnel and freight................. 670,000
Passengers 2,700,000
Air evacuees.................................. 325,000

BIBLIOGRAPHY

A COMPLETE BIBLIOGRAPHY for this book would run to many pages. We therefore confine ourselves to citing below, and acknowledging with gratitude, sources from which actual quotation has been taken.

Arnold, Henry H., *Airmen and Aircraft*. New York: The Ronald Press, 1926.

Rockwell, Kiffin Yates, *War Letters*. New York: Doubleday Page & Co., 1925.

Rickenbacker, Capt. Edward V., *Fighting the Flying Circus*. New York: Stokes, c. 1919.

Air Travel Magazine. New York: Air Travel Corporation, June 1918.

The Medal of Honor of the United States Army. Washington: U. S. Government Printing Office, 1948.

Fraser, Chelsea, *The Story of Aircraft*. New York: Thomas Y. Crowell Co., 1944.

Archives, USAF Historical Division, Research Studies Institute, Maxwell Air Force Base, Alabama.

Hall, Grover Cleveland, *1000 Destroyed*. Montgomery, Ala.: Brown Printing Company, 1946.

Mingos, Howard, ed., *The Aircraft Yearbooks for 1943 and 1946*. New York: Lanaiar Publishers Inc.

Karig, W. and Purdon, E., *Battle Report, Pacific War: Middle Phase*. New York: Rinehart and Company Inc., 1947.

DeChant, John A., *Devil Birds*. New York, Harper and Brothers, 1947.

Lanphier, Thomas G., Jr., Lt. Col., series of three articles distributed by North American Newspaper Alliance, 1945.

Edmonds, Walter D., *They Fought With What They Had.* Boston: Little, Brown, 1951.

Craven, W. F. and Cate, J. L., *The Pacific: Guadalcanal to Saipan.* (*The Army Air Forces in World War II,* Vol IV), Chicago: University of Chicago Press, 1950.

Kenney, General George C., *General Kenney Reports.* New York: Duell, Sloan & Pierce, 1949.

McKee, Philip, *Warriors with Wings.* New York: Thomas Y. Crowell Co., 1947.

Scott, Robert L., Jr., *God is My Co-Pilot.* Blue Ribbon reprint, 1943.

Scott, Robert L., Jr., *Damned to Glory.* New York: Charles Scribner's Sons, 1944.

Craven, W. F., and Cate, J. L., *Europe: Torch to Pointblank* (*The Army Air Forces in World War II,* Vol. II). Chicago: University of Chicago Press, 1944.

Craven, W. F., and Cate, J. L., *Europe: Argument to V-E Day* (*The Army Air Forces in World War II,* Vol. III). Chicago: University of Chicago Press, 1951.

Stars and Stripes. European Edition, London Branch, September 7, 1943.

Fifty Years of Aviation Progress. Washington: National Committee, issued in observation of the fiftieth anniversary of power flight, 1953.

Air Force Magazine. Washington: Air Force Association, June, 1951.

Air Force Times. Washington, Army Times Publications, January 12, 1952.

Newsweek Magazine. Dayton, Ohio: Weekly Publications Inc., May 25, 1953.

Sunday Mirror Magazine, King Features Syndicate Inc., July 5, 1953.

Thyng, Col. Harrison R., *Air-to-Air Combat in Korea.* Maxwell Air Force Base: Air University Quarterly Review, Vol. VI, No. 2, 1953.

Get to know the facts and the fiction from the internationally best-selling author...

LEN DEIGHTON